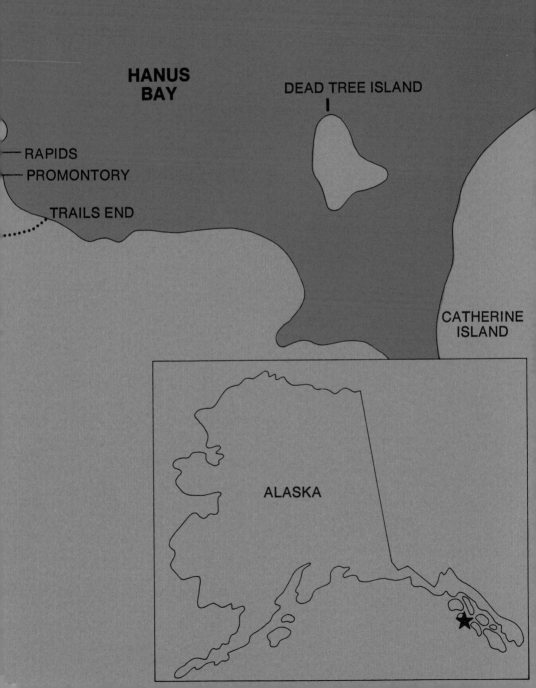

PERIL STRAIT

HANUS
BAY

DEAD TREE ISLAND

— RAPIDS
— PROMONTORY

TRAILS END

CATHERINE
ISLAND

ALASKA

# RED SALMON,
# BROWN BEAR

THE AMERICAN MUSEUM OF NATURAL HISTORY'S

## THE NEW EXPLORERS

GENERAL EDITOR:

ALFRED MEYER

# RED SALMON, BROWN BEAR

## THE STORY OF AN ALASKAN LAKE

BASED ON THE EXPERIENCES OF

## DR. THEODORE J. WALKER

CREATED BY ALAN LANDSBURG PRODUCTIONS, INC.

**WORLD PUBLISHING**
**TIMES MIRROR**
NEW YORK

PUBLISHED BY THE WORLD PUBLISHING COMPANY
PUBLISHED SIMULTANEOUSLY IN CANADA
BY NELSON, FOSTER & SCOTT LTD.
FIRST PRINTING—1971
COPYRIGHT © 1971 BY ALAN LANDSBURG PRODUCTIONS, INC.
ALL RIGHTS RESERVED
LIBRARY OF CONGRESS CATALOG CARD NUMBER: 75-159587
PRINTED IN THE UNITED STATES OF AMERICA
DESIGNED BY JACQUES CHAZAUD

**WORLD PUBLISHING**
TIMES MIRROR

# Contents

# Foreword

I have my doubts about T. J. Walker, biologist, student of the California gray whale, and keeper, from one winter to the next, of a remote Alaskan lake named Eva. . . .

He sat huddled in the stern of a small boat 500 feet below, a tiny, bent figure clinging to the handle of a miniature outboard motor. The boat poked along Lake Eva's southern edge, then swung out in a long graceful arc as we circled in to land, leaving compounding silvery V's in its wake. He cut his motor when we cut ours, stood up, and with an oar nudged his boat toward one of the plane's pontoons. A tail of his red-and-black-checked halibut shirt fluttered in the wind. He wore hip-length wading boots. Assorted gear lay strewn in the bottom of his boat, most of it sopping wet and giving off that peculiar pungency of canvas, gasoline, and cold water. His beard was the color of gray stone and curled perfectly at the edges like filigree sculpture. He reached up and shook my hand, a gesture that changed midway into one of balance. I could not tell much about a smile because of the beard, through which he mumbled. But as we stood there joined—he rocking in his boat and I, somewhat solemnly, rocking on the pontoons of the airplane—he looked at me and I saw in his eyes, bubbling and frothing way back there, a cauldron of mirth. "Why, you old billy goat," I thought to myself. "Either you're a trickster or you're laughing at the world or you've been out here far too long."

Lake Eva, blue as the sky, is a long lake sitting in a long valley on a very large island bearing a good Russian name, Baranof. This is southeastern, coastal Alaska, land of the evergreen forest and of the Tlingit and Haida Indians, those builders of totem poles and fishers of the great rivers. It is temperate and maritime, except at higher altitudes where the glaciers sprawl. To its coasts and up its streams and rivers come the anadromous migratory Pacific salmon, *Oncorhynchus*: the sockeye, the pink, the chum, the coho, and the chinook. Spending most of their adult life at sea, the salmon return to fresh water in the autumn and winter to spawn and die in their parent streams, rivers, and lakes.

Only a few malamutes and huskies hang around the docks and fishing boats of Juneau and Sitka, the region's principal cities. In a bar in Juneau, where I had stopped on my way to Lake Eva, I came across commercial salmon fishermen, several cannery workers, and a free-lance lumberjack from Oregon. A man of obvious backwoods stature and specialization, the lumberjack was a cutter, and his reputation had brought him work for a month on an island in southeast Alaska. The strategy was simple, he explained: cut down all the trees on the island except two or three; leave these for the bald eagles to use as nesting sites. He laughed explosively. "Christ," he said, "they may as well stick up a few telephone poles for all the good it's going to do the eagles." He also told me that a Japanese firm was currently buying vast amounts of raw, unmilled timber. Shipped to Japan, the logs are lashed together and sunk in Japanese harbors where they will be preserved until needed, perhaps twenty or thirty years hence. "That," he declared, with a salute of his beer glass, "is foresight."

In deference to the frontier spirit, I rented a bright red pickup truck instead of a Ford Fairlane; but you can't go very far by road in Juneau: across the bridge that spans that Gastineau Channel to Douglas perhaps, or north to Mendenhall Glacier or Auke Bay. Anywhere else notable lies within walking distance: the docks, the Alaska State Museum, St. Nicholas Russian Orthodox Church, the headquarters of Channel Flying Service. I stopped in at the Flying Service. Topographic maps hung from the office walls, mechanics overhauled airplanes in the adjacent hangar, free coffee was dispensed. But the chief attraction that morning was the roar and crackle of the bush radio. While some people were calling in for supplies, and others to arrange to be picked up by plane from fishing and lumber camps or from the outlying canneries, the bulk of the radio traffic that day dealt with search reports on a downed airplane. The weather was abominable: low cloud cover, gusty winds, heavy rain, little visibility. A flight to Lake Eva was out of the question. Terse, negative reports came from the search pilots.

As the afternoon wore on, all of Channel's planes returned without having sighted the lost plane. Outside it grew even blacker and the rain thundered down. The radio finally quieted. Some people in the office left. I talked to the receptionist, who operates the radio, and discovered she had been married twice to

bush pilots, and had been twice widowed. It was a modern ver-
sion of J. M. Synge's *Riders to the Sea.*

All at once, a tentative, halting, gentle voice, probing the air-
waves, searching in that blind dumb roar for acknowledgment,
politely and delicately interjected itself into the gathering gloom
of the offices of the Flying Service.

"KNX-2, KNX-2, this is Lake Eva, Lake Eva, over."

It was T. J. Walker.

"This is Lake Eva. Thank you very much for answering KNX-
2, I appreciate it very much. I was just wondering, just calling to
inquire about the grocery shipment I ordered two days ago. I
wondered if there was any possibility of its being flown in sometime soon, that is, whether you had any room in your schedule
for a drop shipment. I certainly don't want anyone to go to any
special lengths but I would dearly appreciate anything you can
do on this count, over."

I had admired the receptionist because of the way she han-
dled the radio, the clipped style, the efficient brevity, the gutted,
lean communication. On hearing T. J. Walker, it was instantly
clear to me that this man had probably added a new tone of
unorthodoxy, even courtliness, to the wilderness radio network,
if not to the wilderness itself.

After my landing at Lake Eva, Walker led me down his sin-
uous trail. Hemlocks, ferns, and mosses sparkled in the rain. As
we began to wade the creek to his cabin, he murmured apologies
to the pink salmon. By crossing, he said, we disturbed their nest-
building. Being, for the most part, a considerate guest, I followed
the house rules of Lake Eva, as laid down by T. J. Walker, and
henceforth charily tiptoed across the creek uttering apologies to
the otherwise preoccupied fish.

Walker's cabin is like a diner with three compartments. He
lives and works in the first section, sleeps in the middle one,
which features four bunks and a tiny window, and uses the back
section for storage. It is an unimposing place, stained a creosote
brown on the outside. A potbellied stove in the living room casts
a spare amount of heat. The cabin was built and abandoned by the
Alaska Department of Fish and Game, which had conducted a
five-year salmon survey on Eva Creek. This is the rippling chute
that drains the lake and empties into the estuary. Walker calls
the estuary "the basin in which the tide plays," and that tells you
a great deal about Walker.

To my immense regret and discomfort, I became claustrophobic in Walker's cabin and found it impossible to sleep. I listened, as T.J. often did, to the moisture drops crashing endlessly from the hemlocks onto his tin roof. I also formulated private escape plans in case the Alaskan brown bear suddenly opened the door and walked into the cabin. I was positive, amid tosses and turns, that I heard him out there once or twice. No creature, I am steadfastly convinced, can populate the dark corridors of insomnia more terribly than the Alaskan brown bear.

That five years' worth of salmon data and a modicum of shelter were available undoubtedly figured in the decision to locate the first "New Explorer" project at Lake Eva. Of course, so did the potentially explosive presence of the bear. The generative idea behind the series is to place a scientist who is, or who has the potential for becoming, a competent cinematographer into an area that is remote but also typical of a larger ecological zone. In the case of Lake Eva, we have a glacial drainage system involving tributaries, the lake, the creek, the estuary, and the ocean — an elegant spectrum of habitats and principles. The New Explorer would have to deal here with such phenomena as the mixing of fresh and salt water, the properties of a coniferous rain forest, the geology of a glaciated valley system. He would, if such were his vision, trace food chains, explain climate, track vertebrates, and be sensible of the flowering of plants and the rise and ebb of tides.

Manifestly enough, he would also be rummaging through his own psyche, for another aspect of the series is that the scientist-photographer does not merely commute in and out. Unfortunately, today a great deal of work in the natural sciences is restricted by convenience and confined either to the laboratory or to busy academic (and usually urban) schedules. We do not live in an age where a naturalist or an ecologist is ordinarily content to spend a huge chunk of time by himself looking into a ticking ecosystem. The New Explorer, however, is dropped into his locale and left there — for at least six months, for at least time enough to observe a biological community creak and shift from season to season, if there be seasons.

Food and mail are dropped to him. He has a radio, and if he doesn't answer it three days running someone flies in to see what is wrong. He also has a generator for electricity to light his quarters and to charge the batteries that fire his cameras. Perhaps — since all this filming might appear on television someday — a film crew visits once or twice to photograph the scientist-photographer photographing. But, basically, he is obliged to hoe his row alone. Obliged to document photographically what he sees, with still and motion picture cameras. Obliged to speak his observations and reflections into a tape recorder every single day. And obliged to blend himself into an ecosystem that has its own precedents and is not dominated by human beings.

Walker, man of the amused eyes, documented, observed, and reflected. His life for more than six months (April through October, 1970) was involved in the life of such creatures as the elusive Alaskan brown bear, whose presence haunted Walker constantly. The salmon arched up the falls to Eva Creek, spawned in a reproductive frenzy in front of Walker's cabin, and then died. Otters and bald eagles watched. The hemlock, the skunk cabbage, the length of day, the moisture, the temperature—all exerted their singular and combined influences on this New Explorer.

Walker, accordingly, did not escape the rigors of his voluntary isolation. He brooded and fantasized profusely. His moods swung rapidly from depression to elation and back again. When his equipment failed, he cursed; when he was underwater watching salmon spawn, he exulted, though not neglecting to complain of the coldness of the water. He worked compulsively, driven by what he often dispairingly regarded as an impossible task. And herein lies a crucial element of the New Explorer series—the inner, psychic documentation. Like any scientist, Walker is not merely a disembodied scientific antenna, not pure brain, but a human being being fraught with emotion, vulnerability, and bias as well as with perception, insight, and reason. Like Shylock, does not the doctor of ecology weep and laugh, does he not bleed when his skin is pricked? This record of the life of Lake Eva is as much a record of the observer as it is of the observed.

Every once in a while as I was going over the transcripts of Walker's tapes after my brief visit, I would think that, yes, madness has him. It was too much. The bears, the isolation, the shapes of the hemlock in the weird light of arctic evening. And then, gradually, I began to understand my intuitive doubts about Walker and to define the strange merriment I had seen in his eyes that morning next to the plane.

Walker grew up in Montana and became an ecologist at the University of Wisconsin. He was a mountain person by spirit most of that time and did a great deal of mountain climbing. But then he went west and joined the staff of the Scripps-Howard Oceanographic Institute. He stayed twenty-three years and studied water, fish—particularly the function of the lateral line—

and the gray whale. Then something happened. I don't honestly know what. It sounded from the tapes as though he had been smoldering with discontent for at least some recent years. I think, if I remember our conversation in the cabin one rainy afternoon, that he thought that Scripps-Howard, like so many institutions in America, had changed from an intimate and exciting research facility into an overinstitutionalized, muscle-bound, bureaucratic nightmare. Perhaps I am exaggerating his disenchantment, but I did sense at Lake Eva the relief of a man who has left politics and gone back to a work he had previously loved.

In any case, once he was at Lake Eva, I think his life changed more than he suspected it would, and probably it has changed more than even now he suspects it has. I think the amusement in his eyes came because he was in the cleansing embrace of the physical, elemental world, like Thoreau. He perceived the workings of biological time and of biological succession. He not only perceived these intellectually, but to a certain extent he experienced them as though his analytical abilities were now and then overwhelmed by his synthesizing abilities. Walker must have, at least momentarily and in his way, understood nature in the broad sense, in the way your own brain tissues correlate to and identify with the life and the death everywhere around. Subliminally, anyway, he placed his own life in the context of biological time and succession. The power of such a confrontation must be staggering, for it is your own mortality that you look upon. What else could one be—particularly when seeing an editor from New York struggling out of a ridiculous airplane—but amused? A cosmic amusement at the inanities and ephemera of civilization.

My doubt about Walker is fairly spurious, even romantic. Once, while editing the transcripts, I had looked up the word *pan*, the one that relates to the movement of a camera. The next entry was the proper noun *Pan*. At this curious point I recalled the frequent mentions Walker makes of his recorder, that simple little wind instrument. I vividly remembered his description of sitting down in the forest and playing a song on it. Pan, as everybody knows, was the ancient Greek god of forests and a piper of engaging songs. Somehow or other, I found myself, and still find myself, making the rather ludicrous connection between T. J. Walker and the great god Pan.

ALFRED MEYER
Editor, *Natural History* magazine

# 1

---

# THE
# FIRST DAYS

*April 19*

April 19 and I hope that everything is working. I've been up since six o'clock and taken care of the living chores and attempted to warm the cabin up a bit. I noted that the temperature outside was 22°, and cabin temperature near 30°. Already in the week that we've been setting up here a lot of vegetation has begun to pop up. Of course I'm still viewing the flora from eye level; I haven't scrunched down to the level of the plants yet. Right now, Day One Proper, a magnificent layer of moss sprawls over everything, climbing up over the logs and covering the entire floor of the woods. I am too busy to think much about the next several months, but a few thoughts are floating around. It does seem to me valid to get away and try to see things from a much different perspective — the Lake Eva perspective, if you will.

Here I am removed from cities, the technological cities. I've gone back in time, for now I live in a cabin in the woods, a tremendously romantic circumstance. I suppose there lurks in my mind some vestige, some recollection of the early pioneer days of America when families literally struck out westward, living in clearings, working their way across the Appalachian forests into

1

prairies, mountain areas, the Rockies, across deserts, finally arriving at the Pacific Ocean. So I sit near the ocean, hands in my pockets, a little on the cool side—I don't happen to have my outer shirt on—trying to imagine the great power the land and the waters must have exerted on the consciousness of the pioneers.

I'm well fed, comfortable, anxious to get out and begin my survey of Lake Eva. Right now, spring is beginning to stir and plants are growing and filling the stream banks with an exuberant, life-green flush.

I have the idea that in the city, whenever someone else is talking, your own mental imagery stops and you are drawn into that conversation, unless you want to be rude and butt in and take away from what the other person is saying. Here, I'm happy to note, the only person who can butt in is myself, and I find that I am talking all the time, in one way or another.

Already I'm starting to realize that *being* alone is a much more difficult experience than merely *feeling* alone. Being alone requires you to exercise full ingenuity and judgment. You have to keep on top of what's going on. So much can be negated by accidents or carelessness—overturning a boat, the cabin catching on fire. Today I've had my first dose of the tyranny of mechanical equipment. I attempted my first check in with the radio at 4:30 in the afternoon and made several unsuccessful attempts to call out. Suddenly the radio quit altogether. From the point of view of logistics, the failure of the radio to operate will be regarded by the outside world as an accident. Someone will probably fly in to see what's wrong. It's irritating. I find myself concerned about my resources, like the logistics of fuel. The generator uses up a great deal of gasoline. By being alone, I'm finding myself forced to evaluate and work out some kind of a living routine which keeps the cabin in reasonable neatness. I'm forced also to figure out a means of drying out enough wood to keep a little fire going in my potbellied stove.

As yet, of course, no encounters with Alaskan brown bear, but I can say that an animal that generates footprints that last throughout a winter and into the spring must be a tremendous animal. I have the distinct feeling that if all the signs that I see of Alaskan brown bear are any indication, I'm in no-man's territory. I am afraid the bear is going to be very much on the scene.

I prowled around a bit in the estuary and up through the tributary that comes in from the south and was surprised to find some spanking-fresh bear tracks. There was still mud in suspen-

*Lake Eva, with Peril Strait in distance.*

*Walker touring the lake's frozen
surface at high noon during the short
daylight hours of March.*

*Lake Eva, looking southwest.*

*A frosty morning at lake's edge.*

*Walker moving along the trail
in spring.*

*New shoots of the twisted stalk, a
perennial inhabitant of the forest edge.*

*Coarse grass in seed, growing along
Eva Creek.*

sion in the impressions. It may have been only a medium-sized bear, but it was real and impressive, nonetheless. I decided *not* to go on and follow him any more. I looked around a bit and came to the conclusion that this bear had been feeding on skunk cabbage and had eaten the flowers right to an inch from the ground. It is an awesome feeling knowing the bears are out there.

Today I saw a bald eagle at the beach and then this evening, when I came out of the cabin, I frightened one off. It went flying upstream, turned around, and came back the other way. They're large, ponderous birds. At the estuary this evening I found a portion of a stomach which obviously was from a Dolly Varden trout — it wasn't completely eaten. Why it was left there or what had been feeding on it was anyone's guess. Perhaps it was the eagle.

We had three or four showers yesterday, which introduced me to the water regimen. Rain came down and swept the needles and the bark; then a delay, and the dripping began. The force of the rain is broken by the trees; the coalesced drops which accumulate in the interstices of the branches begin to drop down — and last night I found myself lying awake hearing the dripping of water onto the cabin roof, not in the regular rhythmic way of rain but gravity dripping. It overpowers one. All this rain is first stopped by boughs and needles of the hemlocks. A lot, of course, gets held back by the veneer of lichen — for all the world like old man's hair and whiskers — but a lot, too, in the tips of the trees and along the bark and even down on the deck, on the mossy floor. The mosses themselves hold the rain and release it more slowly. The steady-state effect of all this retarding of the rain from the clouds is to produce a continuous source of moisture which seeks its way to the low points of the landscape: the tributaries, the lake, the stream.

The stream draining the lake is a very gentle one, with a fairly constant flow. I haven't noticed a great deal of fluctuation yet, although there's still a big snow melt in the higher regions. As I look out of the windows I see the snowline retreating rather rapidly.

Since I'm keeping this biological system under surveillance I will at some point have to make my way up to the tips of the ridges. I would like to climb along one of the streams. I want to collect water at these places for my petri dishes so I can test the fertility of the water. How quickly does water pick up nutrients? The water must be tremendously enriched almost immediately as it works its way down through this porous water route and the plant materials. I also have to check the activity of life as it begins to develop along the mouth of my stream and I will, of course, have to maintain surveillance of the lake itself and the tributaries supplying the lake. A lot of space to cover, and a lot of happenings, I hope, will be etched in my mind via the route of eyes and ears and body; the sensation of temperature, for example.

The high ridge produces quite a bit of rain. The closer you get to the lake, the more evident the rain is. As I was standing there, speculating on how to get the boat operative with oars that don't match the oarlocks, an otter popped up on the lake from the marshy area just at the exit of the lake. The otter surfaced beyond me. It had seen me and swum underwater past where the boat was parked and proceeded to come up the lake. I was delighted to see that otters were on the lake. When they're surfaced they create quite a wake, so I should be able to spot them easily from now on, especially as they tend to stay very close to shore, I noticed. I was tremendously surprised at the force of the otter's exhalation and the similarity to whales and seals of the violence of the air release through the nostril of the otter. Of course, it is in the real sense an aquatic mammal. It was also struck by the way the otter swam. It occurred to me that the forelimbs, which are leglike and used in dog-paddle fashion, put the animal high up in order to breathe. I couldn't help marveling at the fact that here is an animal that functions in bitter-cold water. It must be 42° in the lake.

## April 20

The estuary lies downstream from my cabin. It was at one time probably another lake or a series of two lakes. The erosion of the stream cutting into the rock has drained it. But the tide comes in and goes out each day and there is an impounding of water. This is where migrating waterfowl appear to congregate. It probably will also be an area in which my underwater diving will be easiest to carry out and where I will first see the salmon and other anadromous fishes (*anadromous* refers to fish capable of functioning physiologically both in fresh water and in sea water). You can hardly view this estuary without reflecting on the tides, and yesterday there was a 9.3-foot tide indicated on the Sitka Tide Table. The tide is a profound and dynamic process.

I walked down the trail along the estuary and noted that in general the birds were very shy and promptly left the area when I approached. In filming animals, I learned one has to shoot the stage on which the action takes place; it's better to be a middle distance rather than right up on top of the animal, although sooner or later I want to see just how close I can get. Of course this is the major mistake that many nature photographers make, trying to get a portrait which is so tight and shot at the moment when things are static so they record only a vague impression of what's going on. I went on down to the strait and took the water temperature — and also a picture or two across the strait looking north toward Chichagof Island. Catherine Island with its snow-covered peak is beautiful. I waded into the water and discovered that the top of it was fresh even though I was somewhat below the entrance to the lagoon. I should explain here that to a geologist a *lagoon* is a body of water which has no inlet, whereas an *estuary* is nothing more than an entrance of a stream flowing into the ocean, from which the fresh water usually skids over the top of the underlying, more dense, saline water. At the strait, as I have indicated, the water on top was fresh and as I walked I could see the stirring of the upwelling of this dense water, which is probably in a mixing situation with the top water. A number of piles of seaweed floats were neatly stacked by the highest tide. I could see the marks; the tides had generated three or four layers of material. It's hard to understand why this would have happened. You would think that each tide would obliterate the tide before it, except for the high and the low immediately before — unless we are dealing here with tides that are diminishing.

Clouds are boiling up over the ridge all the time. Little tantalizing breaks of blue with a shaft of sunlight throw the estuary into brilliant sun; but the spot moves on, which means if one wants to play with available light, one has to photograph rather quickly. This hide-and-seek game underscores a very important factor: these mountains generate weather. They break the flow of the Aleutian lows which are moving in from the west, and as the humid air, which is moisture-laden from the huge evaporator out over the Pacific, works its way over the snow-covered ridges, it rises and cools. Considerable fog and clouds develop and, depending on the degree of cooling, a fair amount of moisture is extracted from that air in the form of snow or rain.

I heard a raven make its peculiar croaking sound, and at that very moment the bird flew up out of one of these terraced skunk cabbage gardens and lit on a broken stump, which stuck up about 30 feet out of the swamp. The bird tarried only a second, and then flew out of sight, but as it flew off, I noticed that it was carrying in its talons the limp body of a toad. So here was a beautiful example of predation where the crucial act took place very quickly, or at least was terminated abruptly. There are always a number of situations in which animals, and plants as well, are provided with the means of overstocking or supplying the habitat. However, by means of a variety of food chains, nature with equal effectiveness puts safeguards on population; restrictions, limitations. Animals are cropped so that overpopulation doesn't occur, and the population seems to stay at a reasonable, steady state. Of course, catastrophe or overpredation in one part of the environment is usually offset by an increase in the productive capacity of the animals. There's always enough environmental pressure to make most animals move about. Man is the only animal I know that doesn't ever feel — or at least not too much in America — the pangs of hunger constantly. Every other animal is generally driven to search for its food full time.

Two families of common mergansers were perched on the rocks on the upper end of the estuary as the tide went out. I was impressed by the rapidity with which the water level changed. It's always been a mystery to me as a biologist to find a rationale to explain the gravitational interplay of the earth and the moon, how this interplay might cause oscillation in the tides and water depths of the oceans. I've never really been able to understand the mechanics. I like to think that the gravitational force is a pressure effect which is generated in what we call space and for which we are unable to find anything, differentiate anything, measure anything. Yet there must be something; we just can't believe that it would operate otherwise. There must be some sort of a pressure field occasioned by the moon that creates variations in this gravitational force, which is indicated by tides.

I attempted to start the generator and discovered that it wouldn't run. I worked and I worked, but it didn't work, and finally I gave up. I would have to go without lights, without a battery charge on the camera, and without my strobes. I went in and had a good supper, got my fire going, then went back out and decided the problem must lie in the governor linkage, since I found a spring loose; then I tried the generator. It started lamely and I got it running by jockeying the adjustments, but the generator is not quite right. It puts out a rather pale voltage and the light bulbs are medium bright only.

As to conveniences, the john here has no door and has a Women's sign across one side. Kind of a beautiful john with a marvelous view. The seat, the whole contraption, is built onto a pit which is filled with water, which dramatizes neatly the idea that the water table is just below the moss. Only on the steeper slopes is the drainage sufficient to keep matters dry. I had asked some of the people who helped me set up when I first came in, whether they had any tree-climbing equipment, or any paratroopers, for fire-fighting. A naive question. "Are you kidding?" one of them asked. "This is the asbestos forest." True enough. I'm finding that wood takes two to three days of baking over the stove before it is dry enough to burn.

## April 21

Today is my first day to wait and watch, and the site I picked was not Lake Eva but the estuary, which I define as the basin in which the tide plays. It essentially covers a rather extensive area of water, running from the waterfall all the way down to Hanus Bay and Peril Strait. I find this estuary of great interest biologically because it is in this basin that physiological and behavioral orientations will take place in the interplay of salinity and fresh water with the anadromous fishes. It is a transition zone.

The first great shock I had came when I suddenly looked out on the gravel-exposed portion of the upper estuary basin and saw a pair of Sitka deer walking into view. Unfortunately, I'd set the camera position and fixed the tripod and here, without any warning, was a target of opportunity, two beautiful black-tailed Sitka deer. The deer leisurely walked across the flat, proceeding from south to north, and disappeared out of my view, heading right for the opening where the steam poured into the estuary basin. That was treat one and I think I photographed it fairly well with the Leica. With more camera experience, perhaps I could have put the movie camera on the deer. But in a way, I'm up here to learn how to film. I'm not a wildlife photographer and I find myself very much in conflict, being a professional, trained biologist. For example, I'm just as much drawn to the plants, which are static from the point of view of cinematography, as I am to wildlife; and yet I know that when the chips are down an audience identifies nature with subjects that move about. But I'm learning. I've learned that if one sits down and waits, things happen.

Lake Eva is a joy to view. I think the most magnificent views are the ones looking west up the lake, since that's where the snowy peaks are. There is also a rather nice backdrop of mountains on the east side of the lake at the outlet. Of course, the big event of the spring occurs at that moment when the lake turns over. To people who don't think about it, it may be a surprise that during the winter months the lake is cut off from the air, although there is some oxygenated water being carried into the lake from the tributaries. The point is that the lake is quite dead in the winter months. The coldest water has the least density, which is fortunate for life, for otherwise I don't think life would have ever made its way into fresh water. The water at surface is at freezing and forms an ice cover which cuts off most of the heat loss to the atmosphere. Once this happens the air is denied access to the lake, and the lake begins to use up its oxygen. The first area to use up the oxygen is the lower region. There is a large amount of life along the bottom, insects and bacteria incorporating the energy that's available there. I was curious to see if there were many signs of this turnover. The autumn turnover of the lake takes place just before the lake freezes over. It's then that the cold water which accumulates at the bottom gets cold enough to come up to the top and begin to form a layer of ice.

## April 22

With infinite cunning, I decided to erect a blind near the estuary where I might record the activity of the mergansers at fairly close range. I had picked a beautiful, downed log that was covered with a heavy carpet of moss. Although comfortable, it was obvious on second thought that I was in full sight of the birds; moreover, it would take quite a lot of effort to get to it through the brush. One could, I suppose, rise early in the morning and beat the mergansers into the area, but I haven't got around to that as yet. I decided to cut a path through. I thought also that a path would give me more freedom by eliminating the crackling as I walked through and I could use the cut brush to build a fence on one side. So I went to work and cut a path down through the salmonberry, devil's club, and huckleberry and put up a fairly sizable blind. It took me nearly two hours to clear it out, and much to my astonishment when I finished I found two stakes driven into the ground and a couple of galvanized nails driven down just below the log. Whether it was a digging or some sort of a blind, I don't know. It might well have been a hunter's blind at one time. Man has an odd way of leaving his mark, especially in Alaska where hunting is a mobile affair and all one has to do is hire a seaplane to go into any area he wants. Who would have dreamed that in this seemingly virgin, undisturbed area, I would find signs of human habitation when I cleared down a path to the log. I also had the nagging sense that this was at one time a bear trail, but perhaps my imagination is playing tricks on me and I've been thinking too much about the bear whose track I saw. Maybe he isn't really making these tremendous hollows and tracks that persist through fall and winter. But I am still carrying the shotgun. I felt pleased with my progress and thought I had created a fairly good blind. It will be fun to find out whether or not the cameras will operate by remote control from across the estuary. I can see the activity of the otter coming in and out of the water, and the mallards. In the process of clearing this blind I heard a buzzing sound and I looked up. Sure enough, there was the hummer, the male ruby-throated hummingbird hovering over the green urn-shaped blossoms of the huckleberries.

About that time I got ready to wrap up the camera. I had set it on the stationary tripod and left it sitting there, knowing that no one was going to come along. It is extraordinary knowing that there's no one else, just me. Nobody is going to come along, the trail is mine. The trail that day by day I'm growing fonder of and on which I'm seeing more and more. As I was putting away the camera a little flurry of fog came from nowhere on the estuary. There it was. Immediately I thought, my God, it's snowing—and it was, beautiful big wet spring snow streaking down and swirling across the estuary. So I packed up the cameras and slouched my way through the muck back to the cabin to get comfortable. It was apparent to me that my not sleeping through the night because of the magnified, oversized raindrops could not have happened if it hadn't been raining hard through the night. An indication of this was that every one of my footprints was washed down and the trail looked decidedly more mushy than it had before.

My more sophisticated animals give every indication of being very cool, calm and collected, operating in ways that don't advertise their positions and activities. The otter is there, but if you don't happen to be looking at the right place at the right moment, you'll never see him. His passage through the lake and stream is very much like the whale. Much of the time he's under-water and he acts very frightened. How much of this is imagined on my part — the passage and nature of these beasts, the genetic inheritance which has paid off for them and which they do not owe primarily to the predation on them by man, although cer-tainly man has been the cruelest of predators. Is the furtiveness of wild animals a response they need in interacting with each other? I just don't know, it's one of those thorny issues that one can ponder. How in the evolution of the animal were the proper responses built in?

I looked out the window of my cabin at a squall that came up, and the fog clouds around the trees were so beautiful that I thought I was looking at Chinese silk screens. I decided to take one last trip down to my new blind. Walking across the drained estuary, which is now down to about a foot and a half, I explored that section of the estuary to the east and north. I got across and retraced my steps around the estuary, and it was wild hearing the crack of seaweeds underfoot and the fragments of mussel shells and clams in nearly fresh water.

I returned to camp early as a precaution. I didn't want to be caught in the dark wading across the shallows of the estuary, which has a bottom of fragmented rock with a great deal of moss and algae on it. I've also learned to be more careful in my walk-ing along the trail. This trail is a blessing. Without it, I don't think one could cover this mile of ground that lies between me and the lake and the estuary. I could wade up or down the stream, I suppose, but having stepped into a hole without any warning I'm inclined to appreciate the trail. I should point out that every time I want to go somewhere I must put my boots on. If I don't, I'm not going anywhere. The only trails on the cabin side of the stream are the natural trails of the bears and deer, and these trails have a wicked habit of vanishing before your eyes. A huge downed log is all it takes. How the animals get across them I'll never know. The trail across the stream from the cabin is man-made, of course, and is the one I primarily use. The WPA in '32 must have worked long and hard cutting away timber needed to build slats across the marshy areas over which the trail runs. But these long planks and the trappings of trail-making have an overgrowth of moss which lends a softened curve counter to things and hides the ugliness, the sharp angular saw cuts, of man's handiwork.

## April 23

I never before realized how beautifully the snow flakes reflect and define the gusts of wind and the paths they take. By midday the snow gradually gave way to rain—rain with drops so fine that I could see gravity waves radiating out from each raindrop as it impacted. As I waded the crossing from the cabin to the trail on the opposite shore, I watched this downpour pounding away like a tremendous number of little drummers creating craters on the stream with the huge, magnified raindrops.

A new freedom, going to bed whenever the body dictates, impresses me greatly. When my body gets tired enough, my mind just doesn't want to play games and keep going; in other words, I can't outsmart my body. I can't convince it that I should stay up longer and continue intellectual pursuits, and so I go to bed. As a result, I frequently wake up early in the morning. Today it was 3:00 A.M., and I awoke with a start.

The quietness at that time of morning is breathtaking. Every time I move in my sleeping bag it sounds like an army turning over and yet it's just the sound of the goose feathers adapting to my body contour. The only time that I am disoriented in the experience of being by myself is when I wake up. For the moment I actually feel or think that there is someone around me, and that is the one moment of dread or shock. This morning I was even more firmly awakened by two animals hissing at each other, and they sounded as though they were in the room. I couldn't go back to sleep. In fact, I was so alarmed by the hissing that I could feel the hair on the back of my neck stand up. What a fragile creature a human being is: half adrenaline and as easily frightened as other animals. Mink probably did the hissing.

After waking, I realized where I was and what was going on and I decided it would be the perfect time to hear some music. Last night I had laid out some music to play before I went to bed, including a tape of two violin concertos. Max Bruch's Concerto No. 1 is a lush romantic thing and I had been curious as to how well it would fit my mood, so I had played it last night. Occasionally my mind snapped loose and I would be asleep, and then would wake up again and hear more of the music. This morning there was nothing left except the other side, which is the Frank Martin Violin Concerto and not in my judgment pretty music, a far cry from the type of music I've been finding so suited to my need up here. This music is just a little bittersweet and generates a feeling of disquiet and stress, although not violent stress. Last night for the first time I felt so completely rested and so much at ease with myself that I could lie there as though there were nothing between me and the music. Every little facet of it emerged and I was tremendously impressed by the remarkable skill, the craftsmanship, the musical imagery.

In the twentieth century we are inclined to expect a creative event to reflect our own state of mind. I have a feeling that when a great creator, one of the gifted ones, creates music that is truly remarkable, the listener may just not be in the same psychological state of mind, or of repose, as the composer. The result is conflict and discrepancy, and so communication fails. Generally, I'm so enamored with hearing this music that I would stay up all night. But now my ego interfered. I was too pleased with the way things were going here to stay awake. Besides, it's frightfully cold outside that sleeping bag. You really have no idea what a fragile person a human being is when you strip him of his clothes and put him into a cold, cold situation. Getting up to go to the bathroom in the chill of night is a major enterprise; it takes considerable intestinal fortitude, for example, even to push oneself out of the sleeping bag. I also find it distressing trying to get the bag's zipper zipped back up after I've dashed back into bed.

The days are arbitrary here. I'm sure that already, if you were to ask me what I experienced on Day 3, I would confess that it all appeared to be one big romantic fuzzy dream. By the way, the idea that in dreams one compensates for the absence of people, one's family and one's friends, certainly seems to be true. I'm dreaming a great deal up here, and not all my dreams are happy dreams. But I think that over most of my life I've been living and doing things that, if not completely foreign to my nature, represented a way of life that I wasn't enamored with. Presumably, I was aware of it but shoved it into the background. Yet, one's unconscious has a lovely way of needling one from time to time.

Toward 4:00 P.M., wanting to expand my awareness of the new environment around me here, I thought I would walk up the trail that runs along the side of the lake. I couldn't envision getting all the way at that time of day, but I thought I'd walk until I got tired and then turn back. It was my first time on that mossy trail, and it was snow-covered, with puddles of water standing along it, a remarkable testimony to how poorly drained the little pockets are that form in the trail and along the side of the forest.

Mosses are of course very primitive plants, plants that for the sexual period of their existence require a film of water. I've also seen the plant succession that takes place adjacent to a glaciated surface where the glacier is receding, so I was aware that mosses are, if not aquatic plants, the next thing to it. As a matter of fact, most aquatic plants—ignoring the algae which are completely dependent upon water—are land plants that secondarily reinvaded water and somehow manage to make a go of it. The big problem, of course, is how do you pollinate your flowers and raise them up to the point where normal reproductive interplay can occur. In this act most aquatic plants reveal their past identity by poking their little heads out of the water to flower. Then the normal interplay of wind or insects accomplishes the pollination.

This trail has a tremendous amount of downed timber. There is no special graveyard where all trees eventually end. Wherever a tree falls is its resting place, and anyone who has attempted to work his way across downed trees, especially these up here with diameters 5 to 8 feet, has had to do some fancy climbing. A lot of trees have died, but are still standing and are being invaded by living things, most beautiful of which are the wood-conch fungi. I don't know at what moment the rotting of the root system occurs to allow these trees to tumble. Apparently there has been some wind in this area, for in some places a fair number of trees have toppled at the same time and have died and rotted, leaving a glade or a clearing. In these clearings the dominant plants, at least on this south shore of Lake Eva, appear to be salmonberry and devil's club.

I went for a fair length, maybe a half mile, and I was surprised at how much of a shore was in here and how open it was. When seen from the lake, the forest appears to march right down to the lake. I thought that there was no respite. Actually there is a little space in there. I came across some gigantic fresh bear tracks and, again, I can't help stressing the impression that these bears must be enormous. Cold, old prints have a remarkable persistence, lasting through a whole winter, but here were new ones. The bears must like to wade down through these slippery, mossy sinks to the lake, at least that was where these were headed. I didn't bother to proceed in that direction, needless to say.

As I retraced my steps to the cabin I was very much aware of my limitations physically. Every step was harder than the one before, as in a dream, and by the time I got back to the cabin I was totally exhausted. But I got the fire going and warmed the place up, although to do so I went through about a third of all the wood

I had accumulated and had the stove completely draped with pieces of wet wood that were gradually drying.

## April 24

I came in last night again wiped out with fatigue and made the mistake of having one cocktail. Instead of taking the sting out of my fatigue, it sent me into bed. There's something very puzzling about this isolation. I find myself completely obsessed with economizing time and economizing material. I'm losing the desire to eat very much. I know I'm obsessed with all the weight I've been carrying around, including me, and the most logical thing for me to do is to shed 20 pounds. The question is: How soon can one shed it? I'm becoming increasingly aware that one's mind functions in terms of one's body. Of course, I'm slightly embarrassed to discover that there's more to me than just my mind. But it's good to hear from the other parts; you know, the parts that make it possible for the mind to work, to put it where it ought to be and keep it balanced and functioning. It's good to have the feeling of being downright tired, to be aware that this muscle is feeling *ouch* or that that muscle is tight. The sense of one's body, I think, is something that we've lost track of. We're always so comfortable, everything is so easy. All we have is our mind, and the whole strategy of society is not only to provide us with our mind but to reinforce it with everyone else's mind. The result is that we live as though we're in a communal mental trance.

I was concerned with getting out word to everyone explaining why I wasn't on the radio as I was supposed to be and why I wasn't able to function completely the way we had planned it. I also wanted to make sure that there was some reality to my isolation. That is, occasionally I have to touch bases with those who are feeding me and providing me my way of life. I fired up the boat, loaded it with the mail, and went up the lake. It was one of those moments when, although the backdrop of mountains was only partially visible, the little cloud formations coming up over the top and spilling down the snowy slope produced a spectacular effect. Looking up past the mountains, I got the feeling that I could almost see the top. I knew, of course, where the top ought to be, but the blend of white clouds and white snow, muted by the shadow of the cloud, gave me the illusion that I was almost

looking up a stairway to . . . to where? It was a glorious passage-
way. I couldn't help thinking, looking up at those open spaces
amid the dotting of little black pines here and there, what a magnificent place this would be to ski. If one could do it. And this is
always the worst compulsion of the twentieth century—How do
we do it? Everywhere man goes he needs to be with others and
to have all his facilities. So, that if this were more accessible and
one could ski here, I imagine there would be the lovely ski lift
and the lovely ski lodge and the thousands of lovely, sprawling
skiers. . . .

The lake was an absolute perfect mirror. If nature ever deliberately designed mirrors, Lake Eva is one of the prettiest and fin-
est. I was completely enthralled with these mirrorlike images and
found myself photographing them with just enough of the reality
of what was reflected to establish the fact that I was playing a
game photographing a mirror. I wanted to hike to the far end of
the lake once more because I wanted to see what kind of effect I
could get with the alders. The alders mark this deltalike termina-
tion of the stream system that feeds Lake Eva. The alders around
the lake are very low. When I made my first tour of the lake by
boat the other night, I was struck by the fact that the delta alders
made a handsome photographic pattern, or line, and I wanted to
see what it looked like in the morning light.

I can't tell yet if I'm beginning to solve my photographic
problems and developing the habits that one can only partially
exercise back in the city. There photography is so interrupted
and limited by the ugliness of human technology. It's damned
embarrassing how difficult it is to find real naturalness around a
city. The city spreads and spreads and spreads and you have to
make a 30-mile trip just to get out to the perimeter, and what a
perimeter!

I was impressed with the fact that since the lake's length runs
east and west, the north side of the lake is actually in the sun
much more of the time than the south side. So, we have a hot
and cold side to the lake. The wind yesterday must have shaken a
lot of scale off the pines. The debris drifted down to the forest
floor and, of course, was picked up by tiny tributaries and carried toward the lake. As I watched the increased runoff into the
lake, I saw few signs of turbidity, and there's a very good reason
for this. The tremendous carpet of moss functions as a basin or
screen and the only substance that really gets by after passing
through this muslinlike material is pure water. Unfortunately,

pure plus stain—the amber stain of the decaying material of the peat moss. The streams do, however, collect and carry into the lake a fair amount of debris and it was interesting to see the lake surface dotted with debris. It all accumulated on the north side of the lake in the shade, indicating some pattern of distribution which as yet I don't understand.

At the upper end of the lake I was joyed to hear the sound of the airplane, which of course I hear all the time. Three or four times a day it passes overhead, generally running down the strait, out to one of the logging camps. But this time the sound grew louder and clearer, and sure enough the plane flew in, spotted me apparently, and landed on the lake to the east, but then taxied to a stop at the far end of the lake nearest the shelter cabin. Well, I thought, the pilot isn't going to come over and see me; he's going to drop off whatever he has—and Oh my God, here I am in the boat with all my outgoing mail and the grocery list. Now I realize I'm contradicting myself, favoring my isolation but dashing for the plane at the same time. I suppose it's natural for a human being to want to have a stockpile of groceries around. I would hate to abandon this venture at this stage of my ignorance or knowledge for lack of groceries. My son has sent me two marvelous cassettes on how to survive in the wilderness. It's ironical that the father, who doesn't really know how to handle this wilderness situation, is the one that may have to do the surviving.

The plane turned around as if it were going to take off again. The pilot looked as if he were planning to run me down as he came charging up at near take-off speed, which I suppose is around 60 mph, maybe more. Just before reaching me he cut the engine and skidded to a stop. I turned my boat around bravely and headed into the waves that he was kicking up. I gave a rather poor demonstration of seamanship in bringing my boat around and alongside him. He was eager to be on his way, and by the time he got three boxes of groceries on the pontoons ready to give me we must have exchanged all of three sentences. I asked him how the weather was in Sitka and what arrangements were made, whether he was coming in to Lake Eva on a set day or on a variable schedule, and he indicated the latter. I then apologized because my outboard was acting so poorly and gave a few helpless jerks trying to get the damn thing started so I could get out of his way. It did take over after what seemed to me to be an embarrassing two or three minutes. Then he turned on his engine, the propeller began spinning, and away he went. I leisurely sailed back toward my cabin.

On the last trip of the day to the estuary, I took the power saw to prepare the blind, and I was surprised to see how high the tide was, and how full the estuary. I didn't bring the shotgun down on this final trip, assuming that the power saw would make so much racket that I wouldn't be visited by Alaskan brown bears. They may be out of hibernation, but they haven't moved into this area yet. Maybe it's just as well. There were beautiful settings of ducks when I got there — two that I still have to identify, a flock of buffleheads (two males and about five females) and, of course, the common mergansers. Yesterday, I added a new bird which I was able to get a positive identification on, the fox sparrow, a bird that has a habit of scratching and kicking the ground for its feed. They were hopping around just outside my cabin door as long as I didn't move and I got a very good look at them. Fox sparrows are in fair abundance here, as are varied thrushes, which are calling.

I've become increasingly aware of the length of day. I got up the night before last and last night again around 9:30 for a final tour of the bathroom and was surprised to see that it was still twilight, still light enough to see the silhouette of the trees. I was surprised to discover that this morning it was light at 4:00. The sun rolls up this avenue on the stream here east to west as early as 6:00. At 6:10 it is hitting little portions of my islands.

It becomes more and more clear as time passes that walking up and down the trail and moving around is not the way to observe animals. The only way is to go to an area where animals are likely to be and sit — and as yet I haven't simmered down enough to have an overpowering urge to sit still for long periods.

I found myself photographing some more impressions of the vegetation, at the moment skunk cabbage, which I think is very imappropriately named. A skunk is a rather strikingly marked animal, not a very pretty animal in my judgment, certainly not when seen close up, and the smell is bad. I should mention here that I'm beginning to smell like something from a city dump. Twentieth-century cleanliness is great as long as you're dealing with other people, but when there's only one person around, one can pretty well put up with one's smell, I find. Only after the momentary shock of crawling out of one's sleeping bag does one realize how fragrant he is. I'm going on the theory that the more smelly I am the more likely the bear is to smell me. I'm told they don't like the smell of human beings and if this is true maybe they will give me a wide berth until such time as I am ready to come to grips with them.

## April 25

I think I'm still like a pinwheel that you light on the 4th of July. I'm going around with a great deal of vim and vigor but by the end of the day my powder runs out and I find myself just a bit too tired to reconstruct what happened. It is a remarkable feeling, the pendulous swing from fatigue in the evening to absolute power to burn in the morning. And to achieve full-bore when I get up is for me a new feeling. Back in the civilized world, I have to force myself into facing the day.

Yesterday I tried out my blind at the far end of the estuary. I started by arriving too late; the birds were already somnolent, having no doubt had a good morning feed. I'm talking now about my friends, the mergansers. The mergansers seem to feed when the tide is at the upper estuary, at least the mergansers that I'm in the process of filming. I can't be sure that these are the same ones I have seen before but I have a feeling there is one pair at the upper end of the lake, another at the lower end, and a third pair that combs the stream on their own. Probably there are others. I'll know better when I tramp a little more. By the time I got my camera tripod set up I made the horrible discovery that it didn't fit the ³⁄₈ screw on the pans. By the time I fiddled around and got the camera on the tripod as discreetly as a twentieth-century savage could, I saw that my mergansers were beginning to wake up and wonder what was going on up there on the hill. About the time I got everything in order the mergansers decided they had had enough of that and left. I stood there ready to go, but with nothing to shoot.

I decided to leave the camera, but the weather began to threaten and look more nasty so I put a plastic bag over the whole thing. Rather than wait around, I set out to cross the estuary, it being low tide, to see how the view toward Catherine Island would look, and maybe get a still or two of some of the sea lettuce in the estuary. These simple seaweeds develop only in the path of the deepest water, where they grow very well and are attached generally to the stones. There are two species, one a

*Wild garden on a partially sunken
log in Lake Eva.*

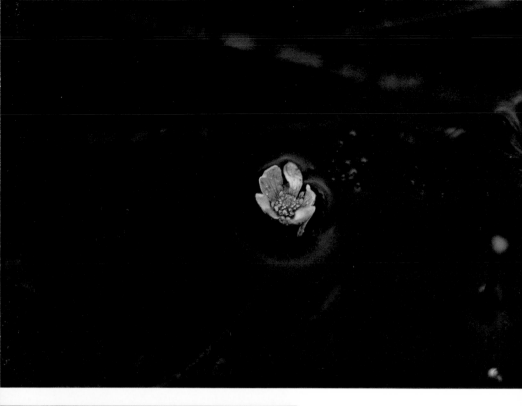

*A crowfoot flower floating on the surface of Eva Creek.*

*A new shoot, or fiddleneck, of the bracken fern.*

dark maroon-red and the other a brilliant light green. The light green one seems to be photosynthesizing at a fairly high rate and there's an enormous amount of entrapped air in the tangled mass of filaments. Later on I will look at this through a microscope. At the moment I'm held up by the lack of a microscope illuminator and slide. I went over the now nearly empty estuary; this requires a certain amount of caution because the tide comes in with a roar when it gets ready to. I didn't check exactly where the rapids were and it looked to me as if I had rapids all the way down to the lower basin, so I decided I had time enough to make the outing and I did. The tide has quite an area to cover before the flood of the basin. I filmed one shot of the promontory where the otter comes ashore and gets up into the timber—a rather pretty spot with red huckleberry showing, especially attractive in the lighting I had then. I went over again to the cloverleaf basin that builds up to the north and back into the trees, where I found a huge log that had been washed ashore, obviously from some lumbering operation. An ominous log, indeed.

# COLD SQUIRMS
# IN THE
# RAFT

*April 26*

Basically, I think, I am attempting to develop an ecological study, not one of great detail or with the sophistication of focus that a specialized scientist would bring to bear, but essentially one that tries to look at this lake, this stream, this estuary, through the eyes of a general scientist, a general practicioner, a G.P., if you will. I'm going into this not so much aware of everything that could happen but with the idea of seeing for myself what *does* happen. For example, let me get down some basics about this place.

I was very much taken the last few days by the fact that the lake and the stream are a culmination of a biological system which involves, underneath it all, a rocky substrate. It is relatively impervious to water except where the rock is fragmented, broken into cracks that reach down into the rocky spine of the mountains, mountains carved and sculptured, dug out by the overpowering weight of glaciers and the prodigious forces of gravity, to produce rather beautiful U-shaped valleys. Over this rocky veneer at present lies an absolutely tremendous forest which extends all the way to the top of the ridges on either side of the draining stream. The lake is a basin formed where the ice found weakness in the rock and scooped out a reservoir. Along the sides and up the slopes have developed a complex of life and a hemlock-dominated forest which thrusts up into the air and supports itself by matted roots. Over these roots lies a certain amount of soil, and over this soil and fabric of roots lies the carpet of sprawling mosses, a kind of blotter, springy to the foot and consisting primarily of muskeg, sphagnum, peaty mosses. This blotter is the first moderator of the weather, which here in southeast Alaska features a tremendous amount of water—snow in winter and rain in summer and fall.

The impressive event of the last couple of days is the explosion of plants pushing their way up through the moss and the leaf litter. Actually, there isn't much litter which is rather amazing; the few leaves lying around on top of the moss are largely under the salmonberry and they seem to be slower in rotting away. Of course, this is temperate forest, a so-called evergreen forest. There is actually a low prostrate canopy of evergreen-type flowering plants and nonflowering plants. But in the last two or three days there have been all types of buds beginning to pop up. The little necks of the ferns are showing and these are very charming. Fortunately, there are microclimates in the forest where small cold patches of air persist and where some things are conveniently delayed by this tiny, vestigial refrigeration process. The spring explosion of things beginning to sprout and all the perennial plants coming up is at least partially temperature dependent, but I'm sure there is an interplay of light as well.

## April 27

I have a reasonably good inventory of how a common merganser spends its day. It seems to be divided between eating, sleeping, feather-preening, and looking around: I get the feeling that the animal is making a complete visual tour of the shoreline of the estuary. The mallards were also in the estuary, but immediately took flight at the sight of me. It is easy to speculate on how man, through the ages, has lived on and hunted duck and how gradually a species has evolved which reacts properly to the sight of him and gets out. The thing that most impresses me about the mallard is his extreme sensitivity to sound. The merganser is a fish-eating duck and not normally hunted, so perhaps hasn't such an extreme fear of man; but even this bird, if you show yourself, will take off instantly.

If all I'm doing is chatting, maybe chatting is my way of fighting the solitude. As yet I haven't felt lonely, deprived, or really the need for anyone. It's hard to realize as I sit here that the raindrops falling on my cabin are not primarily rain coming from the sky but the aggregation of tiny raindrops falling off the trees with a tremendous plop when they get big enough. So the rain that I'm hearing is very loud and gives me the impression that it's raining hard when it is really only a delayed response, so to speak, of rain that has washed over the needles and leaves of the trees above. A little like running through a leaky umbrella.

## April 28

I put the place in better order today, although I must admit that order to me consists in having as many things spread out in as many places as possible.

I was again impressed with the thought of how difficult it is to see everything that's going on along the trail. The forest has limited visibility because of the trees and the shrubs, and one gets accustomed to looking down, a very logical strategy along this trail because it's so thickly covered with fallen trees and holes. Step into a hole and you sink down far enough to require a hard pull against the suction. Of course, there's always the danger of slipping, too. For the first time today I noticed false hellebore beginning to burst out in great numbers. The trailing raspberry plants are all up and there are a lot of new ferns growing, the very delicate ones. I didn't find any new bear tracks, and the old bear tracks definitely seem oldish. It still amazes me that those bear tracks in the peat moss survived the whole winter.

## April 29

As dark-gray overcast as it may be, I'm not cold. I've actually found myself shedding my halibut shirt when I was wearing the brush jacket and I got the distinct impression that the battle between spring and winter, which had been fought at this elevation in the early part of the week, was diminishing. The battleground has moved up the slope. The only puzzling thing to me is a drop in the level of the stream. I assume the higher level that I encountered when I first came into the area was generated by the snowfall of the week before, which was appreciable, probably 6 to 7 inches.

I suddenly realized it was getting dark again and I said, Oh no, not another rain. Sure enough, it's beginning to look that way, as though maybe moving the raft down the river today would have to be canceled on account of rain. My idea was to get footage of me coming downstream, wading next to a raft. Onshore I would set up a remote-control camera and activate it by a transmitter in the raft.

I had set up the tripod station along the stream in order to get familiar with the radio relay and the remote operation of the movie camera. What finally transpired was a miserable exercise in which every error actually was, I think, to the benefit of the company underwriting the Lake Eva project.

I started out planning to shoot at wide angle. When I got down to the stream and looked the situation over, I changed my mind. I decided it would be better not to have the figure—me—so remote, so I put it on telephoto. I got down with the camera and discovered error one: I'd forgotten the pigtail that connects the battery to the camera. I had the battery and a camera on the bank of the stream, but no connecting piece. Of course, that meant another trip back to the cabin. I sloshed up to the cabin and back, and rigged the camera properly. I had also brought the transmitter and now I found it wouldn't operate. I made the remarkable discovery that I hadn't put the antenna on tightly enough, but when I got that on right it seemed to work. I then went back to the cabin to rig the rest of this charade, which involved getting the rubber raft in the water. I'd carry a long pole and at least a two-by-two with a hook on it for the waterfall, thinking that if worse came to worse I could pull myself to safety. I certainly didn't want to go drifting down that waterfall, nor did I want to have to abandon the raft in water that was too deep. I thought it would be smart to wade the route to make sure it was negotiable. There's no obvious current—there is some, but no rapids, no heavy current. I stepped off the bank and made the frightful discovery that it was a soft bottom. With visions of going in up to my eyes and being unable to extricate myself from this deep mire, I quickly hauled myself back on the beach and decided that, for this sequence, I would have to raft down, sitting in the raft rather than walking alongside it. This would perhaps make a more interesting cinematic experience anyway.

I was a little apprehensive. I was also extremely tired, it now being about 5:00 in the afternoon. The sun had been playing peek-a-boo through part of the afternoon—a usual activity up here—but it was getting progressively less peek-a-boo and at the moment was what I would call cloudy-bright with just the slightest suggestion of shadow. The sun glinted weakly through a cloud cover that was becoming uniformly gray as it veiled the sky, so I had a feeling that only with luck would I pull off this venture with the light I had.

So I started out with some doubts about the scene in the first place, some uncertainty in my own mind as to whether I had picked the right day or the right camera angle. How easily a human being, when doing something that he senses isn't quite under control, begins to find all sorts of reasons for not doing it. But I did want the scene and furthermore, since everything was finally "go" with the tripod and camera, I wanted to finish the job and move the equipment on for other projects. I put the raft in the water and jumped in, having first secured the transmitter as high up in the raft as possible. I had placed the shotgun across the bow and made sure I was in the proper costume beforehand. Much to my surprise, when I jumped in, even though it was just 3 feet deep there, I managed to shift a fair amount of water into the rubber raft. So there I was, kneeling in the raft, which encircled me like a skirt of rubberized canvas—a rather flimsy material it always seemed to me—with water well up around my knees. I started downstream and when I reached the point at which I thought I was coming into view of the camera, I activated the camera.

I felt slightly uneasy. It seemed to take a lot of time to get across that viewpoint. I hadn't bothered to flag the limits of the scene so I was relying on my judgment as to when I would sail through it.

I squinted explorerlike, which delayed the action, and then I poled through what proved to be a comedy of errors. I really didn't like what I had to do to get the boat past the tripod, and I wanted to give the illusion that I was looking for things as usual. Keeping a sharp watch was a smart idea anyway, now that brown bear was undoubtedly out on the prowl. In time I looked up and saw the tripod, which encouraged me to think that I was really getting it at last, so I went on looking and squinting. When I thought I had drifted far enough, I released the button. I wanted to shoot that scene from a couple of other angles and shoot two or three scenes so it would give the film cutter something to play with. I pulled the boat onto an otter-run area and tied it up. Looking over at the shrubbery, I tried to figure out the clearest way to get back to the trail. I started off in a generally left direction over the grass, which I found beginning to make a tremendously active growth, and lo and behold, I walked out into the clearing where the camera was. If I do not seem as happy with the conclusion of this adventure as I should, it may be because of what I had discovered when I pulled the boat into the landing and undid the camera that was lashed to the raft: the transmitter was not on. Because of my desire to save batteries, I'd turned it off between the time I tested the camera site and the time I drifted into what I thought was the scene. So here, by luck, I had not wasted the 100 feet of film. I say luck because by the time the scene was being shot, judging from my check of the camera diaphragm, I was at least one stop underexposed and, moreover, I hadn't even been *in* the scene.

Nature is really remarkably the same, even though she has an infinite variety. I undid the camera, loaded up the packsack, and returned to the cabin. I hammered on my wood supply to work out some of the ire caused by my raft fiasco. I got another box of kindling split. Proper kindling must be in a variety of sizes, I've discovered. I wasn't getting it fine enough to burn at first; now I'm very good at making the fine kindling and what I need are some intermediate pieces. I'm on my way to becoming a fairly skillful woodsman, but it's going to take a while. Of course, I could have done a lot of reading about the ways of woodsmen, but there's only one way to learn, by God, and that's to do it yourself. You can read about it and what happens, but after a while your mind becomes fatigued with all the words, and you turn off, or don't see, or don't remember all the detail.

The raft-and-camera disaster was the one cinematic effort of the day. Long ago, in the morning, I had started out with a few letters to put in the bag in the boat, thinking that by this time the Forest Service would be coming in to make a check on why the radio transmitter wasn't operating. Now I finally got the mail to the boat and then I started up the other trail leading along the lake, thinking I would go a short distance to see if there were any bear tracks because that was the area where I had seen tracks before. I found my bear tracks. By this time, of course, the rain and dew in the morning had nearly obliterated them, at least the toe tracks. It's incongruous when you think about it: here is a large animal leaving tracks in the sphagnum drainage areas where I'm always a little apprehensive to walk for fear of sinking down and getting bogged in. I suppose what I really ought to do is walk *in* those bear tracks, but somehow those tracks seem sacred to me. They are a sobering reminder that this is bear country and that I must remain at least moderately alert. I'm not sure that, under normal conditions, the bear is as bad as people picture; on the other hand, there are situations when a bear would attack a human being, and I'm particularly vulnerable because I'm preoccupied with every bit of the environment and not focused exclusively on the bear, like a hunter.

Right after supper, as I went out to dispose of the garbage, I looked up and saw a marten in the feeding tray where the foresters used to put the fish when they lived here. It was an incredible surprise. The animal wasn't really afraid of me. He showed a little apprehension, stared at me briefly, and then went down the post of the feeding platform and licked the bacon grease that I'd put out. He stared at me again and then disappeared into the shrubbery below. Now I'm tempted to try to make friends with this guy by offering him some fish. It's against my religion to interfere with nature, because I much prefer to observe animal behavior without interfering. But in this case, I'm tempted. Those martens are certainly attractive beasts and I can't help feeling a bit unhappy in the back of my mind, knowing that the human female adorns her body with fur coats. I think one can argue the attractiveness of the fur, but it is a sad thing that this material growing and making possible the life of an animal — it's a tremendous specialization — should end up coating some human female who isn't even really cold. The early trappers forced their way across the continent living much more primitively than I am. What made their way of life possible was the furs, and the thought that these furs were caught by traps is harsh. It is a very cruel way to catch an animal. Cruel but effective, I suppose. What happened is history, but it's sad, and when I think of the tremendous thrill of seeing this beast — and here I am an old experienced zoologist — I will say one thing for sure. It beats seeing them in a zoo. Amen, amen.

## April 30

I poked my head out the window once to see how heavily it was raining and found the marten back in the feeder, working on the bacon grease. He looked bedraggled and I don't think he was too fond of the rain, but he was fond enough of the bacon grease to pay my feeder a visit. He was quite sensitive and fearful. I thought that he didn't know that I was looking at him, and I was extremely quiet in the cabin so there was no acoustical cuing from me. There was acoustical cuing, however, from the rain-drops, the secondary raindrops that bang away on my roof. Every time one of these thumpers came down on the roof he'd twitch his ears and turn his head and look in the direction of the noise; he kept eyeing the area above the cabin, over the screens, over his head, as though on the lookout for an eagle or a hawk. He was definitely apprehensive and not nearly as at ease in that sit-uation as he had been when he and I were staring at each other.

Another very exciting thing came about. I again looked out and my pair of mergansers that patrol this area of the stream were proceeding up. When they reached the point at which I wade across on this side, they began to work their way to the other side. I got the movie camera out and poked it through the window opening just to see what image size I would have if I wanted to photograph from the front door. It wasn't a bad image, about the same that I've been using out in the estuary. As I watched them they reached the other side and the female pro-ceeded right into the undercut bank and actually disappeared in the undercut portion of the stream. It made a very beautiful ef-fect, watching her dig in and out of those undercut passages with the reeds poking out. The male seemed quite complacent and stayed in the middle of the far channel. At no time did he join her. A small log juts out into the stream and as she approached it she gave herself a little speed and hopped on top of it and then went on over to the other side and continued on her way. No detouring around it.

## May 1

I got back from the lake at 1:30 wanting to capitalize on the sunshine and shoot that scene going down the river on the raft again to give the remote radio another try. I had the raft in position, so I went down and set up the camera and, lo and behold, I'd done it again—left the battery at the cabin. I had to make another trip back and it's a lot farther down than it looks to the eye; by the time you go back and wade the stream and get into the cabin and pick up the battery and wade the stream and go back down the trail, it's a 30-minute jaunt; not quite as bad as to the lake, which is an hour trip. I got back and then rafted down and pulled to the shore and went over to see how much footage I'd shot, and I hadn't shotten anything, which was very mysterious. I'd be damned if I was going to be wiped out. That was the third try on that scene that I'd laid an egg on. To get the raft back, I knew I couldn't wade it because of the deep water right in close to shore, and I didn't want to flood my boots, so I dragged my raft across the marsh. I got it back into position and floated down. That time I registered about 45 feet of footage that covers my passage with the telephoto fully extended. It should be a fairly nice shot; there was plenty of light, in fact it was just perfect. So then, having discovered that I could do it, I went back and did it a final time, by now getting a little bit of pleasure out of it, too. This time I left the lens wide open so that one could see the general view, and this would give the film cutter a chance to work the same material with two different points of view. Unfortunately, this time down the channel I lost control of the boat a couple of times and went around in a circle. It will take quite a bit of cutting magic to make it look straight.

By this time it was 4:00 P.M. In the process of doing this I had sunk into the marsh and flooded out. Well, I flooded out two places, in the marsh and again in the stream, so I came back to the cabin with boots full of water and of course my pants and underwear and socks were wet. Rather than waste an opportunity, I went on down to the stream, stripped from the waist down, and soaped up. Using a coffeepot I then rinsed the soap off with water; and it was chilly. When I returned to the cabin again I was on the cold side, but no harm done.

The picture-taking didn't turn out well. I got across the stream and up the trail past the first skunk cabbage flat, only to be bogged in mire as I started up a little grade. The trail today is overrunning with water so it's hard to tell where the stepping places are and where the bottomless pits are. The result is that about 50% of the time I'm slipping off and sinking into mud halfway up to my knees. When I pull myself out, the suction reminds me that it takes a pull to work against the weight of our atmosphere. I stepped in with one foot, and as I tried to pull myself out with the other I suddenly found myself flat on my back on an incline slope of swishey, ishey mud. With both feet thoroughly in the mud, I made a very fine back print, especially rump print, in that mess besides getting my camera muddy. I finally got myself clear and after a volley of swear words I decided to hell with it, it wasn't worth it, and I picked up the camera, made sure it wasn't in any great danger of being ruined completely by running water, wiped it off a bit, and put it back in its plastic bag to park it alongside the trail.

One of the delightful things about my wilderness is that I can leave anything anywhere and do anything anywhere and there is no possibility of somebody coming along and lifting it or embarrassing me. I was so irritated by the fall that I decided to go to the lake and carry back two cans of gasoline instead of one, as I had originally intended. I zipped up the trail the best I could. It's not really a zip on a day like this, but more of a slip.

The sun had already crawled back over the ridge to the north of the lake, but it looked as though it was going to clear up, and as I stood there taking in the view I spotted an otter making his way along the edge of the submerged aquatic plants. He went along breathing and then diving. He would raise his head and come up to look around and then he'd dive. He was, of course, on the other side of the lake so he didn't look big—and they aren't big even when seen close up. At any rate, it still reminded me of a little whale, although I couldn't hear the breathing tonight. He sped up periodically and I could tell when he was in a school of fish. He would take off like a shot; I mean, that is an animal that can cover a lot of distance fast. Then, when he got past this area where he had apparently been feeding, he swam over to a point. In the meantime, a pair of unidentified birds showed up. I'm not sure if they were loons or ducks, having left the binoculars home. They kept moving farther away and I continued to watch the otter for about 20 minutes. By this time he'd moved over to the point to the west of the shore, where the planes come in; then I lost him for a bit. The ducks—as I think they were—started coming this way and then the otter came out into the lake and it looked to me as though he were making a beeline for the ducks. Now, of course, that could have been an illusion; I was looking at this from a distance. Then one of the ducks dived and disappeared underwater while the otter was still heading in that general direction. Without any warning up popped both ducks, screaming, and I thought, my God, the otter grabbed them. They started to swim in the most violent, disorganized, confused manner I've ever seen. They just flopped and flopped with their wings beating the water, kicking up a tremendous disturbance. They went maybe three city blocks, then settled back in the water, and everything was normal again. Here I think was a case where an otter was trying to get a duck dinner.

Today, for the first time, I got a good look at a chestnut-backed chickadee. I also got an extremely good observation on the dipper, or water ouzel, this morning and again this afternoon. I'm very anxious to get going on the latter species. The one this morning was singing and I have a suspicion there was a nest near the rapids area. I think the ravens have caught on to my marten feeder. I put out a strip of raw bacon last night which was gone this morning, and there was a raven in the tree by the porch.

## May 2

Spring is starting to get here. When I woke up this morning there was the usual thunderous thump-thump of dewdrops on the roof, more raindrops magnified that collect from the branches. I pushed myself out of bed and suddenly I could tell when I looked out the window that the sun was out. That was good news indeed, so I got up, put on my wool pants, and peeked out. It was a fairyland. I couldn't believe it: the sunlight was dancing on the stream and illuminating the dewdrops hanging from the hemlock branches.

It's unbelievable how synchronized flowering is statistically. A few flowers come out a day or two or three ahead of the mean, and then they are everywhere. For example, the skunk cabbage is nearly finished blooming. They were flowering when I first came here and now they're shedding pollen, although you still see a few new ones cropping up. It's because of the microclimates.

I made a trip to the lake in the evening and brought back another 5 gallons of the white gas, after which I cut some wood, built a fire, and had supper. The first time I had soup here, I discovered that I was ravenously hungry. I also found myself making a slurping sound, and I have a feeling that this has to do with my isolation. One likes to hear one's own person making familiar sounds. That slurping sound is definitely taboo in polite society, but here it's a manifestation of pleasure. In other words, one makes the sound simply because one is enamored with eating and ravenously hungry, and everything tastes extraordinarily good. I should say everything with one exception. I cooked a pot of beans the other day which was just terrible.

## May 3

One of the subtle things about a forest is the acoustics. I'm still a little sticky about bears, so I advertise myself very loudly when I'm walking. I haven't seen one yet and I really don't know how far away he'd be if I did see him, but I'd like to have a chance to at least go the other way. Today, I went into a glade where I've seen bear tracks and started hacking away with the power saw. As anyone who has used a chain saw knows, it makes a lot of racket. When I turned it off and my hearing came back, the whole forest was reverberating with the ugly sound of the power saw, although it had been off for at least a minute. How much natural sound in that area had I completely wiped out by this foreign and very unpleasant noise?

I went back to the cabin to give the ailing generators another look, thinking that maybe something miraculous had happened while I was away. I started to work on the one that, at least until lately, has always run. I was irritated because I thought I knew about the machinery of this operation, and I don't know anything about it. I need the generator going not only for lights but for the batteries for the cameras. I gave up on this generator and then looked at the other one and gave it a couple of healthy tugs. It was an even uglier beast. The fly shaft wouldn't so much as turn over. Then I discovered that the spark plug was undone. It looked extremely rusty and I couldn't imagine that it would be a good connection. I went in and looked at the new plug that I had brought as a spare and decided that it was the same type. I would just change spark plugs and have a nice shiny clean connection. But when I did that and then pulled on it, nothing happened. The instructions are on a decal in front. About one-third of the decal had been scuffed off, so I could read only the back two-thirds of each sentence. Finally I thought I deciphered something about a cut-off position on the choke. After figuring out where the cut-off must be, I tried it first in one position and nothing happened, then another and another, and then, lo and behold, it coughed and kicked over three bang-bang-bangs — and stopped. Nevertheless, I was encouraged by this and decided that the adjustment of the carburetor was wrong. I saw two screws and thought that one of them *must* be gas and one *must* be air, so I fiddled with that a while and made a series of slight adjustments. It worked a little better, and a little better, and to make a long story short, about 30 minutes later it was adjusted and running. *Then* I discovered that the damn thing was smoking like mad and decided they had put too much oil in the gasoline. After I ran the oily gasoline out, it finally began to function pretty well. Finally I had it tuned up to where it was running in the most economical position. Unfortunately, the most economical position provides about one hour of generating, and then it's out of gas. The minute I got the thing running, I dashed into the cabin and saw the lights burning brilliantly. Quickly I plugged in every available battery including the strobe, the three tape recorders, and all the camera batteries available. It reminded me of a Christmas tree with about twenty strings of lights.

I heard a toad call yesterday on one of the two islands in the stream. This morning I heard the pitch pipe sound of the varied thrush go off like an alarm clock. I looked out the window and it was daybreak — a quarter to five. I got out of my nice warm sack and stepped onto the icy-cold floor of this cold, cold cabin. Walking into the kitchen, I got out my exposure meter, which gave me a radiance of 2, the lowest number on the scale. So, for whatever it's worth, I have a light reading on the early morning activity of the varied thrush.

# WALKING AROUND IN A TENT

## May 4

Delighted to have the treat of seeing two flying wedges of whistling swans going by, transforming what I thought would have been merely a perfectly wet situation. It's a rainy day and nature is resuscitating, just keeping the pump primed; in other words, nature's pump: a thermo pump which is pumping water out of the ocean and a pressure system that moves the moisture eastward. The mountains cool it and squeeze it and extract the moisture, while the trees and moss act as a reservoir, so everything isn't washed away. Then we have the consequence, which is life. Life in the stream, brooks, rivulets — even at the height of the rain, which has been coming down steadily and hard for 24 hours, the stream is just as clear as ever. If anything, the springs get clearer.

## May 5

I can't help feeling as I walk down the trail that if every human being could be given the chance every day to walk on a woody trail, 99% of the emotional problems and frustrations would vanish.

There wouldn't be any need for psychologists or for religion. It's just that natural environment, and man was given the sensory things to see it with, satisfies the basic needs. How sad that man still goes through the ritual of professing his sensory need for this kind of beauty in the form of parks and gardens, so man-manipulated, so arbitrary and limited in scope. The dramatic thing about the undisturbed forest is the bewildering abundance of life everywhere, thousands, millions of plants. I must count a square foot of ground to see how many moss plants are in it. It's staggering. You have the dying, the dead things all lying around. Nature moving very slowly; it really doesn't move at all, it's all in a steady state, there will always be another to replace. That feeling of life going on is, to me, the basic geometry for all of us and human beings should see just this, and perceive it. Then I think we wouldn't be panicked by the thought that one's particular ego would not always be there to perceive it. These things go on; the important thing is they go on in a meaningful way. I don't think I was ever really experienced in spring to the degree I am now. This is one of the problems of being a youngster. Then we have so much energy and vitality that we are always trying to find something to occupy ourselves — and we just don't see the forest in the spring in the way it really ought to be seen. So here I am in the time when things are coming and I'm discovering that everything comes up differently. No two sprouts look the same. What sprout is going to be what?

I proceeded along the trail in a reverie. I had brought along my snippers and discovered that the trees had on the whole dropped their branches down to a different level. Ordinarily a hemlock branch points up, but when it is thoroughly wet with water it has a lot of give and drops down. I was constantly hit in the face with branches that dropped down with water so I pruned the trail a bit to make it good for 5 feet 11. I put the branches I cut off into those bottomless pits that my boots occasionally slip into. I may get enough in there to improve the trail. By the time I reached the boat, I realized that I had put my rain pants into my boots, and naturally the rain was pouring down my jacket, down my pants, into my boots — and I discovered the rain was cold. When I got to the lake I found that it was about a foot higher than the sand bar on which I had pulled my boat. The bar was now under 3 or 4 inches of water, and the lake was full. It made me wonder whether or not I would get back. How silly.

As I started up the trail, heading from the stream over to the first marshy skunk cabbage area, I heard a huge crack and a rock

slide came down through the timber, close to where I was standing. At first I wondered whether or not I'd be wiped out, but
then I began to think, no, maybe that's a bear. I really don't like
being in the woods on a day when it's raining hard and my hearing is impaired by the noise and the wind changes so much that
I'm uncertain where my scent is. I'm much more apprehensive
when I leave the trail and have to work my way up and over fall-
en logs and through the brush. It's not an easy task.

## May 6

Cloudy, windy, rainy again. In fact, this is the first severe
storm of two days' duration that I've had up here. I got terribly
wet on the 5th and felt that what I'd learned just tramping
around wasn't achieving anything. There is a lot that can be
learned sitting around, even in the cabin looking out. Yesterday
afternoon I had six or eight tree swallows feeding in the shallow
area here directly out from the cabin. I'm reasonably certain that
these birds like to feed over smooth water, which gives them a
visual chance to see their food as it's coming up. The animal glides
and keeps up a fairly high flying speed and is a very adroit maneu-
verer and high-performance bird that gets extremely close to the
water and takes it's food up from the surface. I note this animal
feeding both here on the lake and in the estuary, so it's definitely
one of the food-chain animals and is taking an extensive toll of
insect life.

I find that the clothing I'm wearing, the kind worn by lumbermen, trappers, fishermen, and sportsmen, is adequate to keep
me comfortable. It's ecologic clothing, so to speak, and if you use
a certain amount of intelligence, like wearing the rain gear *outside*
your waders, very little water will make its way into contact with
your body. Unfortunately, I don't like the hood over my head
because sooner or later I begin to get wet across the top of my
shoulders and I also feel as though I were walking around in a
tent.

## May 7

I came across some fairly fresh bear tracks. They are on the
trail for only a brief moment and appear then to lead down to
one of the peat moss clearings which might have been a tributary.

I mentioned how the downed timber lying across the slopes generates sedimentation basins. Soon you have a whole staircase series of paddies; natural, not like the artificial ones they have in Indochina and the Far East. There is a very pleasing aspect to the situation in that the moss is fairly thick in these paddies and the bear tracks show up from the winter before. This bear had been working along one of these and for the first time I could clearly see that he had pulled up, scooped up, one of the skunk cabbages but hadn't eaten much. It is puzzling. If they are really ravenously hungry when they are fresh out of hibernation and are vegetarians, why wouldn't they eat a lot more than they did?

## May 8

I got up at ten to four briefly and checked the light. It was clearly light enough to call it daybreak. The upper portion of the ridge was lit by the very pale light of dawn. At 4:10 I heard my first bird song, the varied thrush again, and by 5:00 most of the birds were tuned up and hard at it. It's a little tough to respond naturally to the sound of nature when you're in a cabin. This cabin was winterized and I think it's got a layer or two of some insulation, heat insulation. As a result, it is pretty well cut off from sounds of the outside. I can generally pick up the airplane sound as it goes by to the lumber camp, but most of the sounds in nature are isolated. The one sound that gets to me in here of course is the thump of the raindrops as they come dripping down from the trees, and this is a disturbing sound. Other than that, there is virtually no sound in the cabin except the crackle of the fire.

I sat on the island and shot the bird pictures, largely the hermit thrush, the dipper, the golden-crowned sparrow, plus the tree swallow. These birds are mainly working the margin of the stream, feeding for the most part on emergent insects. There's a lot of insect life generated by the stream, and the stream itself has an interesting habit that deserves mention. If you watch it carefully you see that the velocity slows down at the edge and the little obstructions jutting out from the bank create a small eddy, causing a lot of water-bearing debris to be eddied in and hang up around the obstructions. The most dramatic of these obstructions in the stream is that area by the logjam, and here it's exciting to watch the action of the birds on the logjam as they fish out the food that is brought to them. You could almost say it is a conveyer belt. It's odd, how, in the search for words, one uses terms in such conflict with the concept of nature. The idea of a conveyer belt is one of the uglier connotations of the industrial revolution and the idea that parts are moved along and various people do various things is odious. Yet there is a descriptive overlay I think here that makes the use of the word relevant and gets the idea across.

Another interesting thing: accumulating on the upper side of the logjam is an appreciable raft of organic reeds that have washed out of the lake. Apparently these rafts will stay there until they rot and can get through the jam. A lot of the birds actually get out and walk on the jam, looking it over for insects. I assume the insects have pulled themselves to safety out of the water. They could be emergent insects but they're probably terrestrial insects that fell or were washed into the water and then crawled up on this life-preserver. Of course, in nature, animals are continuously hungry and they really have to get out and look for food or they're not going to get enough to make it.

Throughout the day I kept hearing an odd sound, like someone bowling in the woods. I couldn't place the sound. It just didn't seem to fit in. By mid-afternoon it dawned on me that the work crew from Fish and Game had come up from the estuary by boat and were in the process of cleaning up the cache of gasoline barrels that they had left at the waterfall. You would think that the first thought of a human being in isolation would be to hot-foot it down there just to have the fun of talking to someone, but I'd be damned if I would stop filming from the island when I had some light, so I stayed there and worked. When the noise gave up, around 4:00 P.M., I went down to the estuary and, sure enough, the work crew had been there. I could hear the sound of a boat already out to sea, but there was no trace of them although there were still two or three barrels left to clean out. I continued on out the estuary and the tide was very high. It went on up to the waterfall and up the tributary to the south, which is the tributary area where the first bear tracks were. I walked in that general area hoping I might see fresh signs of bear, but there was nothing. It is logical to assume that because of the noise of the work crew no bears would be there.

At least I got the tripod set up on the island and while I was doing that all sorts of birds came by. Two mergansers swam up the stream and I filmed them as they fed. I sat there the whole time in my brown field jacket and black hat without moving, so I was able to watch them. One of them was preening and swimming upstream. He was using one foot to work his feathers into place and the other to swim. I get the impression the female is the more aggressive. She seems to lead the way generally and is a quicker bird. The male is more lethargic. Of course the swallows were feeding. They seem to like this shallow flat area where the water flows more slowly and the surface is calmer. I got a very good look yesterday at four green-winged teal and they are handsome birds. I was close enough so they didn't have that disappointingly tiny look that makes you wonder whether you're looking at a duck or not. They seemed good-sized. I hadn't seen green-winged teal in quite a few years.

## May 9

Essentially two islands develop downstream from the lake, and the stream at this point consists of three channels, since there is a middle channel separating the two islands. They stand up above the water 2½ to 3 feet, so there's an appreciable chunk of land. It completely eludes me as to why those islands should be there geologically, but they are; and they're a useful point of reference and actually provide me my best flower show. There is an extensive bed of skunk cabbages in those islands and the emergent coarse grass is also very pretty. It's blue-green in color. Then, of course, I have a very wild situation on the nearest island. It's bridged to this side of the shore by three downed trees. I don't know whether someone cut them down and placed them to make a bridge or whether they just landed there naturally. They've been there long enough that they reflect the activity of weather and the flow of the stream. The stream often almost covers them and has completely rotted off the bark and the branches sticking down into the water. This generates turbulence and almost creates an illusion of a partial or slight dam. More interesting than that, those logs trap debris that washes down from the lake. After every storm a fair amount of organic debris is flushed down when the little intermittent tributaries overflow their banks. This debris accumulates at the lake. A lot of it is reed material which is filled with air, so it floats and eventually is rafted out of the lake and goes downstream. I suppose a good percentage of it actually eddies about and quite a bit of it accumulates along the logs to form a raft, a conspicuous carpet of floating material. I noted that perching birds were feeding both on the raft itself and on the log jam. Certain of the perching birds do use the stream for their insect food. The fox sparrow, for example, gets down in this raft and kicks around on it. The forest does modify the kind of water that's here and has a profound effect on its constant flow. But I'm not doing a simple study of a forest, so ecologically I'm looking at the forest as a bio-mass of material that ultimately will destroy the lake and severely modify the stream.

I can't rely too much at this stage on my personal knowledge. Of course, one can always fall back on the experts if one wants to. I really can't perceive too much of a difference between this kind of a stream and one that doesn't have a lake, but certainly the fish know the difference. The sockeye salmon come up this stream to spawn and will not come up any streams that lack lakes. Similarly, all the Dolly Varden trout that are drawn to Lake Eva know that there's a difference between water coming out of a lake as opposed to water coming out of a valley system that doesn't have a lake. So there's that.

I sat on the island filming across, and much to my horror I discovered that it was a great day, a very sunny day. If anything, the sun was too hot for ideal filming. I was trying to film the birds on the bridge of logs, the upstream raft of material. While I was setting up to do this and was still in the process of carrying things across the stream, I saw in the channel between the far island and the bank an otter, and he was fairly stationary. He was diving and working in probably not more than a foot of water. Naturally I thought I'd better get over to that island and start photographing. The question was how to get there. The otter was south and downstream from the island, and my walking across the stream on the rocks would probably scare him, but I decided I'd take my chances and walk the logjam. To get to the logjam turned out to be a problem because there was a clutter of lumber on the beach partially overgrown with salmonberry and a lot of what I call downed trash. It was a struggle to force myself through this tangle. When I reached the logjam it was apparent that if I were careful I should be able to get across it. I rushed as much as I could, got onto the island, and grabbed a camera. I didn't have quite enough color differentiation for what was· going on, but it was a fairly close scene. The otter, apparently, was feeding on something underneath the stones. I went through nearly 100 feet of film before I decided I wanted to get as close as

I could. In the process, I must have disturbed the otter. He looked up, saw me, raised up on his haunches — and then took off, heading right for the overhang of the bank. So I have a rather nice sequence showing how the otter evaded me and his normal route of travel in that situation. That is why you rarely see otters in the stream; they're there, but they are not about to leave themselves vulnerable to predation. . . . That was an exciting introduction to an otter, which is obviously a wild one, and I hope it is only the beginning of a long period of mutual observation.

I had supper at 8:30 and I didn't run the generator or build a fire. I was so tired that I went to bed at 9:30, although I woke up again and noted that it was still light enough to move around at 10:30. Now that I have arbitrarily picked a stage from which to study the stream, I think I can work out much of its biology right from the cabin area. It is nice to have that possibility, although there are several substreams that I naturally want to include also.

## May 10

I rose about 6:00 A.M. The cabin was 40°, the air was 20°, and the water was 43°. About 10:00, without any warning, four fellows walked up the trail — my first contact with civilization beyond the pilots who bring the groceries. They were as surprised to see me as I was to see them. They were from the logging camp on Peril Strait and we had a good visit. They were just out stretching their legs and had left three other loggers at the boat. I waded back across to the cabin, picked up a couple of six-packs, and walked on down to their boat. It was the first time I've been down to the ocean in about a week and a half and it was a very low tide. I was pleased to be there, and they were delighted about the beer. We had a chat and then I helped them pull their boat back about 150 feet into the water, and they took off.

Because of the harsh light, I gave up photographing for a while and went back to the lake to find out how badly the boat leaked since I last worked on it. I went on up to camera position A and found it just as I had left it. There hasn't been a thing on that promontory, which brings up an interesting point. This was an extremely mild winter (some of the lumber camps opened up in March). I wonder if the bears didn't have to waste as much of their winter fat in maintaining body temperature as usual and maybe are sleeping longer. There is very little sign of use of the skunk cabbage and the lumbermen tell me that they would probably root out all the skunk cabbage along these streams in normal years. I guess the Alaskan brown bear show is yet to come.

I've had a few moments of depression when I felt overpowered by the problem of finding and bringing into focus the kind of animal life involved in this study. A lot of this animal life is microscopic, and a lot of the larger animals — the salmon, the bear — are not necessarily on the scene. The fire is crackling. It's chilly enough. I've got on my halibut jacket and I'm still not warm.

## May 11

I have the distinct feeling that on sunny days the birds tend to avoid the raft debris up against the logjam and the edges of the stream area. Perhaps they're more conspicuous in the sun. It may be that there has been a marked increase in the length of day and it's quite possible that the birds get all they need to eat in the early morning. One of the negative blessings of photography, depending upon how you look at it, is that you have to photograph when the light is strong. So, unless he's in the tropics, a cameraman generally doesn't like to get out and shoot the early morning or late afternoon activities because there isn't enough light. It reminds me of my days as a gunnery officer in World War II. One of the advantages of being in the gunnery section on a destroyer was that the only time you worked was when you had to shoot — and most of the time you weren't wasting your ammunition, you were saving it, which made it a rather nice section to be in. All the other departments on the ship had to work every day. Cameramen are much like gunnery officers. There are days when they can't work and it's almost like a paid holiday. I find myself, on the contrary, a little irritated at not being able to photograph on all occasions.

While sitting in my cabin I thought I heard a dog bark, so I went down to the waterfall and found four fisherman. They were apparently lumbermen who had come over from the lumber camp, but they didn't appear to want to talk so I went on down to the estuary and saw my green-winged teal, male and a female, and a flock of unidentified shorebirds, and that was about it. The men were still fishing at the rapids when I came back, so I went on to the cabin. The wildness of this area was slightly tarnished by their activity. But, of course, it is a free country — although there is an odd situation here. These people who come up to work in the lumber yards mostly hail from Washington and Oregon and they're all scared to death of the Alaskan brown bear. I got the impression that they thought I was crazy living up here.

During lunch hour I wanted to take advantage of very warm sunshine, so I made close-up pictures of the violets on the island upstream from my twin islands. This brought me a horrible discovery. Here is a tiny island with beautiful vegetation, and I was shocked to discover that in my walking back and forth and around, I had demolished a fair amount of plant material. Human beings are completely oblivious to what's underfoot. We think that dirt isn't very good, but the dirt is so much the life of a plant that a plant can't exist without a place to put its roots.

I just can't help feeling that human beings are so human oriented that the only form of art they recognize is their own, their own weak creative efforts when, in reality, there is such a wealth of design and beauty in nature that goes by the board because nobody knows about it. Somehow or other people won't get deeply interested in things that they don't themselves experience. I think we should teach people to love the out-of-doors, to be sensitive to it and aware of the fact that we're only a small part of it, that in spite of our supposed superiority, our intellectual superiority, we still basically breathe air which is recycled thanks to the magic of plants. They take the carbon dioxide that is toxic to us and it's their bread and butter. They manufacture it into salable carbohydrates and all the rest of the building blocks of protoplasm, the substance of which all life consists. I think it's a tragedy that we *teach* biology, and I don't care whether you're talking about Harvard or Yale or Timbuktu or the lowest and most insignificant of the biology courses in high school. The fact remains that the people who profess to know about these things and to love them haven't the vaguest notion of how to see nature. They don't know where to find it, they don't know how to experience it, and if they demonstrate the existence of it they do so on a field trip which is more a social outing than a field trip. If anything, they do more damage to nature by their activity than they do if they never brought the kids out at all. The point is that people should find these things out for themselves. You shouldn't have to go to some expert to know that if you look here or there you'll find something. You're there—look! It's as simple as that.

Yesterday, psychologically, I was expecting the worst, and I probably got the worst because of my attitude. I actually resented the fishermen—just seeing them, out of context, so to speak, without any orientation as to what they are or where they're from or what they represent. A human being, I'm thinking now, is not a particularly attractive species. But on the other hand, I think I get a real stimulation out of the environment, and it's odd.

In the evening I was working in the cabin with the front door open when I heard a scurrying sound, and out darted the pine marten. He was trying to make up his mind whether to come in or not. I'm sure he would come in; he's a very curious animal and he didn't act frightened. On the other hand, he didn't manifest a great deal of interest in me either, and went back into the brush and disappeared into a hole in the ground. I put out a pan with a couple of eggs, hoping he (or she) would partake, but no soap. The eggs were still there in the morning. Apparently the Steller's jays had tested them, had poked their noses into the yokes and broken them, but they didn't eat them. So I brought them back in, got out a can of mushrooms, and made myself a mushroom omelet. I'm sorry, Mr. Marten, but I ate the food.

# GETTING DOWN
# TO
# BEAR TRACKS

### May 12

I took a long trip along the lake and found another set of bear tracks. They weren't over a day old but, again, the bear didn't stay on the trail very long. I stepped in one of the tracks just out of curiosity and was surprised at the size and the weight of the animal. They walk flat-footed so they don't sink down to their ankles in this stuff the way I do. This bear had also munched the grass. The only portion it seems to be eating is the flowering stalk, and only a part of that.

On this particular trip I also noticed that flies were beginning to pester me, although, as far as I know, I didn't receive any bites as I had mosquito repellent on. Nevertheless, having them periodically between my glasses and my eyes, in my ears, and just generally humming and buzzing was annoying. The one insect that really generates a powerful flying signal is the bumblebee, and the bumblebee has been in evidence practically all the time since I got here. They're usually solitary, feeding on the plants that have been flowering. The conspicuously flowering plants, and the ones that the bumblebee has been hanging around, are the huckleberry and the blueberry. Along with these the skunk cabbage has been in bloom. Now we can add a new plant, the violet, and yesterday for the first time I noticed that the scouring reed's (horsetail's) spore-producing structures were fully out. I haven't yet got a good photograph of that. It's a very beautiful structure with a lot of grace and one I certainly want to put on film.

One has to be careful in the selling of nature not to oversell. Some of these things are fairly fragile and are attractive to flower pickers. Even a biology class going through a field or along a trail will trample down a lot of vegetation. I was reflecting yesterday that the bear doesn't modify the vegetation very much by his walking because he usually has a well-defined trail that's used each year and also the bears step in each other's footprints. I think basically the reason for that is the bear doesn't like getting mired. When he sees a bear track, he figures that the other bear didn't go down—the track is the proof of it. Basically, though, this must take a lot of finesse. It shows you another thing about the Alaskan brown bear: the animal has to have his eyes looking down all the time or he couldn't effect this unique way of step- ping from one footprint to another. The deer is the animal that kicks up the least disturbance, with its tiny short hoofs. The deer trails are remarkably undisturbed, and they scuff the ground hardly at all.

The ground here doesn't pack the way it does in other areas, because there is a very short fermenting season when matter can rot and, also, it's a fermenting situation in which a lot of the plant material, the vast bulk of it, is apparently resistant to rot- ting, particularly the coniferous components, the cone-bearing trees. I would say 80% of the bulk of the plant material underfoot is coniferous wood and needles, which are even more persistent. The loss of evergreen needles is not an annual affair so there tends to be a great deal more plant structure in a coniferous needle. I've never known this to be discussed or talked about, but I'm sure it must be like a cannery; you build it differently, running three months out of the year rather than twelve. The one element thriv- ing on this source of material is, of course, the squirrels, pro- nouncedly a product of the hemlock and the spruce both, and they are certainly abundant. Here they do a lot of burrowing under- neath the ground.

I got a distinct impression yesterday that now the plants have come up one level toward the source of light so that the mosses underneath are more in the dark than they were—not that they had a lot of light before, but again this is their problem and they've adapted and photosynthesized. They're actually occupying landscape, which is evolutionary success. I've been speculating on how one tells how long a tree has been down. I noticed some trees along the trail that had fallen just last winter apparently. It was surprising that when a tree goes there's about 150 square feet of prop-rot surface that goes up in the air to form a vertical wall. It becomes very pretty, canopied with moss. But the bare ground becomes invaded almost entirely by liverworts, which leads me to another thought that I've had in the last two days. I've become aware that the liverworts are beginning to form their spore-producing structures. They come in a variety of shapes and forms and add a distinctive touch to what I call the macroscopic environment.

Occasionally you find some shelf conches, leathery-type fungi, on rotting wood and stumps and on the snags (trees that haven't fallen over yet). This rotting wood is invaded by these picturesque shelflike conches. Some of them ooze a liquid from the undersurface, and I'm not sure what the meaning of this is. I'm going to have to get some help to study this, obviously a book on fungi. I tasted this material and I'm still alive so it wasn't toxic. It didn't have much of a taste but it certainly was a beautiful sight. It balls up in huge droplets underneath. I wiped some clear and noticed that as the day went on these droplets seemed to become smaller and evaporate.

None of the bird books that I have are designed for anyone other than the guy who wants to know what it is and then seems to be perfectly content to rack up another species. He is concerned with how many he can find and that's where his interest stops. He could never spend a whole day or a whole week or a whole month or a whole year just watching one single kind of bird. You have to exercise a lot of ingenuity and a lot of patience to do that. I haven't done too much of this yet and I won't do it except on those species where we are basically dealing with an animal to film because I just can't afford to get lost and keep seeing the forest instead of the trees — all forests look alike until you start looking at the trees.

I just discovered my beard has got all kinds of dandruff in it. Is that possible?

As I see it right now, the principal user of the stream in the bird world is the merganser. They are a much maligned bird, hated by all fishermen as far as I can make out. Sportsmen don't like any predator that preys upon his crop. Again here we see man pushing his way around without any thought of the consequences, and I'm beginning more and more to feel that there is a moral obligation on the part of the human being to respect all forms of life. This isn't to say that we should give up and go back to being savages or limit our numbers to a pioneer population level—far from that. I just think there is an enormous amount of space on our globe that isn't being used by man or is being used in only a fragmentary way. As I fly across the United States in an airplane and look down over the thousands upon thousands of little farms, I think of the trend to move to the city. A farm is lonely. It's a hard way of life physically and the temptation is to make life easier. I think the lesson we must learn is that life is not really easy—if it *is* easy it's abnormal, and isn't good for one.

## May 13

This was one of those in-between days. There were certain indications, in my judgment, that a front was coming in. The wind was out of the southwest again, and toward evening, as it picked up, we had a rather gusty time of it here. I didn't really get at the day until after the Forest Service left, which was around 11:30. Finally they had come to check the transmitter. It had blown a fuse, apparently because the power supply is not adequate. Forest Service said they would send in a new one. The fellow who did the work was a very efficient, personable guy who seemed to diagnose the trouble by poking at all the wires with a pencil. He got the radio transmitter working and called. Sitka and Juneau both came in loud and clear, and he set up a schedule for me. Then he worked on the generator, which, for a variety of reasons, had got out of adjustment. He got it running nicely and then I walked to the lake with him and we said goodbye.

Again I thought I had fresh bear tracks, but I couldn't be absolutely sure. I was fascinated by them but decided to veer off their path for fear that some gigantic daddy bear would come loping down on them. And they're so big and such beautiful tracks. No question that the animal went there, but I'm not sure that I'm reading out all the fine print that an experienced Indian trapper would read out of a track. No doubt I'll get some information out of them, but I'm not terribly aware of animal tracks out here. This is a forest in which the undercarpet is untrackable except in muddy spots, and the muddy spots occur on the trail along the skunk cabbage hollows or skunk cabbage paddies. I'm not sure if there are more than one or two bears along that side of the slope as yet. I suspect that most of the bears are up in the main stream system that feeds the lake. That has a lot more open, bushy country in it and more feeding grounds of grass. I'm also told by the radioman from the Forest Service that this is the time of year when the bears are down on the tidelands. Of course, the kind of area that I have here in Hanus Bay is not exactly unpopulated at the moment with human beings. The signs of bear that I noticed before when I tracked the bear indicated one or two bears; the pilot reported two when he came in. So I was concerned that I might run into bears on that trail. On the other hand, I've been making a lot of noise with my pruning scissors and there is actually an unbroken salmonberry/devil's club entanglement on that trail. Wherever there is a clearing those rascally things will grow.

Fairly tired. Got the generator started at 6:00 P.M. I fired up the radio at 6:30 and at five minutes to seven I noticed that the transmitter was crackling the way it had when the fellow first fired it up. I assumed that had to do with the relay, so I dashed out to see what had happened to the generator, which was going around at a very slow pace. The pull-pully had come off. I fiddled around with it and found that it was jammed in a lock position. That motor couldn't anymore turn over than fly. I fired up the other generator (the one I had changed the spark plug on) and went back in to see if the radio would work. But it was dead, period. I was right back where I started. Let's hope the new one comes in tomorrow and let's hope that takes care of it. But I'm down to one generator again. That took the fun out of the whole evening. I think this society is doomed and jinxed as far as technology and communications are concerned. I had beef stew for supper again—the stew that I can't seem to get tender. I haven't adjusted to this two-week delay in ordering groceries and I've run out of certain essentials. For breakfast I'm eating powdered milk, which I like very much, and egg omelet, which I make interesting with slices of mushrooms.

## May 14

Once again I am impressed by the extreme quietness of the woods. The squirrels aren't particularly noisy. They don't advertise the fact they're around. Occasionally if you get very close to one he may chatter at you, but generally if you're talking, you're talking very softly. In that first big clearing about one-third of the way to the lake, there is a jay or two that seem to be carrying on some kind of a conversation between them, but generally there isn't a great deal of sound. Yesterday I heard a sound — a new sound — in the distance which kept puzzling me. Suddenly it was overhead, and it turned out to be a whistling swan. There was another sound that I hadn't heard before. I suspected it was a loon, and two birds did come into view, close; not close enough for good camera work but, nonetheless, within 200 or 300 feet of the shore. So we have a pair of common loons, maybe more; but I've been working along that shore of the lake now for several days and this is the first clue I've had that there were any loons on the lake. We can chalk up about the middle of May as the time the loons arrived at the lake this year. I was pleased to add a new figure to our cast of characters. The loon is a very wild-seeming animal and certainly one that adds a tremendous amount of charm to any lake. There are loons in Wisconsin and certain parts of Ohio and some in the eastern side of North Dakota and South Dakota, and probably many other places, but the loon is definitely a bird of the mountain lake and its call is well described as "a maniacal screaming." A big problem in describing bird songs is that it all depends on where you're brought up and what your associations are.

I spent five hours on this outing and got quite a bit farther down the trail, but I'm still by no means close to the shelter cabin. I finally turned back because what could possibly be a very fresh bear track suddenly appeared on the trail. The bears have a peculiar habit. They seem to work at right angles to the trail, which they may momentarily hit, turn either up or down it, go maybe 100, 200 feet, and they're off again; once off, their trail's hard to follow. Since I'm not doing a study specifically on the brown bear, I'm not therefore enamored of the thought of trailing him. I'm not nearly as adroit about going through the forest as he is and I just don't want to intrude any sooner or at greater disadvantage than I have to. So I continue to be fairly noisy as I work along the trail with my pruning scissors.

## May 15

I am anxious to finish the exploration of the trail along the south side of the lake, the only trail that allows access to the west end of the lake. On the rainy days, therefore, I have been cutting back the vegetation and salmonberry bushes. I am doing this specifically to find out just how much and how often the bears use the trail and I would like the advantage of a clear view in front of me. I understand from the forest rangers that a bear, when surprised, will sometimes charge rather than back away or investigate what it's being surprised by. Also, bears are generally afraid of people because every time they've been around them they have been shot at or irritated. A bear will take possession of a source of food and hide it. He will protect it and not wander too far from it. If you happen to run into one of his caches, the bear is likely to charge first and ask questions later. Increasingly, I find, I have a certain reservation about this animal, and I'm a little disinclined to wander along any of the game trails. I'd rather stay in the more open area. I certainly don't know how abundant bears are.

I finally made it to the end of the lake. I have the trail brushed out, which is the term that the Forest Service people use for this menial task of cutting back the vegetation that very quickly overgrows a trail, especially in this luxuriant forest. As I worked, I realized that my pruning scissors were beginning to prune badly. I thought, well, I'll just force my way through this tangle to the end of the lake and then return, because I had a desire to get back to the lake in mid-afternoon in case the plane came in. I got to the end of the lake despite a couple of sticky spots where spruce trees 3 or 4 feet in diameter had fallen across the trail, almost completely blocking it on a very steep slope. I had to do a great deal of crawling and climbing to get around them. Of course, the whole upper end as it appears from the water is a delta with a tremendous tangle of alders, salmonberry, and devil's club. Situated in this mess is a picturesque Forest Service lean-to cabin, which is not on the lake and is open on one side. It's fairly new, well-constructed and, unfortunately, littered with the usual garbage of the twentieth-century American, which in this case, was dominated by beer cans and the polyethylene covers that all the people use now in lieu of the canvas tarp which we paid so much for in the old days and couldn't afford to throw away. It was a much more durable product, but one of our twentieth-century attributes is to improve on the state of the art and gain a little less bulkiness, maybe a little less weight, in order not to inconvenience a sportsman who is carrying a lot. On the other hand, the fellow can afford to go off and leave it. Here I was by a pristine lake that had been visited by sportsmen. I don't think anyone but the adventurous sports type would be here—

*Fiddlenecks of the deer fern.*

*A bed of crowfoot in bloom.*

*Monkshood in flower. Root stalk yields a highly toxic alkaloid substance which is used by Eskimos to kill whales. It is so deadly that a dried smear on a harpoon will kill the largest whale in minutes.*

*A young Alaskan brown bear feast-
ing on salmon.*

*Shelf fungus growing on still-standing snags of spruce. These fungi begin the decomposition of the dead tree.*

*Toadstools ready to reproduce by release of spores. Main body of toadstool extends throughout rotting logs.*

and they've messed it up a bit. Along the trail I occasionally find evidence of their visits, and along the stream I find a great deal of evidence in the form of discarded bottles of salmon eggs (bait) and whatever other hardware fishermen use.

Having arrived at the upper end of the lake and satisfied myself as to it's condition, I looked over the size of the stream. Coming into the lake, it is very narrow, very swift, and very deep, and in many many places could not be forded. Movement around and through the delta area will entail a great deal of frustration. I could clearly see that bear were plentiful in this area. The alder thickets would be a natural place, for an animal that has some desire for security and freedom from harassment would make use of an alder thicket. A lot of the attacks dealing with the Alaskan brown bear indicate, as they were described, that the animal generally goes into a place where he's protected on three sides. This brings me around to a very interesting point. On the way up I didn't see any signs of fresh bear track. Occasionally I saw a sign of a bear track maybe a day old. I've made a rather careful observation of this and I find if it isn't raining too hard, if it's just a typical Alaskan drizzle, one's footprints along the trail carry a full imprint of all the fine characteristics of the boot's undersurface for about 24 to 36 hours. Then gradually the water oozes into that fine print which then begins to disappear. But a sizable, recognizable print will remain for three or four days. The only time that the entire print is obliterated is when we have a heavy rain, so I carefully watch the bear tracks along this trail. Each time I go up I will—as much as I don't like to—I will step in the bear's footprints because I don't want to count that track a second time. By this technique I've hoped I might get some idea of how many bears are working along that trail.

On the way back I found two sets of bear excreta along the trail and I got down and squished my fingers in it to see what it was made up of. It was almost all moss with just an occasional shred of grass. I had been told that when a bear comes out of hibernation he eats grass and skunk cabbage, so this doesn't fit the book. The excreta smells exactly like mildewy wet moss. I went under a log blockage of two or three trees. Here, I should explain, when one tree comes down, it topples two or three others because of the interconnecting root system. Young trees have an unusual way of growing up over an old stump, so the mature trees share the same stump site. Thus, if one falls, all go. Crawling under this low-lying log tangle, I found myself looking down at a piece of bear excreta which had been dropped within 24 hours. Now, how did the bear get under this concoction of trees and go to the bathroom? It was just too wild to believe.

I'm getting so tired of seeing nature studies on how birds mate and feed their young that, as an ecologist, I want to get in the food-chain angle. Instead of finding nests I'm looking for what and where birds are eating and what they're doing. I feel that I have just about as much as I can get on the mergansers other than the feeding of the females along the bank. That's something I've got to get. I'm getting a feeling for the weather and the light I have to work with, but most important, I have mapped out in my mind where we shall play our games and set our stages. I'm thinking primarily of the island area at the foot of the rapids and the logjam, which is a constant source of food; also the waterfall and, of course, the rapids itself. I have to spend days with each species on its timetable: to see when it wakes up, when it naps, etc., and I have to learn where I can view these intimacies without botching it up. This kind of activity is the science side of behavior and I think will give us real insights into these species.

I've pretty well marked out the stream and worked on the estuary, which I still find fantastic and, of course, the lake. It is about the lake that I have my most serious misgivings, because there isn't a great deal of activity on the surface. Ordinarily, in any water habitat the biological activity of the system can be judged by the amount of animal activity occurring at the surface. As yet I haven't done any underwater photography. The coldness of the water necessitates real protection and until I get a good footboot and gloves with which I can operate the camera, I don't propose to go underwater. Also, I still haven't received a life vest and this is an absolute must.

The plane came in, but as soon as the pilot saw I was still among the living, he departed, without so much as even a how-de-do.

## May 16

A Saturday—a nice day, with reservations. It was raining in the morning, but toward late afternoon the weather began to break and we had a beautiful period of sunshine from 6:00 until 8:00 P.M., when the sun dipped below the mountains on the north side of Lake Eva. There has been a definite warming trend. I find myself leaving the cabin door open occasionally. Already I would say that May is clearly workable until 10:00 at night and if one were eager in the morning one could be out in nature as early as 4:00. I usually get up around 6:00.

I was somewhat relieved to notice that the stream is beginning to subside a bit. As a result of a three-day warm period this week the stream came up about a foot and it was hard to cross it. I also noticed that the water temperature was beginning to "warm up" to 45°. The trip to the estuary didn't reveal anything new or different. The tide was out and the waterfall looked impressive. I did notice one sign of bear. It looked as though the bear had been digging, investigating a burrow close to my blind. I'm getting to the point where I can spot a place the bear has been even though the moss doesn't look torn up by the impact of a bear print. If you look carefully you can tell that the claws have dug up a bit of occasional moss. It requires close looking, but nonetheless it is there.

At 3:00 o'clock a plane came directly over the cabin. The pilot seemed to rev his engine, which to me means: I've got some business with you. You never know, maybe there is an emergency and they have to get in touch with me. All kinds of thoughts run through my mind in such a situation — someone in the family is sick, or the film unit has a point they want to make, or maybe even the new power supply for my transmitter is here at last and I can get back on the air. So I sped to the lake. Normally I dawdle along the trail looking at this and that. It's ironical, I find myself contemplating, intellectualizing a lot when I'm going along the trail. . . . I think it's the utter flood of sensory impressions. After a while the mind just won't take more. We're thinking animals now and not completely sensory, we're not operating with the full flood of sensory impressions, and I can't keep myself stirred up all the time wondering behind which tree a bear is lurking. If one did that, one would go crazy up here. There are so many moss-draped logs that look like gorillas or bears or God knows what else. So I do a lot of thinking along that trail and it's sad in a way, because I am supposed to be finding things and rubbing my nose into Mother Nature, and yet this is the way it is.

I reached the lake to find that the plane was not at the edge of the landing — I shouldn't say landing, I mean the bar where I have my boat pulled up — but was out in the neck near the half-submerged logs. It was raining hard, above average for Alaska. A fellow was standing on a pontoon, fishing, and as he looked up and then down, I thought: The pilot is waiting for me to get up there, so he's killing time by fishing. I hung around a minute wondering why there wasn't any communication. Then I thought: If someone is going to talk it will have to be me. I hollered out to him, saying, "Did you come up here to deliver something to me or just to check on me?" . . . "Just a minute," he called. "I'll ask the pilot." Whereupon the pilot opened the door and, after a minute of consultation, the fisherman yelled back, "No. I'm up here fishing." He added that he was from Sitka and asked if there was anything they could do for me. . . . "You might tell Channel Flying Service that my transmitter is broken and I have lost one of my two generators," I shouted back. To which he said, "O.K." And then he said the fishing wasn't too good there and asked where I fished. "I don't fish," I said, still yelling. When he asked if I had any recommendations, I told him that the people who work Lake Eva feel that the best fishing is at the mouths of the tributaries which come into the lake, and that there's a nice one on the other shore about two-thirds of the way up the lake. With that, the man crawled back into the plane and they taxied on. It was raining vigorously by this time.

I came back to the cabin about 8:00. The sun was shining by then, so I left the cabin door open. I was so pleased because the afternoon had gone well after the rain stopped that I decided to go to the estuary. At 9:30 at night, mind you, I went down to the estuary. There wasn't a great deal going on, but I did see about twenty tree swallows gliding and flying and picking up emerging insects. And there were four bachelor common mergansers swimming in formation. There was no female around them but they were still swimming in formation. They have a sawed-off, stubby tail that sticks up as they swim and they're very, very handsome. After I watched them for a few minutes, I went up the trail a ways and noted a pair of green-winged teal. It was beginning to get dark. When I left the cabin at 9:30 there had been a suggestion of sunset color in the clouds to the north, and it was charming at the estuary to have these pink clouds peeking out through the pines. I don't know exactly what went through my mind, I just know I was at ease and happy with the world. It was just one of those delightful experiences, where one begins to feel that he is a part of the real world and not the arbitrary world of man with all its pettiness and restrictions.

## May 18

How unprepared a human being is to act quickly and in the right way. One of the few benefits of World War II for T. J. Walker was to force him to act and to react. Until that time I had been a student. I really wanted to know, to experience, and to learn everything, and I did it to the best of my ability. One of the dangers with this type of training is that you are dealing in situations in which, because of the mechanics and the way the material is presented, you don't have to react very quickly. The only time you react quickly is in an examination. This educational system of ours drives me stark raving mad. The teachers decide to give an examination and put it on a grade curve. All that says is that the group is going to pass. So you praise the brilliant ones whom the system was designed to interest. Unfortunately, all the teachers are drawn from people who understand the material easily, and so they are more interested in the few brilliant students when they should be catering to the average majority. I think we should draw our teachers from the average and not from the brilliant ones. Hell, the brilliant ones are only interested in brilliant ones. In a nature situation such as I am in now, you must react very quickly and not sit and figure out a solution. But in nature even the solutions aren't readily apparent.

When I went up to the little tributary today, right at the mouth and about 5 feet away from me, I saw a male harlequin duck. It was absolutely beautiful, an almost milk-blue color, and I hope it will be on the lake all summer. He is not afraid of me and didn't take off until I was only 5 feet away.

## May 19

I theorize on working this trail essentially from the lower end of the lake to the upper where the bear tracks are. It appears to me that the bears, when they come down on the trail, don't go for more than 100 feet and then they're off it. Yesterday I saw on this trail a mother bear trail with her cub track running alongside. These were fresh imprints that continued for quite a piece and then went off the trail to the left and down to the river. On the way back I heard an enormous thump. All I can tell you is that a log had either tumbled over or something had pulled or pushed it over. It really sounded as though a bear had pulled a log over. I was definitely a little nervous, between that and the bear tracks.

Around 5:00 P.M. I decided to see how things are going at the estuary. I keep thinking that the otter, who comes in here occasionally, comes when the estuary is high. Perhaps this otter is actually living on the estuary and not in the stream. I want to check this theory out, which means I'll have to wait and see if it's true. It was a good outing. By the time I reached the estuary, the tide was out. I went up the tributary to the south, and there is now one of the plantain family blooming. The buttercup, which has been in blossom for a while, is still blooming down there and I saw young salmon. The one that strikes my fancy the most is the one with the orangy tail. I'll have to get out my salmon book to look this up—they probably all have orangy tails.

My venture at Lake Eva is significant for me because it's giving me a chance to experience the thing for which I was trained, the study of life—life in various forms. I'm no longer studying it as a superspecialist by virtue of my research requirement to work on a single animal or a piece of an animal or a function of an animal. I'm free-wheeling, I'm out and seeing the total, and this is essentially the study of ecology. I think there is a reality to the idea that man in his tampering with nature has unlocked a hornet's nest and the hornet's nest is pollution—pollution of his water supply, of his atmosphere, and pollution and destruction of his ground on which most photosynthetic processes should take place. But even more important, and the thing that I'm going to hammer at constantly, is that man has gradually lost the ability to survive except in his very specialized urban environment, which is, in itself, no damn good. It's an environment that is driving our children to drugs, our older generation to alcohol and on through all our aberrations of religious cults, etc. We have all these abnormalities which we not only have but constantly advertise. It's sad to think we dwell on crime, we dwell on the shortcomings of man. We make these things appear to be meaningful, and as a result civilization is going down the tubes, so help me.

You know, there is an odd thing about human beings going on vacation. Let's say you have some growing kids and you think, wouldn't it be great to have a summer in the woods. Or there's a possibility to send junior off for two weeks, four weeks, or six weeks to summer camp. But these experiences, although in the environment of the woods, are still ineffective because you have a group reaction. All these people brought together interact with each other, and in a rather bad way because the environment is a new one. The natural reaction in such circumstances is to fall back on each other, and this takes on the aspect of a military operation. You've got to deal with a lot of people, so you put them in barracks and boss them around. It's all very up-tight. To keep the kids from going crazy in this environment, which they understand very little about and see very little of, you map out their hour-to-hour activities. The most exposure the kids will have is a hike or two or during which they may tear down part of the landscape in the process of some project. What we need, of course, is opportunity to be alone with nature. Each of us needs to have a place for contemplation. Maybe part of the charm of religion is that you go into a rather beautiful building and sit in a pew and think—the only problem is that the thinking you do there is probably society-dependent. It just isn't going to work. You've got to be able to feel that you are capable of standing on your own two legs and doing your own thinking, and the few people who survive the beating that they take in our educational system and manage to learn to think independently are the leaders. These are the ones on top. They have learned that you've got to be yourself. You may identify with the group, but I'm sure when the chips are down each one of these fellows is a cold, cruel egotist and knows full well that if he's going to succeed in what he's doing he has to rely on his own judgment. . . .

I was very much taken as I worked along the stream yesterday by the growth of the bracken ferns. The new growth is still developing and looks like a clenched fist or an animal that has his hand up protesting. I was also struck by the accumulation of trash along the high-water mark—in fact you can tell where the high-water mark is by the amount of vegetation, which eddies around and gets trapped on the stems of the plants that overhang the stream. Primarily the overhanging plants at this point are salmonberry, which presents a nice effect with the color. The fresh leaves of the huckleberry, blueberry, and salmonberry all have a lush yellow-green translucent color. They are alive and fresh. I also noticed that a lot of moss gets carried away and accumulates in tufts along the stems of the salmonberry, marking high water. These tufts remind me of ballet skirts. So you see, even though I'm deeply enamored of nature, I constantly reach back for some visual identity with the life I've left.

I explored one of the animal trails off to the side and I came across a skeleton of a deer. There was no trace of fur, but he must have died during the winter. The bones didn't appear to have been chewed on and the skeleton is there, except for the skull—there's only the lower jaw.

# 5

# NATURE'S STOVE AND THE FOREST

## *May 20*

I can't help thinking every time I see the gray fog rolling in that here is water in motion. It's eerie to watch. I find that when I get into a forest where the vistas are very close and similar — until I start looking at the fine detail — I have the feeling that the world is my size, has my sense of space. The fog is coming in at 10 to 15 knots now and I can see the rain dropping out of the clouds. It gives me a very powerful feeling of motion. I have a delightful feeling of seeing, as the fog scrapes along the tops of the trees, that the forest isn't made up of uniform trees. There are big trees, medium-sized trees, and little trees, and the backdrop of the over-steepened valley in which I am nestled is not just a uniform slope but has a tremendous amount of space. The trees seem to recede in the distance and the irregularities on the slope suggest little tributary, subsidiary valleys. . . . I wish sometimes that English had the diminutives other languages have.

The idea I was struck by was of an enormous "stove" in the Pacific Ocean, the Japanese current, which has all the hot water that was heated thousands of miles away in the tropical zone and then put into motion by wind, creating an enormous river of warm water that flows northward. This huge "stove" is heating the air above and as it does so, of course, moisture is evaporating out of the ocean into the air. Since, interestingly enough, nature abhors a vacuum, the colder air around this heat sink begins to move in that direction, and that generates a lovely wind which makes the ocean such a rough place. The wind comes spiraling into the center of the stove, and as it does it begins to turn. Thus you develop a rotation system in which the air is not going into the whole from all directions uniformly but appears to come in obliquely, giving a rotational effect to the wind. The wind spirals around at different velocities depending on how close you are to the center of the system or how far out you are. It gathers up moisture and so is self-perpetuating. What I'm experiencing today is the inboard side of this gigantic wheel. I'm sure if *you* were on the ocean you would appreciate it here, nestled among the trees, but you can tell the wind has been out over the ocean because of all the water it has gathered and which it is currently spilling down.

So we have the rotational effect and we're seeing it now. For one reason or another, due to the slippage of the earth's atmosphere, the rotational effect, and the impact of solar forces on the outer atmosphere, periodically these huge eddies of circulating moist air are carried eastward—we're rotating eastward so there is a tendency for this heat sink to slip, and it begins to slip eastward—and lo and behold one of these gigantic wheels moves across the mountains that flank the mainland. As this wheel begins to move eastward, we experience different degrees of wind and rain and the subtleties of weather.

I couldn't help thinking this morning, what an interesting anomaly. Here the air is clearly scooting across the sky at about 15 knots to the center of the wheel, spilling all this nice moisture, with the consequence that here you have a tremendous body of water with the gravitational drainage of this water going in the opposite direction: the weather system brings it eastward, the drainage system brings it westward.

Last night when I went to bed, the stream was very low as the storm was approaching. This morning it's over its banks in sections, but not the whole length of it. So we have in the stream itself the main channel, which carries the water most of the time, and when the situation gets a little out of hand the stream adapts to a sudden influx of water, either from the melting of the snow or from the rain, and rises. Thus those sections of the stream where the basin is flat will be subject to flooding, and every stream has similar flooding sections. When man needs space and builds in one of these flat areas, he gets into trouble with the water.

I've always been, in the back of my mind, opposed to the logic of trying to catch all the water that's on it's way to the ocean and holding it back and letting it evaporate someplace else or letting it become loaded with minerals and say that it is good drinking water. The water we get in Los Angeles has been artificially held back into artificial lakes in areas where lakes couldn't exist and manipulated in a way to create a lake where there shouldn't be one. This has profound effects on the biology of the stream below, a situation that is usually blithely ignored.

About pollution of the stream: up here nature pollutes the stream royally with all the plant material, and yet Lake Eva isn't a polluted lake simply because the water flows in and out of it so quickly—in about ten days, I'm willing to bet; but I'm not a hydrologist so I don't know what the turnover is. You see, here we have a very real undisturbed situation and a force that has not been tampered with. It's in a steady state with the environment and in a very wet area, and here is a stream that doesn't flood because of the wonderful blotter, this carpeted blotter that lies below the forest, catching and holding and delivering the water at a reasonable rate. A beautiful system—and the streams reflect this.

It is important to realize that this is a mountainous area, and in mountainous areas there is not very much space for streams. Normally a stream is at the bottom of a valley, and the valley is cut by the stream itself. Here we have a glaciated valley, a tributary valley, and I'm willing to bet it is 600 to 800 feet above the main valley floor, which is filled with seawater and called Peril Strait. Above the lake we consequently have a certain meandering and this area is crowded with plants that don't mind being flooded—alders and thickets of berry and plants that can put up with occasional flooding of their root system. A plant doesn't have a circulatory system to pump the necessary oxygen to all the vital tissues, so generally the root hairs—the tissues that are involved with the movement of minerals up to the plant body—are the only parts of the plant sensitive to oxygen deprivation, so drowning the plant with too much water merely means that you deprive the root hairs of oxygen. The water in the soil, incidently, is lacking in oxygen anyway because the bacteria fail to develop.

Here of course the soil is less compacted and is opened up by all the plant fiber, the mosses, etc. Therefore, it's soil that is porous, so the flooding tends to be ephemeral.

Here today we have one of those dramatic scenes in which we can actually see the flow of the conveyer belt of clouds along the rim of the wheel and we know that it's going to continue to rain. It's good weather for the plants and bad for the human beings. Human beings are the most poorly designed creatures I can imagine. Put us out without any clothes, without any bedding, and without any artificial heat, and the only thing we can do is keep alive by the heat that we generate by shivering. Most of us wave the white flag and we're not around very long. So here I am once again with my hands in my pockets. Springtime in Alaska is not like springtime in Kentucky, but on the other hand, I take cold better than I take heat, so. . . . You know, it just makes you wonder. The only thing that man has in his favor is that he has man, and because he has man he has the ability to communicate and build a tremendous technological society and it's all very great. But somewhere along the line we've slipped—as we grow more skillful at doing what we do, we become less and less skillful at involving human beings in our mechanistic schemes.

T. J. Walker up here is still ruminating over some of the musings of civilization. In other words, I haven't really chucked it—and I don't think I want to. There must be more to the reality of nature than putting it in books or zoos or newspapers to save it. Save it for what? We've got to learn to use it. Whenever you put a group together, the people who are willing to get in and do something or have a gift of gab, usually by default become the leaders. But then they have to stay in power somehow so they walk a tightrope between the issue of doing what to them appears logical and what to their constituents appears logical and what to their board of advisers appears logical. The reason they want to put themselves into this situation is the desire for immortality. It's odd that we make such a fuss of putting people into history books. I've never been able to understand completely why normal, functional human beings would want to experience someone else's experiences secondhand. In other words, why just read about it; why not go out and experience it? Well, it's easy enough for me up here to babble on and on and act like a pope, because nobody can fight back at me. This is, come to think of it, the beautiful thing about being by yourself.

# May 21

All day long the air flowed westward and we really had a rainy day. I went out on a couple of safaris. One was to the lake with my notebook. The wonderful thing about ecology is that you can't really look at what's going on in the water without asking how come the water is still there. There is a pump that keeps pumping the water into it. The stream was full and went up about a foot. This was really a big storm, and the one thing I want to emphasize is that it is the Japanese current that brings the heat into our gigantic atmospheric stove out here. Also, I want to nail down once and for all the fact that this particular place happens to be in the mainstream of the Aleutian lows which are these violent oceanic storms. You can see that there is a two-way process here: water pumped in and then drained out. These water molecules, when they get on the ground, gravitate to the lowest point and the lowest point is the bottom of the valley. From there they move to the level of the sea.

If the camera crew were here today and took a look at the rapids they would no more think of going down them than of going over Niagara Falls. There's a vast lot of water flowing down those narrow channels, and it's mighty swift. The rapid areas of a stream are where the stream gets a big injection of air because of the churning.

On this trip—I went out at 11:30 A.M. and back at 2:30 P.M.—I noticed that the bank plants are underwater because of the flooding. Two of the requirements of being bank plants: they've got to be able to withstand large doses of sunlight, and they have to be able to hold fast to the bank until the water goes down. Here it's about 12 hours before the stream recedes and then the water flows out quite rapidly, and things settle down to the way they were until the next rain. The water that goes into the stream from the mossy carpet is nearly free of minerals, so this stream and lake are carrying water that has a superb taste. The lack of minerals, however, makes it rough on the animals and plants that grow here. The water is relatively clear but it does have a very marked golden stain, which comes from the decay of wood and stagnant moss from the fallen dead trees. Now, the plants growing along the stream bank are very important because their root systems retard bank erosion. They prevent the stream from tearing away and eating out and extending itself. This confines the stream to a narrow channel, which causes the water to move swiftly and the bottom to be gravelly.

The wind yesterday pruned nature's ornaments adorning our trees. As you look up at the trees, you see hanging down from various dead branches a lot of plant growth, like the lichens growing on the branches, and pieces of this, along with dead branches, were torn loose by the wind. A lot of it landed in the stream, which carried it down into the ocean. In a sense the wind tests the tree, determining whether or not it has a right to be there. As you go through the forest you see some areas where the wind has actually ripped several whole trees out, forming a grove of what is left.

I feel so bad when I realize that in the twentieth century, although we have more knowledge and can do more things, we are damnably close to catastrophe. The reality of hunger and of not having good air are dominant, but they in turn are dominated by the educational system and propaganda. Too many people are seeing the trees and not the forest.

I have a whole notebook of things I saw and did. I found a strawberry, believe it or not. At least I thought it was a strawberry. It looked like a strawberry but as I bit into it, what a shock. It wasn't a strawberry. It tasted like juniper berry. It was the driest berry I've ever eaten in my life. So *there* was a sensory impression, and once I get that plant identified I'm sure I'll never forget it. (Note: It was the green male cone of the spruce. They are red and cut from the tree by squirrels.)

## May 22

When spring really arrives here, the air masses shift enough to bring the warmer airflow off the Aleutian low, and that warm air rains instead of snows. The water temperature is 45°, which is 13° above freezing, and I'm taking baths in it and hoping to build a temperature tolerance to it. I took a five-minute bath from the waist down. It lasted that long because it takes that long to get the soap off. I was red from the waist down and my toes felt frostbitten. I took that bath in the morning, but by 9:30 P.M., after chopping wood, I was so sweaty that I went down to the stream and got in up to my waist for my second bath of the day, taking again about five minutes for the top half of my body. I splashed and worked the water up with my hand to my chest and armpits, the way Red Cross Lifesaving prescribes for taking the shock out of cold water.

The irony of the bath was that it so invigorated me I couldn't go to sleep. I must confess I'm beginning to feel a little left out. I know there are people working around fairly close to here, not on this island but on the island just to the north of me. These people of course go home on weekends. The flying service is very busy on Friday night coming in and picking people up and taking them out to the bright lights or to home or wherever. These are people who essentially don't realize how lucky they are to be out here. Nevertheless, I always feel a tinge of nostalgia and homesickness, which is aggravated by the sound of those airplanes.

The irony of work in the twentieth century is that it really isn't work, it's just a way to keep everyone busy and occupied. Much of it is paperwork, repetitive busywork, especially if you are with the government or any large organization.

Alaska and the people in Alaska are essentially just out of the pioneering age. They came up here to get away from it all, and having got away, they gradually became indifferent to their environment. They now look at their environment as does a typical human being, namely, as something to conquer, to make money from. An obvious money-maker is the tourist business, so they advertise that they have better scenery than in the lower forty-eight, and they probably do. The sensory impressions I have had of Alaska would certainly indicate that this is a beautiful wild country. But the Alaskans haven't made very much money with their tourists and part of the reason is they are catering to too small a segment of the population. You can't make money unless you have hundreds of people coming in. If you want to see how to make money on the country, just look at Hawaii. It's got a lot of people coming in but, God, did it ever ruin Hawaii. Up here, of course, the big business is hunting, and hunting is great because everyone wants to have a big Alaskan brown bear that he shot himself, with great danger to himself. But why shouldn't the bear be dangerous? How would you like to have someone put a bullet in you in a place that didn't put you out of your misery by killing you immediately? What would you do about it? You would charge. Of course, that ever trusty Alaskan guide, in the business to keep his client from getting killed, usually kills the bear before the bear wipes out the hunter.

The real interest in Alaska is this lovely thing called wood. The forests here are fantastic. There is tremendous need in other parts of the world for wood. One of the wild things about the twentieth century is that we have developed the power and technology to go in and cope with getting wood trees cut down and moved out and processed. With ships functioning as they do it's also perfectly possible to move the trees of Alaska to all these places in the world. But when the forest goes, all the things that weren't involved in the harvest of the trees are left without adequate moisture protection: they no longer have the humidifying canopy, they no longer have the protection from the heavy rain, they're overburdened by light. And that, I think, may produce a permanent modification of the forest floor. You may be able to grow *some* kind of tree on it, you may be able to harvest a forest product *called* a tree that is perfectly adequate for man's need, but it is no longer the same forest. The water supply and the heating of the water in modifying the stream and the animals that live in it—all are gone. There will be an alteration of the system and something else will move in. The question is: Is that which moves in as valuable as that which was there?

I vacillate on the horns of a dilemma: the need for wood and the needs of the forest. Come to think of it, I'm a very privileged fellow sitting here experiencing the real wilderness, the real unspoiled rain forest. It isn't going to be that way very much longer. Occasionally, when the sound is right, I can hear the lumbering going on across Peril Strait 20 miles away. I know that those powerful machines are crawling around up there. I spent one summer around a lumbering area and I know how violent an upheavel lumbering is.

Back in your mind you hope that maybe the computer, the new wonderful electronic machine that man has dreamed up, will do away with our need for paper. Yet we continue to require newspapers, for example. The names change but people do the same things and it's the same news year in and year out, decade after decade. You know what percentage of a newspaper actually gets *read* in a metropolitan area? The newspaper serves many, many interests but it's pathetic that we have to sacrifice all this lovely photosynthetic tissue which is so essential in keeping our atmosphere clean. I have a strong feeling that the purification of our air is done in these forested areas and it's here that our water is purified. Maybe eventually we will realize that we have to save these woods, that we can't arbitrarily keep cutting them down. There are so many people in the world today who are so man-oriented that they have no feeling for this area. I'm willing to bet that 50% of the people who live in Alaska are completely oblivious to it's real charm.

The difficulty in building roads here means that there aren't many yet, and so there aren't many cars. Travel has to be largely by air, so there are many areas the average person hasn't been to yet. Unfortunately, this does not prevent lumbering interests from getting in. Although, as I have said, they are not widespread, they are nevertheless in. And so gradually this wonderful air conditioner and purifier of nature is going to go by the boards, and what a tremendous loss it will be. It is such a pity that these forests are experienced so imperfectly. I have no confidence that any writer, no matter how skillful, can possibly generate a feeling for the tragedy that is beginning to unfold.

# 6

---

# THE
# BURNISHED
# LIGHT

## *May 23*

This past six weeks has been mainly T. J. Walker, casting director, in search of a cast. So far most of the potential cast isn't here. We have the mergansers, the waterthrush, the dipper, and now other bird users of the stream, such as the sandpiper. . . . But this sounds like a bird show and I don't want it to be. Then we do have the otter, but it has already been kicked around and is emphatically not tame. It has to be cautious, perhaps because of that big bald eagle sitting up there. . . .

I'm also of the opinion that the otter should be on his toes around the brown bear in the water, because the bear sees well and fishes the water; so there is a possibility of the brown bear being a predator of the otter, although in nature's design this probably isn't often true. It's puzzling. There isn't a great abundance of otters around here, but the number of otters may be a reflection of what little food is available for an otter; it could be as simple as that. If an animal doesn't have a food abundance, there isn't a Carte Blanche credit card that says to every animal: Go propagate yourself.

The wind is so strong that it's kicking a lot of water out of the trees. It's still rainy and the wind is still moving to the west. The wind just blew my door open. It's the kind of day that makes me want to go for a walk, although I have indicated my reluctance to walk far in the heavy wind. I think both the Alaskan brown bear and I are deprived of hearing because of the noise. Of course, the brown bear really enters the scene when the salmon are here, and they will be here soon. First the sockeye, or red, then the pink or humpback, followed by the chum or dog and lastly the coho or silver salmon. Oh, the confusion of common names.

## May 24

I have a lot to do and I'm so anxious to get out and capture some of this world that it keeps me from feeling lonely or dealing too much in the past. Why should I keep going back to the past when the only thing that matters right now is *now*? I don't have to alienate myself from things that are happening and the environment doesn't hamper me. I have a tremendous library here and I could really become profound if I absorbed all this information, but I'm inclined to feel that instead of putting a name on a plant or an animal, I'd rather go out and see it myself. It's a game of discovery and I have somehow to create a visual and an acoustic record of my feelings and my observations and my thoughts. We aren't dealing with a cut-and-dried experience here. Of course, I could show how much of the rest of the scientific world works by relating the background and literature review. Then, of course, I could launch into a stream of facts, which I find terribly hard to digest, and scare everyone away. But I'm not doing that, and it's great to be unfettered by the limitations of a specialization. We've all been led down the wrong path, to the point where we are no longer willing to go out and experience things ourselves. I want to create the feeling that I'm a guide and a reporter.

I just saw a dipper sitting on the logjam with a wiggling little salmon parr. *Parr* is the term scientists used to define the salmon of 2 to 3 inches in length. In fact, as you walk along the stream, you can see all the tiny salmon parr swimming along the edge. It's here that the dipper fishes, along with the female merganser, so I'm beginning to establish in my mind an understanding of the bird life, the dipper and the merganser, their food and how they get it.

I went for a walk in the evening along the bear trail and was just amazed at how saturated the forest floor is with water. Every depression is full of water and makes a pond anywhere from a foot to 8, 10, 20, 30 feet across. It's difficult to go along the bear trails without being in water periodically, and there are little streams running from one pond to the next. I'm not sure that I will go in there once the bears are in the area. Maybe I could build a high enough observation platform in these trees so I can survey this trail.

## May 25

It was a rainy day, a dark day, a windy and cold day. I went to the lake in the morning to get some still pictures of the clasping hands of the devil's club buds, but the growth of the buds has been such that they're beginning to leaf out and the buds are no longer buds. They don't look like clasping hands now, so I had to settle for a different view. Actually, I have a dislike for this plant, even of photographing it.

You may wonder why I don't go further into the woods, and the reason is that the woods repeats itself. As the trail goes in and out by the stream it samples the forest. The only thing you don't get a feeling of is the contrast between an animal trail and a human trail. The main difference here is that an animal trail is less distinct, it comes and it goes and has many branches, so it's hard to know which one to take. Down at the estuary, I found there wasn't much going on at the estuary proper. One female merganser swam along on the little shallow that develops when the tide goes out, and the tide was out. It was rainy and windy and a damnably bad afternoon. I went to the estuary to get the buttercup picture. Why do I want a buttercup? It's a real gem and brings back many memories of my graduate student days in Wisconsin, which was crawling with oozy wet places such as this. I did get that buttercup picture and also a plant that I remembered was a shooting star. It had a slightly different look here than in the Rockies. I walked on down the trail to the bushes. The tide was halfway in and halfway out, and I noticed a cabin cruiser which had just hauled up anchor about a quarter of a mile away. The people were on their way back across the channel and I will say they were friendly; they waved to me, which is more than most of the fishermen do who come along this stream. They were in there fishing, and there was no way for them to get over and see me. Furthermore, it's against the ground rules; in other words,

I'm supposed to be up here seeing how well a human being fares without another human being. The truth is, he can fare. He won't reproduce, that's for sure, and I don't recommend that a human being who has a thought toward perpetuating the species go off and be a hermit.

## May 26

It's absurd that I'm so frustrated by a simple little thing like a generator. One of the first things I'm going to do when I get back to civilization is to learn all that needs to be learned about how to disassemble and repair one of those monsters. I'm never going to allow myself to be caught again by this dependence.

On the way to the boat after supper I was startled to see some extremely big and extremely new bear tracks, which were laid down sometime between 3:00 and 7:00 P.M. I don't know exactly how they got there, except that I got the impression from looking at them that the bear had just preceded me down the trail when he sensed that I was there and scurried off the trail in a place where you wouldn't expect a bear to go—it was an overgrown area. About that time I heard a crackling sound below the trail, but I didn't pursue it.

## May 27

I went down in the morning to get some water for the breakfast. I always dip the water out just adjacent to where I have the underwater thermometer attached on a wristband to a stone and, lo and behold, the thermometer was gone. I thought, my God, how could that be, it is impossible, the current isn't that strong. The instant reaction was: Where could it have gone? And the only thing I could think of was that the band had rotted and come loose, and the thing had fallen down among the stones in the water. I went down and noticed that everything was scattered and out in deeper water, as though some animal had been in there at things. I got in, groped around, and found my stone with the watch still on it. I can only conclude that the otter came in and worked those stones over for food, kicking them around a bit in the process. But he didn't take my watch—that would be a wild thing to see an otter with a thermometer watch. It gave me a sense of how strong otters are and how they work over the stony parts of the stream. What impressed me most as I searched for the watch was how bitter cold the water was. I had pushed my shirt way up so I could put my arm down in the water almost up to the armpit. I did want to recover the watch, so I groped around and retrieved all the stones, and my arm grew red, purple, blue cold.

There is a warming trend, though, and I find myself overheating on the trail in my present costume sometimes. This generates a little problem when I come back into the cabin because I'm damp from perspiration and it's chilled in there, about 32°. I find myself just a bit on the cold side. When I first came up here, I was making a fire in the morning and a fire in the evening. More recently I've had the fire in the morning to take the chill off the place, but I've skipped the evening fire. I have been tempted to go to bed a little earlier in order to get up earlier. As the days lengthen, I find it's breaking down my sense of time and I'm a little disturbed inwardly by the thought that it's still light very late and I could be operating.

At the estuary were four female mergansers taking baths, and it was the wildest thing in the world to see them go through the water flapping their wings and kicking up a horrible disturbance trying to get the water all the way through their wings. The tide was out, but not very much, and I think they were cleaning themselves with fresh water which, I think, tends to pile up on the surface. Abruptly, one of them jumped up out of the water onto a log that is half buried and began preening herself. There is a lot of work involved in getting all the feathers back in place. Each feather has to be rubbed by the beak, and this caressing of the body by the bird's bill and neck is the bird's way of working the oil from the oil glands at the end of the rump over all the feathers so they stay waterproof. I noted that she had a very prominent crest and red feet, and then suddenly one of the other females jumped out of the water and began to gesticulate with her mouth and neck toward the other one on the log. Was this, I wondered, some signal of submission or signal that the other one was dominant. Yet I've always had the impression that these mergansers work as a group, and the more I watched the more I realized that what I was seeing was last year's young still with the mother. They have black feet whereas the mother has real orange-red feet. The crests of the young ones are not nearly as ragged as the mother's and it's conceivable that some of them are males, too. I think the black plumage of the male comes in only with the spring molt when the animal is in courtship. It was great to see that again, and I felt privileged. It was an exciting moment.

## May 28

Today the salmon are starting to come in. I just saw two and they are fast and big. I can see them clearly in the shallow water and they're tremendously nervous and easily turned back by imagery that they're receiving. They are very big, almost four feet long, at least they seemed that big. I ran on down to the estuary hoping to see some of them jumping, but this is apparently just the beginning of the run.

Later on, I did have quite a thrill watching a bald eagle circling up about 600 to 700 feet. When it wanted to come down it would stall in some current, and everytime it stalled, it fell, then would pick up enough speed and convert it into another circle and glide. As it got over the treetops it would level off. How magnificent!

I may have to use the stream for refrigeration because the weather is getting milder and milder; but there's the risk of my stores being turned up by a bear or otter and raided, which would set up a food chain that I don't want to have. Also, it might be a source of bear attack.

When the plane came in today it sounded almost like a sonic boom. I feel my hearing has really become very acute because of the stillness here and maybe the bear, in this same situation, is just as startled by his acute sense of hearing. Maybe that also generates a bear attack.

## May 30

It's one of those wild days that Americans are so fond of. I don't know why. It's supposed to be a day in which we commemorate our loved ones, and there is something very touching about death and the realization that we're all brought down to the same common denominator. Having devoted most of my life to being around life and liking it, I think I'm in a philosophical state of mind where death does not appear to me to be a serious problem —why should it be? I find repugnant the point of view that there is a resurrection, that life will go on somewhere else, and that if you have botched up this life you are going to get another chance. I think if we didn't have that foolish notion—almost like Santa Claus—and if we really looked at the world around us and all the creatures, plants and animals, we would sense that we are all the same. We are, after all, little more than an accumulation of organized biological material that undergoes sequential phases of birth, growth, maturation, and death. And we face accidents. I don't worry about this generation or the next, but in the back of my mind lurks a very ugly thought: the sensory joys that we've all experienced, and that our children will experience, will not go on indefinitely. If we could only be content and not constantly push ourselves into more and more of the limited environment in which we live. There is a loss of ego and a loss of being which comes from being too crowded. I can't possibly enjoy being in New York City or any other big city for more than a day or two. I go into a state of violent depression. You learn not to see all the people streaming by you; you just don't see them and it's abnormal. A human being should want to be with another human being because a human being is a reflection of a human being, and they interact. At the same time, I'm particularly distressed by the idea that man must constantly seek out a large group to be at ease in, as if he were afraid—and in a sense I guess he is.

Well, it would appear on May 30, which is a national holiday, that T. J. isn't thinking very much about those who have gone before. But in a way I do, although I know they're at peace and, God, I hope it never changes.

Two men came by, and as I sat at my window watching them, I resented their being here. When they came back, I resented myself for not wanting them here, so I went out and waved at them and took them three cans of beer. One was an Army captain engineer from Santa Barbara and it was just great to talk to him. He was about ready to get his Ph.D. He seemed shocked when I wished him good luck and told him I had intended going into teaching about 23 years ago, but that I was fed up with teachers. . . .

## May 31

The salmonberry are three-fourths through their blooming period, so there goes another very conspicuous landmark. The buttercups are still very much in evidence in the open areas and the skunk cabbage leaf is huge now. These areas are quite pretty. To me skunk cabbage is a very special, attractive plant. The flowering spikes of the skunk cabbages are supposed to have red berries, but exactly when this happens I don't know. The flowering spikes are almost prostrate on the ground. The lily of the valley should be the next big show, if the flowers are anything.

Because of the plant blotter through which the rain must fall, the amount and kinds of nutrients in the water are in rather short supply. In consequence, the lake does not develop a tremendous plankton growth and the microscopic plants don't get out of hand. So the lake stays clear in terms of organic cells, since algae are one-celled. The water does have a marked reddish stain, and the stain is, I think, one of the reasons that the lake warms up as it does. The stain absorbs heat although I wouldn't say that 47° is particularly warm.

## June 1

I had a brainstorm today. I've gone over the fact that when the air temperature is colder than the water we visualize that water is evaporating. We're aware that the water is flowing rapidly to the ocean and lake, carrying along a certain percentage of the debris that goes into the stream as a result of the wind or what the animals drop in. Nonetheless, the idea occurred to me that a lot of debris works it's way to the overhanging shrubs that bend down to the water's edge, particularly when the stream is up. I began to notice that a lot of the branches that are in the water when the water rises are actually carried downstream bowed, bent back, in the direction of the current. The current and buoyancy and other things interplay here so the branches always spring back into their normal position until the water catches them again. There are a lot of harmonic motions, motions which are repeated over and over in a definite way.

## June 2

I'm finding it progressively more difficult to sleep, partly, I think, because I'm not working hard enough any more since I don't have the camera to work with. Without an operative generator, I can't charge the camera batteries. I do have a still camera with me all the time, but if an Alaskan brown bear came along I probably wouldn't be able to get a picture of it because the trail alternates between dark and very dark—and one can't take pictures and fiddle around with exposures along the trail without giving some thought to the bear.

I really have no orientation of time any more. I'm never really very hungry and I eat whenever I happen to be in the cabin, that is, when I'm not busy outside. I'm anxious to get out and away from the cabin. It is not a prison and I would certainly hate to be doing this without one, but on the other hand it is in the cabin I think that one develops the feeling of being alone. It's just natural to associate a cabin with family or with social life and people, and there aren't any people here, believe me.

The tide is moving up every day; high tide comes in a little earlier, and the low tide is later.

I think now we can begin to develop the three different levels of the understory; the lowest story is moss, then coming up through the moss I find dogwood, false lily of the valley, and the smaller twisted stock. There is also a smaller unidentified plant that looks like a strawberry, but I know now that that isn't so. Above that are the twisted stock and the fern and above that the shrubs, and where the shrubs are you don't have too much of the other understory.

About mid-afternoon the wind came up and it was obvious that a frontal passage was coming in again. The wind was a high wind and I was surprised about how fast this storm came up. The wind moved at about 30 to 40 miles per hour, and five bald eagles came in with it. They were really riding that wind, obviously searching the upper reaches of the forest for food; birds, or maybe, squirrels. They would dip out of sight and sail into the trees on the ridge. It was wild and beautiful and I could see the white heads and tails so sharply. It all conjured up some immense, indescribable emotion in me.

## June 3

The parents and baby dippers have been feeding all around here. The parents are beginning to sing, which means the male is courting the female again, and this means it is longer between feedings. Today is the first day I've noticed the babies in the water and swimming, putting their heads down and looking.

They know there is something in the water that they should be catching, but they don't know how to do it yet. They're running around a lot with the parents, and, as I say, the parents are beginning to abandon them.

## June 4

It's easy to overdrive yourself here. The light is so permanent and *you* decide when it is dark because it is twilight for a long time, until about midnight, and there's a lot of light at 2:00 A.M. You have to know exactly how much you can do and not do.

The stream has gone back to 45°, so from the time the snow melts until the time it gets to this cabin it's warmed essentially 13°. I don't know how much of that warming takes place in the lake. I should check the temperature of that tributary that goes into Lake Eva.

The rapidity with which things progress here is absolutely astounding. I've been here seven weeks and now I hardly recognize places that were favorites of mine, because they're choked with bracken fern and skunk cabbage. I made three trips to the lake to cart back my supplies, and just about have a complete grocery store here. I got some fresh meat and fruit, but I don't think the temperature is low enough to permit me to keep anything perishable. I can keep bacon about a week, and on this day cooked about two pounds of it which had gone moldy. I've discovered that if I cook it all the way down, leaving no fat on it, I can eat it.

It was again one of those nights when I couldn't sleep. I guess every now and then you get a big tug from civilization and the tug is a very overpowering one. You suddenly find youself alone and wondering why you haven't noticed that you were alone and why you haven't done something about it. I really don't know what another person would do. I'm doing the very best I can, and that is to continue to find what's here. It's ironical that I'm a little hesitant to wander off the trail for fear of hurting myself.

## June 5

The dippers were singing at the stream so I jumped into action. The babies were practicing swimming where the current is the roughest. They'd walk along a log, put their heads into the water to look, and occasionally one would come up with larvae that was attached to the log. It was exciting seeing them first hand. You can read about this, but it's not like seeing it yourself.

The whole feeling of the lake and shore today is that of summer. The first time I approached the lake, I could see about a ton of golden debris going into it and I didn't know what it was. When I got to the water I discovered it was pollen from the spruce and hemlock. A noticeable amount of pollen falls into a lake during the late spring and it's possible to date the age of a lake by the number of pollen layers in the bottom sediment.

I found some more bear tracks on the trip to the estuary, and they were about 5 inches wide. The one other set of tracks that are always on the trail are the deer tracks.

## June 6

The one thing that I thought would keep me stable in this environment is the knowledge that in the past when I have been out in the field I would always go to the end of the trail or to the top of the mountain. It has always been a source of great pleasure to me to be out and doing things. I began to look over this environment with the idea of picking stages on which life's activities could perform, and in the process of doing this I discovered there are really slim pickings. Nature isn't flagrant. Nature is in effect playing cops-and-robbers and is not exposing herself. Animals do not lie around, but are endowed with caution. I began to realize that the animals are here, but I am an intruder. Human beings have camped this place and fished this place and trapped this place, and the only animals left are the ones that have this built-in caution.

The tragedy for an area like this is that as man develops mobility, it becomes profitable for him to erect lodging for people who take advantage of this mobility. The first thing you know, the area becomes a vacationland. As soon as that happens here, people will come in droves and see only a sliver of what's here. The Forest Service is logging the trees with the idea that the only important thing here is the tree and its products for mankind— people have to read their newspapers and magazines, they say. Nobody really reads anything any more, but they still keep cutting down trees instead of thinking of ways to eliminate the necessity of using timber. The question arises: What happens when we cut down all these lovely trees? The Forest Service says that in 30 to 40 years new trees will be up, though they won't be so big; but then you don't need them that big. They were rotten in the middle anyway, they say. So, you see, already you have abused and destroyed the entire forest. Not only the trees; you've also thrown away the humidifier and the umbrella that keeps this place from washing away, so the streams will change too. They will be much hotter and there will be a marked change in the animals that can live in this water. The whole thing is going to hell. For what?

## June 7

One baby dipper is all by itself feeding at the waterfall. The dipper is a very curious bird and will fly to you if it doesn't expect you're up to something. The mergansers don't seem to be in evidence any more and are probably up in the trees nesting.

In the afternoon I was going up to the lake to bring down some gas. As I crossed the stream I was a bit puzzled about its color. There seemed to be greenish streaks in the water and I discovered that the stream was now also carrying a tremendous amount of pollen. The pollen behaved like a dye and I thought it was a great opportunity to film stream circulation. It was a beautiful sight. The pollen has a gold-green color and is not affected by wind. In the same shots I was able to get the young salmon that haunt the embankments of the stream. The salmon were living within the eddies produced by the irregularities of the bank and the interplay of roots and overhanging branches. Otherwise the fish would have to swim continuously against the current which would soon sweep them into the sea.

## June 8

The incoming adult salmon were feeding, and it was almost frightening to see them break out of the water with their mouths open, because they give something of the feeling of a shark.

It was a very windy, cold day. I amused myself off and on trying to write some poetry and did a fair amount of exercising. I didn't sleep well again last night and that's beginning to be a very irritating problem. I went to sleep about 10:00 and much to my horror I woke up about midnight and couldn't get back to sleep. So today was kind of a drag for me because I couldn't get any sleep. I'm not too inclined to reminisce or talk of plans for the future up here or even to think of civilization. It's toward the end of the day and I've had a demanding day. The kind of day that doesn't lend itself to a place like this.

## June 9

I went to bed early last night and had a great problem sleeping. The fact is that it's light out, and the only reason I'm not out enjoying it is because I'm tired. It's hard to turn off the light and go to sleep. I got up at 4:30 and it was a sunny day with not a drop of rain. The trails are beginning to be less muddy.

This week there is a tremendous downfall of pollen. All the leaves on the bottom of the plants are flecked with it and the toadstools are flecked with it. It's on the camera lens and in my nose.

I took a boat trip and noticed pollen along the edges of the lake. There tends to be a divergent flow of water laterally and toward the edges, and this tends to move the pollen along the edges of the lake.

All at once a plane zoomed in and landed on the lake. I drove my little craft over to the plane and chatted with the people. It turned out that Boeing owns planes and flies aircraft executives who are interested in their planes up to Alaska. The executive and I had a fantastic conversation about conservation and we learned a lot about each other in a short time. He made me wish I could keep going on to other things and to other places rather than stagnating on one lake. I keep thinking about the hunters and trappers who are constantly moving around, and I think it's a normal instinct of any organism to move until it is at ease or has security. For most organisms security is being in an environment in which they are not stressed beyond their capability. And so one of the reasons you can say that there aren't many people here on Lake Eva is that basically it's a hell of a place to make a living.

Anyway, it was interesting talking to this fellow. He had two other men with him who were fishing. He made an interesting comment when he said that these men had caught a lot of fish and were good fishermen, but they strongly believed that anything they caught they should throw back, and they did. You see, basically, no matter what anyone says, a human being is another environmental force on fish. If you're catching them all, obviously they're in short supply, so I was intrigued by this idea. I'm terribly depressed by those human beings who put our resources into short supply. Fishing is an enterprise which cannot be continued at the present rate without a lot of regulating.

I've been worn out by the experience of the long day and cannot help drawing the conclusion that the animals in this area have a tremendous advantage because they have a lot of time to gather food. I'm willing to bet that the success of many of the plants up here is due to the long day and the relatively mild weather. It's getting warmer all the time. It is 46° and a clear night.

## June 10

I would like to point out that I do brush my hair once a day whether it needs it or not, and I decided to use the deodorant, which must be just as odious to the bear as my personal oils.

## June 11

I've finally found out how to lick my insomnia. When I feel a little tired after supper and when I have everything put away I no longer force myself into another round of activity, reading or something—something right now is nothing, really. I came up here with language tapes to study my French and cassettes of music, which is mostly Mozart with a little Beethoven and some odds and ends, but I haven't been able to listen to this because of the lack of power. So I've been going to bed a little earlier. I may wake up once or twice and I may have an occasional dream, although the dreams aren't meaningful enough for me to ponder them in the morning.

## June 12

I saw the marten again. He was along the edge of the stream on the opposite side and he nearly got my baby dipper, which seems to be the only bird on the stream right now. I don't know what's happened to the adults and I think when they leave the nest and forage for food they only forage near rapids. The marten apparently would have eaten the dipper—it's easily accessible to the marten there now because all the embankments are leafed over by overhanging branches of salmonberry and bracken fern. The bald eagles came down the stream twice, about one-third the way up the height of the trees, and they are really quite large.

In the past I was an avid collector and I liked to have a specimen of each thing I photographed, preserved in the format in which scientists collect specimens. If we're talking about plants, we generally collect them for use as dry specimens. There are some things that aren't readily dried, such as toadstools and mushrooms and the wood fungi. Flat structures like leaves and stems don't require a great deal of additional flattening; these dry specimens are usually taped on or glued to a piece of white paper. An herbarium is just a collection of these. One can learn a lot of botany in short order and identify a lot of plants just by going to a university and asking to see the herbarium collection. But it's almost like going to a morgue, you know. Here the dead bodies are and they don't look lifelike. There is an unpleasant aspect to specimens and it is, I think, a necrological idea, of seeing the body.

But I don't want to do that any more, and the reason is, if you think of all the people in this country in real life, damn near every last one of them goes through an educational system. Most of them are taught biology at some time. Biology shouldn't be *taught*, because it deals with things that are alive and are really there; they are not phony, abstract things. How do you get the reality across to the people who are taking the subject? This depends upon the skill of the teacher in talking, and here is my complaint. Basically we teach kids all the parts of the animal, and they are given a formaldehyde frog. You begin to wonder, wouldn't it be nicer if we made biology a study of living things so that our people would be drawn to the beauty and mystery of living things? Why create this barrier, that all of biology is a formaldehyde frog?

Another aspect of the problem concerns cities. As they grow there is a fair amount of subterranean activity—excavating, which brings up a lot of dirt. The dirt has to be carted off and it usually ends in a dump station, filling in a stream bottom or tide land. Soon it is all flat and you wouldn't know there was or is a stream around. The plant life associated with the drainage sys-

*Maturing skunk cabbage. New
sprouts are a spring staple for the
omnivorous Alaskan brown bear.*

*Bear tracks on the shore of
Hanus Bay.*

Adult Alaskan brown bear scrambles
ashore with 7- or 8-pound female
red salmon in his mouth, which he
will eat immediately.

*The view from Hanus Bay from the estuary at high tide.*

A coral fungus growing near the estuary.

Tidal flats provide a temporary bridge to an islet in Hanus Bay.

tem is gone, and once it's gone you've lost the animals and the charm. All you have left is the flat land to build on. The process is repeated endlessly, and finally if you want to get out to where nature is, you have a long drive. We are now far withdrawn from the reality of nature, but finally people are beginning to realize that mankind is becoming too abundant and can completely destroy the water supply. I don't know why we say "water supply" in particular. After all, the stream is an integral part of nature and any disturbance of it has biological consequences and climatic consequences. Basically, all waterways are polluted. How do you pollute one of these streams? Actually, you not only pollute it, you prevent the normal flow by dams.

Now I'm getting into a treacherous area and I'm not sure that I can get the idea across. A stream carries a certain volume of water to the ocean and this water is not transported uniformly. In other words, a stream is a collecting system which collects water from tributaries, and the collecting of this water gives you the volume of water which arrives at the ocean. However, this isn't the total volume of water that was collected, because the stream evaporates the water and absorbs oxygen and gives off carbon dioxide. In addition as the stream flows along it is slowing and has a certain amount of leakage. Not all of the water reaches the ocean. Some of it is hung up in passage, evaporated by the trees and the plants along the stream. You can sense the work of evaporation when you see moisture rising off the water as mist. Trees along the banks provide the stream partial shading from the sun, so the stream is kept cooler. The stream is also cooled from the evaporation of water into the air. Thus a stream is generally colder than the air around it and that's why we like it recreationally.

In addition, the stream receives water from its tributaries, however small, and the tributaries receive their water from the snow or, indirectly, through seepage. The water coming through seepage may have been in the ground for a considerable length of time—and here is where you get into trouble. The subterranean source of water in the stream undoubtedly passes through an area in which man is in active enterprise with the ground, meaning, essentially, farming areas. The farmer has learned that by doing this or that he has a better growing condition for a particular crop, and so he fertilizes the soil thoroughly. The surplus fertilizer is carried off into the subterranean water supply and reappears in the drainage system of lakes and streams. Now the lakes and streams have a greater source of nutrients than before so the plants thrive and tend to make the water turbid and odoriferous. Whereupon we go to considerable expense to filter off all the algae and purify the water. The stream has not only the fertilizer but also the sewage of the towns along the way and that of the grazing animals, and so it goes.

Here in Alaska, if you have a stream you have hydroelectric enthusiasts who make electric power by allowing the gravitational force of water to work against a wheel. If you want to use this power you have to store up (in other words, dam) a lot of water, thereby destroying the drainage system that normally collected water for that area. The other threat to this lovely country, as I have mentioned several times, is timbering. If you cut down all the trees they will eventually grow back, but it takes a long while and in the meantime they aren't there to conserve the water and, by holding it, to cut down erosion of the ground. So as this land is cut over it will gradually reduce the natural fertility and we will have a completely different kind of stream and effect.

We don't yet know beans about each plant's function in terms of total genetic significance. We seem to be throwing them away before we understand the system. I think the basic fault is that we haven't learned to appreciate the beauty and the necessity of living within our limits, and we won't as long as man is obsessed with the idea of being created in God's image and assumes that he has a ticket willfully to destroy things in order to make money.


## June 13

Just above the waterfall, two men were fishing — and they were very tiny men; one was crippled and only came up to my navel, clearly malformed, but very friendly. They were either Eskimos or Indians but I wasn't sure, so I asked them and they were Tlingit Indians. The Tlingit, essentially a fishing people, were native to this island and built the totem poles. I was glad to see them and talk to them and spent the rest of the afternoon with them. I shared a beer with them and got further background on the Alaskan brown bear, their way of life, and so on. They turned out to be half-brothers, originally from Yakutat. I've been told that Yakutat is a typical Indian community where everyone makes his money in the summer months and then spends the rest of the time doing nothing. They were fishing for what they called bluebacks, the sockeye salmon. There were about fifteen of them, 10-pounders, all poised in the middle of the stream in a little basin above which the water shallowed, which the men were trying unsuccessfully to catch. They finally tried to snag them with a hook, but the salmon wouldn't take spinners, and the men didn't have flies.

Both men work in Sitka and had come from Sitka by boat. This was the last part of their vacation before going back to work. George Ramon is a baggage handler. I was very impressed with his straightforwardness. The other Indian, Peterson by name, is a bookkeeper for the public health service. He owned the boat, which was a cabin cruiser, that they had anchored out in the bay. They had rowed ashore in what I think they called a yak-yak. They hadn't had much luck at the waterfall so they came back and fished the rapids above the cabin where they caught one cutthroat trout. I think they also had five or six cutthroats that they caught on spinners.

I don't know what to say about the brown bear. The brown bear is like a shark — most of the time it avoids you, but if one wants to run into you it will. The Indians told me they had just returned from a trip to Hubbard Glacier where they went into the ice field and ran into a glacier bear — the blond grizzly. The grizzly, of course, is nothing more than an underfed Alaskan brown. Alaskan browns have some heredity isolation by virtue of being situated on these islands, but for all practical purposes they are about the same. Apparently the grizzly is nearsighted. They fight a lot with each other and maintain territory along these streams when the salmon are in. There is always a possibility that the bear will mix you up with another bear. George Ramon was of the opinion that the best thing to do when you find one is to stand still, hold your ground, and talk to the bear. The bear will become curious as to what you are and will stare at you and then usually back off and go his way. It was interesting to get his point of view.

Then I talked to Peterson, and he said he's never encountered a bear on the trails in all the years he's been out (he is forty years old now). He told me about a fellow walking along this very trail that I use and, as he came around a tree, standing 5 feet from him was an Alaskan brown. He shot from the hip and brought the bear down with the second shot. George then told me of having to shoot a glacier bear to save his brother, who was in the direct line of the charge. I must admit that they sounded like very calm people. He wanted to save the head for a trophy so he shot the bear in the hind legs and the front legs to cripple him, and then in the heart. One of the other stories I have heard somewhere is that the bear's hind legs are larger than his front legs so he can't run down hill. Therefore, if you want to get away, always run down hill. But I think that's likely erroneous.

The Tlingits said that the bear is a good swimmer perfectly capable of taking care of himself in the water. There is a general feeling among hunters that they should never shoot a bear in the water because the bear will charge. He will dive and then spring himself up out of the water and actually onto the boat.

I hope George and Peterson come again sometime, because we really did have a good talk. I'm a little upset that I don't have a pocket-sized tape recorder so I can record people as they talk. If I'd had a mike with me the details of our conversation would not have been lost. The Indians were a delightful interlude and meaningful to me because here were the people who really owned this country, it was theirs. They live in harmony with it. . . .

I forgot to mention yesterday the bear tracks I picked up going to the boat. The bear had walked up the trail to a huge log and apparently hopped right over. There isn't a mark or scratch on the log.

## June 14

The skunk cabbage hollows are completely dominated now by the bracken, which tower so far above them, that you are no longer aware of the skunk cabbages unless you look closely down through the bracken ferns. A lot of the things that were previously easy to photograph are now buried under grass or reeds and other plants. A week ago I was photographing full-grown plants that stood no more than 6 inches above the ground. The grass-type plants are up about to my knees now.

The bear have been traveling through and have heavily tramped down the grass. It was not a tremendously fresh track although it must have been made that day.

I was delighted to see that my school of sockeye salmon, which numbered between ten and fifteen when they were pointed out to me, had grown to a sizable school of forty or fifty. The one thing I'm a little puzzled about is that the information on the sockeyes suggests they migrate by day and rest by night, but the behavior of these fish doesn't suggest that.

## June 15

When I reached the waterfall area I was distressed to find that my school of sockeyes had completely gone. They just weren't there. Apparently they've gone on to the lake, so they must migrate in the evening hours. Because of that I went back around 7:00 P.M. to see if any more might have come in; but none had, so I made two trips to the estuary and one trip to the lake. The baby dipper was still at the waterfall looking very lonely. Fortunately, that marten didn't get him that other day so he's still in business.

It has been so dark and oppressive today that the varied thrush were singing all day long. Normally they're turned on just before daybreak and at dusk, so it was a pretty dark day.

## June 16

Evidently a young varied thrush was killed on the trail yesterday. There was no trace of the bird left, just the feathers. It was apparently done by an otter or a marten. Also, the bald eagles began to mate. It's done in through the trees and there is a fair amount of hitting of the wings on the trees. A male mounted a female right behind my cabin, but I was down on the landing when this happened. During all this activity there is a melodic calling. There were five or six bald eagles. When I went to bed last night, an immature bald eagle looked right in through the window. He wasn't very pretty and not neat, but what an alert bird. Their eyes are darting every which way all the time. He stayed there about 30 minutes and urinated quite a while and then dropped his feces. Then he apparently saw something and took off.

I went down to the estuary twice and I almost got into the water to see if the salmon would panic. There was a new school today, numbering about twelve, and they weren't as large as those of the previous group. The build-up of the bald eagle movements along the stream suggests that the stage is about set for the final phase in the life history of the salmon.

## June 17

I happened to notice a toad sitting along the trail in full view sunning itself. This is the third occasion on which I have seen a toad here. These toads are totally untoadlike in that they don't vocalize up here, or if they do, they have extremely soft voices, to escape predation by the raven. He is a very pretty toad with yellow patches on his head.

On up the trail past the boat I began to pick up a fresh bear track, and I had decided earlier that as soon as I run into a fresh bear track it is time for me to turn around and start heading back. There's no reason to bump into one or to overtake one. I did get my shot of the elderberry and I came across my first maidenhair ferns.

On the way back down the trail I saw a huge pile of bear dung which was about 4 or 5 inches across. How I missed seeing it coming up the trail I don't know. The bear had backed its rear end into a cul-de-sac up a steep slope in among the bushes.

## June 18

I was quite taken by the absence of the eagles this morning. They are still not able to make a living on the stream but they sure expect to.

Two salmon went by in the early morning. I turned up some more bear droppings and rechecked and photographed the dung I found on the 17th, which was well dried out. The moss on the trail is almost completely dessicated and the side tributaries into the stream and lakes are dry now — only two or three are running.

The Alaskan brown bear snaps it's teeth when you get near, I've been told, and today I heard this sound for the first time. It was eerie. I'm sure it was a bear. There was no crackling of twigs to show that the bear was running, and this was a nice thing to know. I've been pondering the eating habits of the bear when he comes out of hibernation, this business of eating plants. I think the bear eats material that digests poorly, judging from the droppings which look for all the world like mule or horse droppings. The reason he eats plant material, I think, is to get vitamin C to prevent scurvy.

My spare time is spent working on French. I also find myself intrigued into reading all the fine print on the label of each tin can I use.

## June 19

I have quite a collection of salmon parr around my landing now. Their population is growing because I'm making an artificial food chain where I dispose of my empty cans of shrimp and salmon, which are the main protein foods I eat here.

I have the impression that the ocean temperatures have gone up. There is apparently enough heat on the ocean to cause warming of the air directly above, so that the cloud layer which would be fog at water level is raised to an elevation 6,000 to 8,000 feet. This means there is a layer of overcast that makes things seem unusually dark here. Whenever the varied thrushes start singing during the day you know that the overcast is thick.

In the evening I wanted to see just how long it would take to run up to the boat and back. It took ten minutes each way. I'm not sure I'll do this every night, but it is a tempting idea.

## June 20

I noted a school of salmon just above the waterfall again, about twenty-five of them. An otter was keeping them upset. They swam up and back again and again. When I went back later in the day they were gone.

At night I noticed a big gravity wave, which, it turned out, was generated by the fish. There was no wind blowing at the time. Twenty-five or thirty of these salmon, even more, travel three-four abreast. The schools are slender, columnlike platoons of soldiers. They move fast, 5 to 8 knots. Their backs show a green color and their mouths are very big. It was an exciting finish to this day. Again I went to bed feeling that the salmon in this stream is very insecure and fearful for its life. Again the bald eagles were not in evidence. It makes me wonder whether or not the group in here was migrating.

## June 21

It rained all morning and until around 2:00 P.M. The temperature — 46° — is the warmest it has been. By 2:00 A.M. it was daylight, and I got up at 9:00. I was cabin-bound until about 3:30 in the afternoon and then I decided to film the outgoing tide in a time-lapse. I took along a tape recorder for music and French, and every

30 seconds I shot the time-lapse. A trio of harlequin ducks, one male and two female, came down to feed along the edge of the shore. As I was working there, I heard the voice of a little boy. A pair of Indians and a little boy were going up the trail, apparently to fish, but I didn't get over to talk to them. I think they were fishing without a license because when I saw them at the waterfall they immediately vanished into the woods. I had quite a bout with the mosquitoes while there, which showed me that there is more animal acitivity going on than I thought.

On the way down to the estuary I noted about a dozen salmon schools in the depression where the stream shallows out, but I didn't see any wave action on the stream during the day. There were salmon in the estuary and every once in a while they broke water. They skim just along the edge of the water, sometimes 6, 8, 10 feet before they go in again. They're obviously after something. The one thing about the salmon that I can't get used to is the slender shape. Is the shape a consequence of its requirement to operate and spawn in the stream? I suppose so.

This is June 21, the longest day of the year. I am quite tired. I got back to the cabin about 8:30 and fried some pork chops, the last of my fresh meat. I lay down to sleep in the burnished light.

# 7

# PEANUTS
# AND
# LULLS

## *June 22*

There was some activity on the salmon breaking water again, but it didn't begin until the tide started to run out. I had three passages of sockeyes which came in on the low tide. They come up tight. Also, two or three bald eagles came in toward 7:00 P.M.

There is an interesting situation that I hope to film. A raven has a crow as a constant companion, and the crow occasionally gets angry at the raven and attacks him. But they are always together.

I came home absolutely bushed. It was a nice day with only two or three light rain showers. Nice to have a bit of dampness in the woods again. Sunny weather can be harsh in a forestry situation.

## *June 23*

The battle for space along the edge of the stream is proceeding apace and I have no desire to go in and flush anything out. I saw a female merganser with a brood of ducklings in the evening just below the waterfall. She went up onto the bank and saw me. I went back to the estuary after supper and the tide was still coming in. There were no ducks in the estuary then. I had taken the power saw down and I cleaned out more of my blind. The mother merganser is extremely hard to get close to with her ducklings.

My jays are still coming around for free handouts. I haven't been able to find the dipper recently, but I am finding more and more of the large slugs on the trail. I also found a different kind of slug starting to feed on the bear dung along the trail. There appear to be three types of slugs here: one, gray with black spots, that grows up to 5 or 6 inches long; the little garden slug that is about 3/4 of an inch in length; and a gold one, which is the one I saw feeding on the bear dung.

I'd love to get some underwater stills of the salmon, but they are quite nervous and I don't really have high hopes.

I took a bath tonight and the water is still bitter cold. I don't know that I'm going to enjoy the diving too much.

## June 24

Three common loons. I was too far away to see clearly what was going on, but it was either mating or two males fighting. They would run through the water flapping their wings and making a wierd sound. After about five minutes the gravity waves from this disturbance began to reach the shore. The loons then stopped and moved toward me. I'm fairly sure they saw me, so they turned back. Big fish in the lake were jumping now and then. They seem to be jumping primarily close to shore.

## June 27

The amount of bird life I'm getting on the stream is starting to pick up. There were several bald eagles feeding. I came across a man who was fishing and he said he was a biologist who was surveying the bald eagles. I'm afraid the bald eagles are doomed in Alaska. Supposedly, the lumber people are to leave some trees for the bald eagle; but my impression is that the eagles roam the forest proper in search for food until the salmon appear. A lot of good one tree in the middle of a barren, denuded hill in the hot sun will do.

I decided to dive to see if I could get some pictures of the sockeye. I put on the wet-suit, and after five minutes or so, I began to feel a little cold water in the midsection. As far as filming salmon underwater goes, I might as well forget it. The salmon form is barely visible, and it became apparent that I am too light. The current began to move me toward the waterfall. It was an unsuccessful effort!

## June 28

In the afternoon I collected water samples in empty cranberry bottles. I took one sample at the waterfall and that area is completely overgrown with alders. Then I went on to the upper end of the lake where the main stream comes into the lake and got a water sample there too. I also wanted to check the gravel area there for spawning fish, but it was too rough to see. I turned up a leech, which is a new animal for the lake, and brought it back to the cabin. The toads are certainly plentiful and the underwater plants are coming along very nicely. They will be flowering shortly.

## June 29

Last night and this morning I started putting into order the first of the hydroponic experiments involving germination and growth of a variety of materials, essentially vegetable seeds. Seeing which ones grow the fastest should reveal the phosphate insufficiencies of the water. I'm doing this by germinating the seeds along a pad of fiberglass cloth which is laid in the bottom of a dish. There are a number of variables: whether or not the cabin temperature is sufficient to ensure germination; if there is destruction of the seeds by fungi. I cut out pads for a dozen dishes and have a good collection of garden seeds. I've placed ten seeds in each germination tray, and am using ordinary stream water which I collected today. I will check the experiment about every three days. We should be able to get right to what's in the water, I hope.

About noon it was apparent the weather wasn't going to improve. I chose to make another dive above the logjam, working up to the logjam. I got in the water and for some strange reason the suit was more open and I very quickly became chilled. I worked my way up to the rapids, filming the stream, largely, and

I saw no fish. I decided to try floating back down the stream to the logjam. On the way back I was annoyed to see the film wasn't moving through. At the present time the stream is very low.

By the logjam I found two 12- to 14-inch native cutthroat trout and filmed them. I have now finished two rolls of film with the underwater camera. When I came out I felt great. I had lost a lot of heat. I went in the cabin and slept for about two hours. When I woke up I was still cold. I guess the sleepiness was due to the loss of heat, so I blew the afternoon.

## June 30

A windy, cloudy, dark day. The cabin was 53°, air 36°, and water 47½°. I was up at 6:30 and made a trip to the estuary at 10:30 to discover if salmon were collected above the waterfall. I found about twelve, so I came back to the cabin and made preparations for underwater filming, hoping to use an overturned tree as a blind. The water around there is about 4½ to 5 feet deep and the current is strong. The big problem in underwater filming is maintaining a camera position. You really have to hang onto something for support, and about the only available thing is logs. I was in the water approximately 45 minutes. I brought along two thermoses of warm water with which I flooded my suit to fill the spaces. Unfortunately, I have lost so much weight that now my suit is too large for me. I attempted to film with a three-fingered glove on the right hand, but it was awkward to find the shutter release. I think in general the filming went fairly well.

The salmon were very much aware that I had gone into the water and they retreated. I spent nearly half of the 45 minutes waiting for them to come back into position. They moved in and out of sight rather quickly. It was a very dark day. There isn't a great deal of behavioral activity manifested by salmon stationary in a pool, but they do appear to be extremely disturbed and move about in sort of a race-track mill whenever they feel there is danger.

## July 1

I've been somewhat annoyed recently by the presence of a mother raven with three young ones. A tremendous amount of conversation goes on between them which is very complicated and has a great deal of musical tone.

Today was cold and gray with a lot of wind, and the first day in quite a while that I haven't had any sockeye salmon at the waterfall.

## July 2

This evening I broke out my germination experiment I had started on the 29th of June and was delighted to find that the radishes had sprouted and the beets were sprouting. Both the radishes and the beets showed 100% root germination. This experiment is very amateurish but I hope it will give me some knowledge about the water coming into the lake. The broccoli appears about ready to sprout, so I decided to try a few more radishes and beets and I set up two more dishes of each. Experiment 1 involves eight species of plants, a couple in duplicate, and I hope the additional dishes of radishes and beets will give me an idea of how long it is before I have to give the plants light and, then, the response of the root system to the light.

## July 3

I filmed some footage of T. J. Walker walking down the trail, coming toward the camera, filming my approach by pushing the transmitter button as I came into view. I shot it twice, but the second time through I varied the action as I proceeded toward the camera by stopping to inspect the cow parsnip blossoms. I continued toward the camera without realizing that the cow parsnip I was sniffing was directly opposite a small tributary planked over by a boardwalk — and I promptly slid into the ditch. On film I simply drop out of sight and then come crawling up into view again and walk on past the camera rather sheepishly.

I was unable to verify if the salmon came in on the high tide. I suspect rather strongly that the sockeye salmon just swim on through the rapids and don't have to jump.

## July 4

I got out the different species of vegetation I had started in my water experiment, but I couldn't tell whether the standing water had in any way impaired their vitality. One of the problems is keeping the roots in relatively dark light. I placed some species outside by the feeder where we have the most light and the warmest location and am anxious to see how long I can keep the roots moist so they aren't damaged. It will be interesting to see the effect of light on them. The carrots and onions are just beginning to sprout, along with the spinach, and two of the bean plants have sprouted. The peas and lettuce have not sprouted. The question arises where to go next. After six days I have seedlings, which is good sprouting time. It probably would have been wise to have included a germination evaluation of a variety of ornamental flowers, but I think a plant that produces an edible material is a little more appealing than a flower. It's too short an effort to discover which plant would do the best job.

The next order of business is to discover what the response of these plants would be in dishes open to the light. I could do this in a glass bottle with a cover, I suppose, but I haven't any of these. Well, this is all trial and error, and the ultimate solution is anyone's guess.

## July 5

I made a couple trips to the estuary earlier hoping to verify the presence or absence of my sockeye salmon. Although they weren't around I decided to dive anyway. Around 5:30 P.M. I suited up and lugged everything down. It was raining very hard. It was dark enough that I couldn't ascertain if there were any salmon, so I decided to go on down and try some underwater filming at the brink of the waterfall. I took along a piece of rope with the thought that I could anchor myself in one place and not be swept into deep water and over the falls. The light in the pool seemed O.K. and I opened the lens all the way, thinking I would rather have it too light than too dark. I watched six or seven trout, all cutthroats except one Dolly Varden.

## July 6

I had planned to dive today but by late afternoon both the wind and the rain were so intense that I felt I just couldn't. There were only five or six salmon above the waterfall. The sockeye run seems to be diminishing, for I'm now seeing sockeye only every other day, and there are seldom over twelve. I did reexamine the petri dishes with the germination experiment and am happy to note that the carrots have all sprouted, along with the onions. As it stands now, radishes and beets appear to be the best adapted. I must gather some water from this storm to see whether or not there is a discernible difference in the fertility of this water as opposed to the water I collected from the lake and tributaries last week.

## July 7

Slim pickings today. I was up at 7:00. The air was 33° and the cabin was 52°. The day was one heavy, continuous downpour, the heaviest I've seen, with the front coming in from the west. I did a little filming on this most torrential of days, but most of my time was spent in the cabin drying out. Included in the mail was a package of sheet music for the recorder my family had sent me earlier. I had quite a bit of fun with this.

## July 8

Early this morning a plane flew in, so I fired up the generator and checked with Channel Flying to see if it had something to do with me, but it didn't. Apparently a fishing party had come in. Sure enough, a trio came down the trail.

The stream was very high and I thought it would be fun to see if I could film the subsidence of the stream. First I went down to the landing and attached a red streamer to mark the height of the water. In about two hours the stream had dropped about an inch but didn't show further signs of dropping. I also felt that I didn't have enough cloud formations. The cloud formations that one sees hugging the trees result from pockets of supersaturated water, which of course the plants have created by virtue of their transpiration.

About this time Mr. Blankenship, one of the foresters, yelled across the stream, saying he had come by just to say hello. He said he had never seen the stream so high and he didn't have any desire to come across, and neither did I. Shortly after this the fishing party came back. Finding myself a little reluctant to get involved in a conversation, I went back into the cabin and busied myself. In the process of cleaning up the cabin I discovered I was nearly out of wood. The 50-pound keg of ice I received the other day crowds the refrigerator, but it enables me to keep butter and other perishables so I will have a greater variety of diet.

There hasn't been anything new or different on this side of the stream for the last couple of days. It's been irritating, the last few days, to have been cut off from my usual outings to the estuary and lake, but I haven't felt like talking to the fishermen. I know that the fishermen's presence on the stream disconcerts the mergansers which are on the estuary, the stream, and the lake. They are very versatile creatures indeed, capable of sampling all these different habitats.

I have looked over my hydroponic experiment a little more carefully and have come to the conclusion that there are a number of serious shortcomings as it is presently set up. I should provide some sort of rooting space for the seed material and I'm presently toying with the idea of aquarium gravel along the bottom for the roots to work in. I'm also wondering if the petri dish will afford adequate drainage for them. They are presently exposed to the rain. I did drain the rainwater off, but haven't bothered to replace the water on them as yet. It's amazing how many little details evade you when you're doing something of this nature. I have some plastic petri dishes and am anxious to try these out. I do want to get these roots covered.

I think that summarizes another typical cold, rainy, not-too-bright day in southeastern Alaska. The biological activity along the stream is really peanuts.

## July 9

Once again a rainy day. The stream continues to fall but it is still about a foot and a half above low level.

I made a trip to the estuary in the late afternoon, to get out and stretch and to see how things were going. The trail was wet and soggy but there were no animal footprints, and mine from the day before were washed out as well. On the way back, I heard a rattling sound that I haven't heard in a long while. It was a kingfisher, another fish-eating bird, sitting on an overhanging branch. The only other bird close by is the raven, who is clacking his head off by the feeder.

I worked over the germination dishes and am strongly enamored of the radish because it is the strongest of all those plants I tested.

## July 10

I had a good steak supper and felt very content, although there was an accident in the process of cooking the steak. I splashed up some grease on my left thumb, which necessitated the use of codeine.

## July 11

I woke up at 5:00 in the morning to the sound of the thrushes and I thought it would be a good time to try out the small microphone. It generates enough power to record bird calls very nicely, so I recorded a full hour of the 5:00 to 6:00 A.M. calls. I have had a chance to play it back and find that the background sound of the rapids by the cabin is so strong that only the louder bird sounds come through. There are some rather nice varied thrush sounds and jays on it. Later I recorded the raven, whose calls, naturally, are loud and clear. I am anxious to get the calls of the merganser and the loon. The young mergansers, by the way, have doubled in size and are beginning to look like the adult mergansers.

I notice that most of the plants, including the false lily of the valley, are beginning to show a great deal of rust damage and destruction of photosynthetic materials. They are being destroyed by some diseases.

A trio of fishermen walked by the cabin on the opposite side of the bank and I decided to go out and talk to them. They told me that they regarded the run of the sockeye as only nominal. They seem to take the sockeye as a meat supply and not merely for sport. This man just dropped a hook into the stream, snagged the fish and pulled it out, so there is no actual sport. I check the stream daily and sometimes twice daily. Salmon apparently come in on the high tide and in a year when the run is big the stream would be jumping with sockeyes.

## July 12

Today I continued the collection of the first set of water samples from the tributaries. By the end of the day, I had a good collection of the types of water involved in the Lake Eva system. I went down to the estuary and included one sample of water from a collection of rainwater which will sink into the forest floor within a day or two, so this is essentially standing water. I also collected a sample from the pollywog pond which has a very dark red color. Ever since I've been here I've indulged myself by drinking cranberry juice for breakfast or whenever I feel thirsty. I've been carting down three bottles of cranberry juice a week and hoarding the bottles when empty. There are quart size and excellent for hauling and storing my water samples.

I still wanted to collect samples from the tributaries on the south side of the lake, and doing so gave me a chance to reassess the biological material along that trail, which I hadn't been down for a couple weeks. I was curious to see if the bears were still working the trail, but I did not see any fresh tracks. I brought the samples home and for some strange reason I was somewhat depressed and really didn't enjoy the preparation of the evening meal nor did I feel up to seeing through the rest of the project of setting up the petri dishes.

## July 13

At 6:30 in the morning I called to inform Channel Flying that I had, on Friday the 10th, severely burned my thumb and needed medical advice. It looks very ugly with large blisters and it's beginning to pain. I suspect that I will be getting an extra mail drop this week. It is this kind of accident that makes you think of the danger of operating by yourself; and you feel very stupid to have let such a silly accident happen.

The huckleberry fruits are about ripe. The fruits are pointed up to the sky, and I wonder whether or not this display entices the bear and squirrel and birds to come and sup. Assume an animal does. When it later defecates it drops some of the undigested seeds back into the environment, and by this means the species probes its opportunities for living space, widens its range. I have sampled a few huckleberries but they are not quite ripe enough for me. This begins to herald the time when the brown bear come out to reap this fruit.

I had a good time filming a young female merganser. This bird is extraordinarily keen and alert, and maintains a sharp lookout all the time. I find that the animal very commonly sights me and, rather than panic, continues what it is doing, pretends, and works itself into an escape point where it can then get away. It doesn't let me know that it knows I'm there. This immature bird did exactly that.

## July 14

I reached the lake around 11:00 and rather then sit around waiting for a mail drop I decided to take the boat out. By this time the sun had come out and the whole lake was extremely beautiful, while the mountains at the far end of the valley were in a storm.

Toward late afternoon I decided to go on down to the estuary. I hadn't been there more than a few minutes when an otter surfaced. For a moment it became confusing—because there appeared to be more than one otter. I then noticed that I had a mother with two babies and they were feeding on rocks in the shallow water. They all submerged and swam across the estuary with one breath, then emerged from the water on the opposite side of the stream and went up an otter run into the forest.

## July 15

I did a lot of sound recording in the early morning. Birds seem to do their calling with respect to how dark it is, and they do most of their calling when the overcast is thick. Each day for a full week I hope to make a recording of about one-half hour in the early morning. This should give me a little more insight into the activity of the forest at night. I have seven one-hour tapes of biological noise, primarily of birds, which I have made between the 11th of July and today. I now wish I had two of these Big Ears so that I could go into the Sony, which is a tape recorder with a higher-quality fidelity. I have a very strong desire in my mind to capture—as much as I'm capturing visual images—the acoustic envelope that goes with it. I now have these sounds and I have to go through and work out some kind of recording system to edit the sounds and organize them.

A lull in biological activity has lasted a little over three weeks now, and I'm getting terribly impatient to get at the salmon run and the animal activity which will be associated with it.

When I came back from the cabin in the late afternoon there

was an immature eagle perched on the tree by the cabin. The eagles are becoming more and more oriented to the stream, I think.

I noted a tremendous change in the tastiness of the huckleberry, which brings to mind that the next order of business for the bears, as soon as they get off the grass, is the berry. The berry is still a bit on the tart side, but they should be fun to play with in my oven. I cooked up a number of biscuits and a cobbler or two, and I must confess they hit the spot.

# THE
# ACTOR

## *July 16*

The antibiotic I took for my thumb yesterday was a little dis-
quieting to my stomach. After I had taken a pill I went out to
make some sound recordings when suddenly I was seized by an
upset stomach and I threw up rather violently. I then realized I
had the Big Ear going and had recorded the entire episode. . . .

Certain kinds of plants are just nasty because nature has been
successful in the engineering of a plant and, as a consequence, it
undergoes a genetic explosion and generates a great many similar kinds. The result: a lot of closely related forms which haven't
sorted themselves out and none of which has really crowded out
the others. The identification of such plants is troublesome, even
to the botanist, so I have deliberately shied away from, for example, fiddling around and trying to identify the willow that's up
here.

When I got down to the estuary there was only one raven,
which was turning over the seaweed, and it wasn't happy that I
was sharing the shore with it and kept a watchful eye out for me.
The tide was going out. I walked up to a small island that was
accessible to me, set up the tripod, and watched the raven. While
turning over the seaweed, it would jump up and jump back, re-

coiling as though it had turned up something that was attacking it or exciting it. I don't remember whether or not I got this on film, but I enjoyed it immensely.

Each raven is different. I had one at the feeder that flew off, landed in a tree, and looked at me. I turned on the camera and stood there, and much to my surprise the raven approached the feeder. But when it heard the camera noise it took off, only to land on the pine tree directly behind the feeder and peek up over the top of the feeder at me. I'm convinced the bird was attempting to wait me out.

In mid-afternoon when the sun was out, a school of twenty-five or thirty sockeye salmon sped up the stream, which was very high then. They appeared to be followed by a run of Dolly Varden trout. I think the run for the Dolly Varden has begun as well. I was surprised to see both these fish together. They appeared very cautious of the shallow water and sped up on into the logjam area.

As I sat myself down to supper in the evening, I saw a gravity wave at the logjam area so I opened the door and looked out but I couldn't see anything. I went back in and looked out the window and saw a full-sized otter swimming in only about 3 feet of water and heading on down the stream. I could see the fore and hind legs moving in the swimming motions with exquisite clarity.

Today I felt a little depressed and I really don't know why. I guess it's the lull and the pressure of having a wounded thumb.

## July 17

I noticed salmonberry lying in the water. A lot of the salmonberry had already been plucked. I took in some cups of huckleberries and tried to make jam, using up some of the sugar that was brought in for coffee. The jam, alas, was not a great success.

The natives, I gather, are very upset with the terrible spring and virtually no summer they are having, which is due to the comparatively light winter. The hemlocks and spruces have long since shed their male cones, and there was a period of time when these were floating down the stream in regal abundance. At the tops of the branches now are the beautiful female cones which are being pulled down by the tremendous number of little cones, especially on the hemlocks. The cone is the seed, carrying the structure of the coniferous tree — and the principle users of these cones are the squirrels.

I've been taken aback that the principal user of the stream is not the sockeye but the Dolly Varden trout that have been at sea since the ice went out of the lake. The Dolly Varden trout winters under the ice of the lake and *not* in the streams of southeast Alaska. The water in the stream flows at a very low level in the winter months and the trout begin to show up in October and November, migrating upstream to the lakes, apparently spending the winters there and not feeding at all. In April when I was first here they were all bunched along the edge of the lake, apparently beginning to leave the lake. It's interesting to note that here we are in the middle of July and the Dolly Varden trout are making their way up the stream during the day, not at night. They travel in schools of five or six up to about forty or fifty, and it's an exciting thing to see. When I got up to the pool above the waterfall there were four or five sockeyes but the principal attraction was a school of forty or fifty Dolly Varden trout. I also saw the kingfisher on the stream, and I really have to get some footage on him.

I continue to fret over my thumb.

## July 18

At the lake, I was amazed with the color change occurring in the sockeyes around the delta. They had changed from the green color to a striking purple and I was really impressed with their beauty. Later, I went to the estuary where I found eight or so sockeyes with Dolly Varden swimming around them. Again in the stream later that evening I was conscience of a small school of Dolly Varden swimming upstream. The fish seem to be very conscious of the current and swim diagonally to it.

I must not fail to note the five loons diving on the lake, and, about the same time, a mother merganser with young hugging the edge and disappearing into the side stream of the lake.

In the late evening after supper I was chopping wood and heard a single note that reminded me a little of an elk. I looked up to see a bald eagle surveying the stream. I should point out that I had put the head of a sockeye I had caught on the feeder for anyone who would take it. There have been a few ravens looking it over, but no one has taken it.

## July 19

I read in the Sitka newspaper while I was in the john that Charles A. Lindbergh thinks that man has grown apart from his environment. Well, I think there are two ways to be aware of our environment. One is to be a farmer. If you're a farmer you are conscious of weather, insects, ants, disease, rust—you name it, the farmer gets his nose rubbed into it and, even though domesticated, his animals and plants are part of the environment. It's true that he has created a semiartificial environment, but nonetheless it's functional. So a farmer is very much aware of his environment and has time enough to be aware of it since he is alone with it. His neighbors are far enough away that he and they aren't fighting—at least not at close range. But now, unfortunately, we build roads and the boys can get away from the isolation and go into town. We've got more and more disenchanted with being by ourselves, and have become more interested in being with the herd. I think a city person has no awareness of his natural environment. He's in a completely human environment. If you are going to live in the city you are going to reflect the city. Certainly people who work out-of-doors are aware of their environment, but very few people work out-of-doors now.

The second way to become aware of your environment is to become a nature lover. A lot of people, including me, are nature lovers. You don't have to know what it is that you're looking at, the important thing is to experience a delight in it—of feeling, of smelling the air, of experiencing things. I think the basic error is thinking that man is the center of the universe. He is not. He is just as much an ecological derivative and dependent as the other organisms, and his success or failure is beyond his control. His anthropocentrism, in fact, is a little embarrassing.

## July 20

It was a very confusing day for me. I prepared for the arrival of the camera crew at 2:30 in the afternoon. They have come to get pictures of me doing things. I'm slightly agitated by this visit, naturally. I feel seriously depressed for the first time and worried about performing in front of a cameraman. The reality of interaction with people can be a beneficial thing but has certain implications. I think maybe a person is better off limiting the number of contacts and involvements he has. . . .

By the end of the day I was bewildered by all the talk and almost numbed by it. I found myself lying in my bunk wondering if what I was doing would be better carried out if some team came in here and did it. Also, much to my horror, I discovered

that I was lacking "wrap-up" on most of the subjects by not getting in close to the animal. Wrap-up? There's no way to do it. So
I went to bed feeling much dread over the next day when the
crew would film.

## July 21

We (camera crew and I) went down to the estuary and the
only animal around was the bald eagle. We spent the morning at
the estuary filming, then returned to the cabin for lunch and
packed the diving equipment. After finally getting it up to the
lake, the photographer (the one who was to film this sequence)
and I put on our wet-suits and took a long ride up the lake in the
boat. By the time we got up to the point to film, it was 5:00 P.M.
and the plane was coming in. We had to go back to the landing
to pick up the tank of air, which took time. It was all a very
drawn-out business.

Much to our horror, when we finally got to the delta to film,
we found the sockeyes were starting their excavation of the delta
for their nest. A tremendous cloud of muddy water surrounded
the delta. We snorkled for a while and got an occasional glimpse
of a sockeye, but no chance for the cameraman to film me looking
at sockeye. Around the other side of the delta it was also dirty all
the way down. I was tremendously impressed by the steepness
of the delta slope and the barrenness of it, although there was a
fair amount of trash accumulating there and some aquatic plants.
After the dive both of us were fairly cold, having been in the
water a little over an hour with about a 20-minute dive. I was
glad to have made the dive although I was a little overweighted.
With five of us in the boat and the mosquitoes buzzing, we started back. It was a demanding day, working two habitats—a very
wild day.

The blister on my thumb had reopened slightly and I re-
dressed it in the evening.

I feel funny performing in front of the camera, but I suppose a
film of this type would be dull without some action.

Everything is blurred. I am quite upset, possibly even feeling
my territory has been violated.

I wonder why the salmon and the trout are much harder to
approach in the lake than in the stream. A fish has, along it's
body, a series of current receptors which measure the water flow

along the side of the body. The fluctuations of the pressure in the stream, generated by the irregularities of the bottom, accompany the turbulent flow. The fish needs to have a certain awareness of how the current is flowing, and the only time a fish is frightened is when the current system changes. When a diver enters the water, if the stream is turbulent, the fish pays no attention to the diver. However, if the water is still, the diver moves the water by his motion and the fish flees. There are two aspects of the fish that I am most intrigued with: one is their reaction and sense of smell, and the other is their lateral-line function. Both of these systems I have previously studied quite extensively, though not in the natural habitat.

## July 22

It was a day of utter confusion and a very tiring day. Bill was shooting topside and Jeb was shooting underwater at the logjam. The water depth was only 4 or 5 feet at the most and I finally got enough weight on me, 35 pounds, to keep me down. It was peaceful swimming in and out of the logjam. We also shot a few sequences of me walking down the trail and then we headed back to the cabin.

I was quite concerned about my thumb and dressed it again.

When one is on camera one feels one is moving too slowly and so tenses up to get it out of the way. I find this with myself now that I'm on the performing end. It seemed the cameraman was hard to please, and we had to do everything at least twice. I think it reduced my efficiency.

## July 23

Right now I'm trying to remember the day, a day in which I didn't have a chance to experience anything for myself, other than experiencing the ugliness of going through play-acting. To me routine things are meaningless. I do them like breathing, I don't do them consciously. The mechanics of doing dishes and sweeping the floor, and, God knows, this place would drive a woman out of her mind. It's the wildest place in the world. You have to sweep your floor every ten minutes.

We did some takes of me getting up in the morning and pretending to go into the kitchen. That isn't too hard to do. I'm a sleepy guy anyway and not having had a haircut in three months makes me look like the traditional wild man of Borneo. So I went into the kitchen and washed my face and we filmed me walking over to the stove. One of the realities of being up here is that you know in the morning you're going to be chilly, and if you're so inclined you will start to make a fire and shave some fine kindling, which is about a 15- to 20-minute job. Sometimes I do it at night and sometimes in the morning, so we had to do some shots of T. J. Walker making kindling.

We also had a sequence of Walker going to his bookshelf to get the scientific information he wants. The way I get scientific information is by going out and taking some pictures of the plant or object I'm drawn to; I facilitate my observations by camera work. This is where I'm different from most scientists, who measure the plant for graphs and charts or chemical analysis. Very few scientists are photographers. So I pretended to go through a book. Then we have a scene where I pretended to look through a microscope. I haven't used those microscopes much.

How is a person supposed to go out and experience new things? That's a full-time job. What I'm trying to do in the filming is show how much beauty goes by unseen, unfilmed, unappreciated simply because we have become city folk. We have lost the knack of knowing how to see. There is a lot of experience up here new for me: the salmon, the bear, and so much else.

## July 24

This was the final day for the camera crew to be here and I again play-acted.

We filmed the suiting-up scene at the upper end of one of the two islands near the cabin. They also wanted to do a scene of me playing the recorder that my family sent me.

I had the recorder here and someone thought it would be a good idea to have T.J. sitting in the woods playing it, the lonely explorer. Playing a wood flute in the woods is all very well as long as the wind doesn't blow. When the wind blows it begins to play tricks with your instrument. The wind wasn't blowing and I pointed out a very pretty place which is a bear trail that leads to an overlook of the upper rapids. It's idyllic here and it isn't overgrown with shrubbery. I have often gone up to this place and we went up and shot a scene. Next they want me to pick out an appropriate piece and master it so they can tie it in with the film.

They also wanted a scene of me going off the trail into the woods. Then, of course, they wanted a scene of me coming down the stream, tying a ribbon that identifies a collection site.

I was then given a fishing pole and told to go fish. You've never seen a more clumsy and awkward fisherman in your life. I have a real sensitivity to fish, and I don't like fishing and I'm irritated when I see people fishing. I can see the reason for it when there is a food chain, but the reality of a food chain is pretty well removed. I was asked to fish. I cast the line out and hung up the line and got it all fouled up on the reel.

Every now and then I get the feeling that I'm smiling my smile through all this play-acting.

## July 25

The plane was about an hour late and I was a little upset that I didn't have the still camera because the light was good. We did get some aerial shots of the lake, making two low passes and it was thrilling to get that orientation. In a sense I felt as though I had abandoned the lake. I was kidded about having hijacked the plane. We then made one high pass and I was surprised at the clarity of Lake Eva. I was particularly taken by the valley wall to the north and the tiny tributaries that look like nothing from down below. It was very exciting seeing this. For the first time it dawned on me how truly wild my little universe was.

In spite of the seaplanes that are able to come here, there is a tremendous amount of impassable, inhospitable terrain. When you look at the map there is a ratio of about one glaciated valley to five or six that do not carry lakes.

On the flight I saw some minor lakes that don't even show on the map, so there is a lot of work to be done to put on record, on map, the total number of minor lakes. The thing that always intrigues me about this total concept of a wilderness area is how to get people to it. Once you get them to it, what can they do there? What is the best way of actually using our natural wilderness? On the flight I suddenly realized what a tangle — all the space and me so isolated, I really am a prisoner of Lake Eva. I didn't realize I was a prisoner of Lake Eva until I got up in the plane and discovered what a distance there is to any way of escape or route back to society or to the other world about me.

The flight left me sad and uncertain of myself, and the uncertainty was generated largely by the tension of the film studio which I think began to push some of the panic buttons. I'm sure that bear will put in an appearance. However, in unraveling the ecology of this system, one has to take it as it comes. One can't order the experience he has.

I found myself absolutely and completely exhausted and I found I had lost the knack of being in a crowd and unable to unravel the confusion of a crowd of five. It was a frightening experience in a way, but I'm sure in time I will come back to where it will be all right to be in a crowd. Nevertheless, I think the last man on earth will not necessarily be an unhappy man.

# 9

# PALE
# AS
# GHOSTS

## July 26

There was a raven at the feeding station about 11:00 A.M. and I suddenly discovered it was quite hot. The raven was sitting with his beak wide open because of the heat and I really began to feel the sun pouring down. I decided to open the trunk and get out the "summer" costume. I was still a little hot but I'm sure it was due to the flannel underwear. I changed underwear and discovered this gives the mosquitoes a chance to go through the pants and drill at my legs, and later I discovered that it was a little chilly.

The mother merganser and babies came down again but I wanted to get a scene of me eating salmonberries, so I shot myself wading into the stream to where the salmonberries were and collecting them.

## July 27

The impression you get when you see the sockeye salmon in its mating colors of purples and oranges and reds is that it looks for all the world like Japanese koi.

The delta was flooded by surface waves but there were not too many sockeyes, which was a little puzzling.

In looking at the stream I find that every day it looks more olive in color. The rocks are becoming mossed over, which not only gives the stream an olive-green color but also an odor, and I'm wondering if the odor would attract the fish. I was going up the stream when I saw the mother merganser with her babies, and the babies took off. It appeared to me that there was quite a bit of commotion and that I had two mothers with babies, so I followed them. As I got closer I saw a single mother with thirteen babies. I can't help admiring and liking this bird, but they do have many problems in keeping away from predators including man, otters, martens, and so on. They eat the salmon parr, which keeps the number of the salmon down. Which brings me to realize that I have to wade on up the stream to where the sockeyes are possibly spawning. I'm pretty sure the sockeyes will spawn around the delta. As it turns out, the young sockeye make their first year's growth in the lake itself, feeding on plankton.

I got back to the cabin about 6:30 and it was a nice evening to sit out on the front porch, so to speak. A single raven sat nearby on a tree talking to itself and working some food it had carted along from somewhere.

## July 28

I discovered that the air bottle for my Mae West was empty and I wouldn't have any flotation, so I decided to make a snorkel dive. I was aware of the current around the delta and it was quite hard keeping a position. The visibility was still very bad and I couldn't see too many images but maybe I didn't stay around long enough. I then started swimming and investigating the various angles and saw a few images of the sockeyes, but as soon as they saw me they put space between us. I found that the solution to this problem was to swim very hard and rush them. This didn't seem to bother them too much although they always managed to outswim me.

I entered the water about 12:30 and I didn't come out until 3:00. I was beginning to experience some fatigue. I wasn't so conscious of how cold the water was because trying to film the salmon took my mind off it. The wave structure of lake surfaces is much smaller than the wave structure of the ocean. In the

ocean the waves send down pillars of light, and they are gravity
waves, so they're moving rather slowly. You get the feeling that
the water is penciled with the shafts of light. In the lake, gravity
waves indicate the wind has come up. The gravity waves here
were small, about 2 or 3 inches apart, and I was delighted to discover that as you look down through the water there are thousands of little pencils of light criss-crossing each other. I couldn't
resist the temptation to point the camera down and shoot that.

I worked my way toward the shore, trying to discover if there
were any sockeyes there as compared to the delta, and in the
process I got exposed a bit to some of the underwater plants. I
was in about 4 or 5 feet of water. In the process, I came across a
school of baby sockeye salmon. The fish, in its first year or two
of growth in the lake, before it moves to the ocean, is called a
parr and when it gets ready to go into the ocean it's called a
smolt. At the present time the baby salmon that are here are of
two species; one is the coho salmon, which is found in the
stream and is distinguished by some orange coloration on its
head. It is the principal salmon in the stream. The other is the
sockeye and is apparently found mostly in the lake. Although
eggs may be laid in the tributary, all the young are going into the
lake. I was delighted to see these young sockeye, and they school
very tightly. I know they are being preyed upon primarily by the
merganser. I don't know to what degree the loons are preying. I
haven't seen them for a while now; maybe they're nesting.

I then came upon a sockeye nest, but the sockeyes immediately left and didn't come back. The sockeyes are accompanied by
schools of Dolly Varden trout. The Dolly Varden trout came in
from the sea the same time as the sockeyes, and the first clue that
there is a school of sockeyes coming is that you see the Dolly
Varden moving upstream. The Dolly Varden are the ones that are
afraid of people, and maybe they alert the sockeyes. It's interesting that the cutthroat trout, which is also in the lake, is not afraid
and comes right up to me. These trout are anadromous fish also,
which means they divide their life between salt and fresh water,
laying their eggs in fresh water but spending most of their lives
in the sea.

Around 6:00 P.M. I went down to the logjam and for the first
time saw sockeye accumulated there. I also had a fall. I was walking down to the landing and one of my feet went off the edge of
the log. Thankfully, I didn't hurt myself. The only way to fall is to
fall limp. I learned that a very long time ago. I'm very aware of

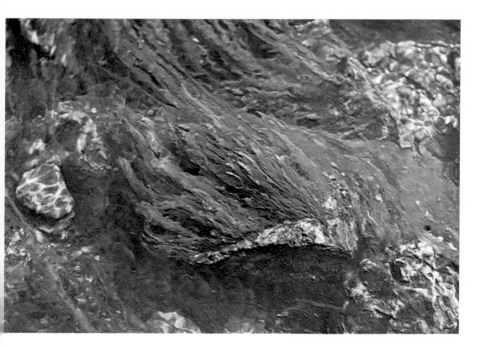

Sea lettuce anchored to gravel in the estuary basin.

Sea lettuce festoons a log in the exposed estuary. The primitive marine algae tolerate drying at low tide.

*A salmon head left in the estuary*
*basin by an Alaskan brown bear.*
*Remains provide immediate food for*
*marine isopods which swarm up out*
*of the interstices of the gravel.*

*Looking up from the estuary to the rapids at Eva Creek.*

*Twin Alaskan brown bear cubs leaving stream.*

*Walker, almost ready to dive.*

how much demand this job puts on me, so I'm going through the Canadian Air Force exercises and I'm also doing some yoga, which I think will give me more agility.

I got some cookies from my daughters at home and I'm trying to ration them and not eat them all at the same time. I also have a bottle of sherry, and I wish I had a case of it up here.

## July 29

It started out as a cloudy day and the contrast between the three previous hot and sunny days, days getting up into the 80s, was terrific. It felt like a cold day. I went back into my long-johns and flannel shirt. I get the feeling that the seasons are beginning to move from summer to fall. There aren't many plants blooming, but I'm not beating the bushes to find each and every one that is.

I wish I could have been two or three people. You can cover more that way. I was a little disturbed thinking that the thrush and robin are no longer singing in the morning, and it seems that many plants and birds are going through a period of withdrawal. The Oregon crabapple is beginning to drop it's leaves, which have now turned a bright yellow. The false lily of the valley is gone. There are some plants, like the dogwood, which will continue to carry a green leaf through the winter.

I got up at 12:00 midnight and made some recordings of the final chirping of the birds at night. I then read about the salmon.

In the morning, I set up the stream watch to film the salmon running upstream. I put the camera on the cabin roof on a tripod, which was quite a chore. I still have to go up and sweep away the litter of leaves and pine needles on the roof. I have a ladder set up now and can shimmy partway up the tree to the roof, and do it in pretty short order. I think, in the case of salmon, the availability of spawning sites is in accordance with how many salmon are spawning. I don't think the reason the salmon come up the stream one species after another over a period of one or two months necessarily means that nature has given them different timetables for arrival. I think the reason the salmon come up the stream sequentially is because they come different distances. (The same applies to the gray whale.)

You get the impression that the salmon stock in the world is in limited supply, being canned and all. A survey to find how many salmon beds are in evidence is nothing more than a direct expression of how many salmon there are, I think. I get the feeling that the salmon do fight for the better beds. They kick around the gravel trying to make it smooth, and the things that come loose are drifted downstream and into the lake. The water in the lake is a coffee-brown color and this may be the reason. I hope I can resolve some of the questions as to how many salmon beds there are, and where they are, with my diving.

I went to the estuary around 2:20 when it looked as though the overcast would burn out. Several hundred salmon were in the pool above the waterfall. These fish were beginning to show secondary sexual characteristics. I could see the difference between male and female and very quickly realized they were pink salmon, so this was the first of the salmon run of the second species. They were somewhat bigger than the sockeye, and their behavior in the pool was somewhat the same.

I rushed back to the cabin, thinking I would work from the log blind which is the only place I can really work these fish unless I wade into the pool and scare the living daylights out of them. The coho and sockeye are salmon that leave their young in fresh water. When they hatch they are no longer fry, they are parr. The coho young are in fresh water for one year. The sockeye young are in fresh water anywhere from one to two years and have the longest record for being in fresh water. Right now, the sockeye young are in the lake and the coho young are in the stream. I photographed the coho young extensively and they are the prettiest of the young. The coho are in salt water three years, sometimes two, and when they come back to fresh water their bodies have to go through changes.

I suited-up at the cabin except for the weights, and I wore some boots over the wet-suit so I wouldn't damage it. I was in the water about 4:45 and the sun was out. On two occasions rather large schools of about thirty Dolly Varden swam by. I think fish generally school according to size because of their tails and the propulsive motion of their bodies, which they screw through the water much the way a snake does, but a lot faster.

Unlike the sockeye, the pink are already in spawning color. I also noticed the animals nipping each other, already territorially minded, and I observed several jumping.

In the evening I went down to the estuary again and I was delighted to sit down at the waterfall and watch the Dolly Varden jumping up the cataract.

## July 30

I checked with Channel Flying and learned that the weather was taking a turn for the worse. It was a gray overcast day. The pink salmon were beginning to come in. The first thing I did in the morning was go down to the estuary to see if they were there, and they are. However, I decided not to dive because it was too dark. I went back to the estuary around 4:00 P.M., trying to get there when the tide was high, hoping to see the pink jump.

The pink were milling at the juncture of the estuary with the stream proper. It was apparent to me that the pink are blocked by the shallow water as they get to the waterfall, much the same as they are blocked by the shallow water near the cabin. For every pink that makes it across the shallows, there are a dozen that turn back. A lot would go up the stream, and a few minutes later they'd come back down.

When I reached the waterfall, I found that I had missed the high tide and the water was going back down, so there was a little depth. Apparently I was watching the tail-end of the passage of the pink across the waterfall for that day. The passage of the fish is regulated by the depth of the water. The salmon has to have water at least twice as deep as the height of the jump it's going to make, I've read, but I'm not really too sure of this. This may be true of the big jumps but not of the jumps in the rapids. I'm drawn up with the mechanics of the fish working it's way up the waterfall. The smaller pink came by. I waded out into the stream just to see how swift it was, and I must admit it takes a good deal of care when wearing waders not to be swept off even though the depth is shallow. I came back filled with the excitement of having seen for the first time how the salmon negotiate these rapids and the waterfall.

## July 31

I had the impression from the sockeye run that they generally come up the stream in waves during the night so that they aren't observed. At any rate, I went down to the estuary and the tide was just beginning to come in and the island was flooded. As the tide comes in, you can see the tidal water flowing up if it's carrying any debris, and generally the visibility is better when the salt water is coming in as compared to going out. When it starts to go out, it begins to tumble against the rock and you are aware that you no longer see the bottom. When the tide is up it invades the last segment of the stream at the bottom of the waterfall. I always thought that if I were a fish wanting to jump the waterfall I would jump it at high tide. I realize now that to get into fresh water, the fish stay in the salt water as long as they can, and traverse the estuary only on high tide. I was able to watch the pink coming in on this wedge of water, and they do a lot of milling (a term we use when a fish starts to go around in an oval pattern). The tide got into the bottom of the waterfall and a few pink made it, but I didn't see any jumping as I had the day before. The jumping is done mainly by the smaller fish. The larger fish have the power to swim right on up the waterfall, and the water is shallow enough that I can actually watch them swimming up the waterfall. I waited and waited and I was again impressed with the Dolly Varden that were coming in with the pinks. I notice that oftentimes Dolly Varden will jump from as far as 15 feet away from the waterfall, and by the time they are through the jump they either collide with the vertical wall of the waterfall or are swept down under the wall of water. Some don't even get to the waterfall. This prompts me to think that maybe they are being preyed on by other fish in the waterfall area and jump out in a form of escape; but, again, in this area it is hopeless to get any underwater observation because of the swiftness of the water.

## August 1

The stream continues to drop in level. It's interesting that these salmon are dependent upon the streams of southeast Alaska to spawn, since they spawn in the summer and early fall when the stream is in the lowest ebb, and the only water the stream is receiving is the runoff of the rain.

There was no activity at all in the estuary today that I could see. I am now of the opinion that the Dolly Varden and pink get up to the stream area when the tide is high enough. Thus the passage of the animals may be regulated by the tidal flow. I'm also of the opinion that a great many of the animals succeed in getting over the waterfall by not really exposing themselves.

On the trail I found a brand-new bear track, just one track and it hadn't been made more than five minutes earlier because I had just finished walking the trail. It made my hair stand up to think it was so close to me, but I never heard or saw him. A lot of events seem to be coming together.

A puzzling thing about this day was the absence of raven and I suspect this is due to the tidal flow. When the tide is low this gives the raven a chance to search for food.

At the lake is a rather wide delta, created by Ratsniep Creek, with a grassy meadow, and there was a Sitka deer grazing on this. I started away from the area to the south shore of the lake and a common loon began to call. I have a feeling the loons call whenever they are disturbed by something. The loons didn't let me get too close but I had been intrigued for some time by what appeared to be an open clearing on the north shore. I pulled the boat up and went ashore. It was an old muskeg in which the trees had tried to grow, but it was obvious they weren't going to make it. Through the peat moss muskeg were situated various ponds about 4 or 5 feet wide with a bundle of aquatics in them.

A bird I forgot to mention, circling around the stream area while the camera crew were here, was the red-tailed hawk. It is a very striking bird. After circling around the stream, it left, but in a little while it came back, carrying what appeared to be a squirrel. It proceeded to sit on a tree and eat the animal.

All the Oregon crabapples are dropping their leaves and the twisted stock are dying. As I stated earlier, not all of the plants bloom in any one year, the reason being that they are all perennials and some aren't quite as far along in the perennial growth curve and so are not producing flowers. It's better not to have all your eggs in one basket.

The deepest part of the lake, incidentally, is 70 feet and is just opposite the delta. I'm still very interested in the little flowerpots that bloom on the logs sticking out of the water. I should mention that the lake has a way of resisting the encroachment of vegetation: by the wave-generated gravity waves and the current; but in general the vegetation is winning. I think the lake is doomed. It seems that this is an old lake bed.


## August 2

I didn't get down to the estuary until nearly 10:00 A.M., mostly because there were a fair number of chores around the place. The trip to the estuary was to learn how the pinks were doing and see if any of them were jumping over the waterfall. The pool above the fall was filled with pinks. The water was very clear but the light was poor.

I continued past the waterfall down the line, and while I was standing there watching, three or four Dolly Varden jumped out over the last little bit of the waterfall at the south bank. Then I noticed the water-soaked fur of an otter. Sure enough, he was there, and the Dolly Varden kept jumping in that area. The otter looked up and then slipped up over the waterfall. I knew the otters went up the waterfall but I didn't know how they did it. They seem to go around the edges much the same as the mergansers and the Dolly Varden. The tide was out and the pinks were all down in the basin at the juncture of the stream and the estuary, which suggests they like to avoid the current.

This is the season of fruits, of course, and, unless the bears will come through and take these out, a lot of the fruit will be wasted.


## August 3

Around 2:00 P.M. I got down to the pool where I have my log blind and made a 45-minute tank dive, using about 300 pounds of air. It was pretty cold. When I'm wedged in under a log and hanging onto a couple of branches trying to see the shapes of the pinks, I'm not exercising enough to stay warm. After a while I began to realize that the water around was exceedingly cold. I did a number of things on this dive. I mounted the tripod on another tripod, pulling a thread to operate it. I noticed the pinks were very nervous about the air bubbles from my air tank, so I held my breath while I was making the shots. I suppose in a sense I've made a major mistake, because I have a hunch that the difference between a stream that has a lake on it and one that doesn't is the clarity of the water. Again the water isn't very clear, even though when I look down and see the stream flowing by, it looks crystal clear. Actually, it is dirty. I got a rather pretty view of three Dolly Varden trout which looked like the line drawings the Japanese make. The Japanese are hung up on two very interesting animals: fish and heron, which feed on fish.

Two very nice cutthroat trout tried to outstare me. It was interesting to see them hold position with very little muscular activity. This is the remarkable thing, of course, about fish that live in the stream. Either it is a bottom hugger, down among the rocks, or it fights the current. The current can be fought in two ways: by outswimming it or by staying in those areas where there is enough irregularity in the flow of the water to cause the water to turn back on itself. The latter is essentially what the pinks do in the pool. I see a fair amount of damage on the fish, particularly the pinks. The important observation on this dive was that when I got out, my pinks, who normally mill back and forth, had all evacuated the pool and gone on upstream. The tripod at the head of the stream was disturbing enough to them that they had made two or three mills and, when the object didn't disappear, they just cleared out.

It's quite apparent that the pinks are going to spawn all over the stream. I can see the little areas where they're beginning to build. They build their nests to lay their eggs where the stream shallows and the upward projection of the gravel bottom provides a filter, so that the water, instead of going over, goes through it. This ensures a flow of water through the rock sufficient to aerate the developing embryo bodies of the salmon. It is possible to determine more or less accurately how many spawning areas there are in the stream by finding these conditions.

My trip down the middle of the stream disclosed several pink salmon spawning. It is wild to watch the male go up alongside the female and throw his body into a series of high-frequency shivers. These shivers are supposed to cause the female to shoot her eggs. I had the impression that the salmon really dig up the gravel and send it flying. I wonder if one can induce spawning by moving the gravel around.

I think that there are still a lot of pinks running in the mill, or herd, that haven't got down to the serious business of spawning yet. The salmon don't spawn when the stream is high. They may be induced to come into a stream when the water is up, but it is highly essential that the salmon use the stream only when the water is at low level; otherwise they will spawn their eggs in many sites which will subsequently no longer be in water.

On the way back I noticed some bracken fern and coarse grass smashed down about a block from the cabin. It was a bear stomp-out, made sometime between daybreak and 4:00 P.M. You could see each and every place where he had put his foot. It looked as though a Sherman tank had had an exercise there. I also noticed some otter dung and right alongside it there appeared to be fruit from the twisted stock, but it wasn't that at all.

They were salmon eggs from the pink salmon that the bear had apparently caught. So there is Bear One's dining table and fishing area.

In the evening I thought it might be smart to go down and check the estuary for signs of bear, but I couldn't find any more. The big excitement was that, although the tide was way out, pink salmon were running up to the basin, wriggling in water that was too shallow to swim in, but they weren't out of command of the situation. I then went up to the waterfall area and found some Dolly Varden jumping but no pinks.

One other observation that I want to be sure to get in: while I was down at the estuary, I looked across it and saw what appeared to be a seal going up the beach. When I looked again, it was my mother otter with two babies.

I was impressed with how dark the day was. The clouds were really floating by. It looked as though it were raining too, because now the hemlocks are beginning to shed some of their older needles and the plants under the hemlocks are covered with them. Also, every bush is covered with a draping of spider webs. These are three dimensional webs, not the two-plane webs that form a smooth surface. The hemlock needles are not very heavy and they have fallen onto the webs so, for the first time, I am aware of the nets. It's incredible to see so many spiders.

## August 4

Yesterday I speculated on the possibility of digging out some gravel to produce more spawning sites for the salmon. Forget it. As we manipulate nature more and more to arrange things for our convenience, it all becomes very dull.

The development yesterday that generated all this activity was sun, along with the fact that the stream is continuing to drop. I went down to the estuary to see if pinks were running up the shallow area. I was there about 9:30 and waded around, but there were no fish.

I left the camera there and walked on into the estuary to see if there were any signs of bear. Negative. On the way back before I quite got up the trail, across the estuary flew a V-wedge of seven Canada geese, and about the same time a bald eagle flew across.

About 12:30 I had everything on my raft. I wanted to look at the pool at the top of the waterfall because there seems to be a regrouping of the Dolly Varden, which jump the waterfall singly. It is believed that the Dolly Varden scavenge the eggs that didn't make it into the gravel bed. I got so involved with watching them that I grew bolder and bolder, and before I knew it I was all the way out on my tether, on the brink of the waterfall, watching the fish as they came up. When they come up over the brink and suddenly see me, they are frightened and speed on to a deeper section instead of stopping to rest. They are seriously exhausted by this jumping effort and afterward lie literally panting, pumping their gill covers (operculae) back and forth vigorously. You can judge the state of the fish by how much they move their gill covers. After about 15 or 20 minutes of this, they school.

They come through those watery slots very quickly, almost climbing, and this reminds me of a bullfight or rodeo. The animal is frightened while it's in a chute and comes suddenly out of the chute into this huge arena. For the first time in my life, I think I've seen, face to face, a terrified fish. I was impressed by both the fatigue and the fear in the fish. I find it frustrating that fish don't have facial expressions. However, when they are afraid they generally match their background or become very pale. Nature selects organisms which provide food chains for other organisms on the basis of making them as inconspicuous as possible. When the fish reach the top of the waterfall, they are as pale as ghosts.

The Dolly Varden have a lot of injury, tooth marks. So the passage of the Dolly Varden from the sea to the estuary is not without mishap. Speaking of the estuary, the animals are grouping up there to come into the stream, but you see very little evidence of predator attack. The predators in the ocean don't follow the Dolly Varden and salmon into the estuary.

When I was at the cabin I looked across the way and there was my mother otter and her two babies. The otters were chirping like birds and I'm sure this is the way they communicate. I was sitting there and suddenly I heard a coughing sound. It coughed and coughed and then it started to growl. This was coming from a hole in the bank and it was another otter.

Now the bears have enlarged their fishing area at the creek so they now have a turn-around and come in and go out the same way. Also, much to my surprise, right at the log blind, where I filmed the pinks, was another bear walk and there were salmon eggs on it as well. So the bears are beginning to move in, but I haven't seen any. Last night at midnight I thought I heard a splashing sound in the stream, and I think that maybe the bears are beginning to work that area.

The life of T. J. Walker at Lake Eva has finally become excessively demanding of time and energy, but I can't complain about it. It's exciting to see this upturn in biological activity, in life.

# 10

---

# COURTING
# AND
# SPAWNING

### *August 5*

The stream has gone down about one more inch. The stream was really dragging itself and was so low that many Dolly Varden and pinks turned back when they reached water too shallow. If they went across they would have had to tread water with their backs showing, so it was very low indeed. The coarse grass that was underwater is now completely out of it.

I spent enough time watching the upstream migration to note that the fish are much more alarmed when they go upstream singly than when they go in a group.

I was up at 5:00 and when I opened the door to go down to the landing to get some water for breakfast, it created enough sound, apparently, for the salmon to hear it. They were just heading downstream in an explosion of water. It was an enormous wake of a group of thirty to forty salmon and a dramatic demonstration. The salmon prefer to migrate when the light is down.

I went to the basin at the bottom of the waterfall to see the pinks and Dolly Varden. I get the feeling that the Dolly Varden are moving on upstream to the lake and not planning to stay at the top of the waterfall with the pinks.

Fishermen were in again from the logging camp and they

hooted and hawed and were unnecessarily noisy. They seemed very thrilled to hear their echoes in the forest. One caught a salmon I had filmed not three hours earlier and the fish was squirming and frightened stiff. The guy put him back but I was absolutely sick. I'm totally puzzled by humans.

I went down to the estuary hoping to spend the full day getting some eagle action, along with the bear. The tide was out and there was no action at all. I got there about 11:00 A.M. and it was deserted. I thought it would be fun to walk over to Peril Strait to film the ravens and the sea gulls. I thought it would also be interesting to show the plant growth along the estuary because it has developed two distinct regimens, one in salt water and the other in fresh water. I have a suspicion that the reason these plants are able to take their odd environment is because they're more fresh-water than salt-water plants, and the effect of the salt water on the plant is modified by the high velocity of the fresh water. In the process of pondering this, I looked down in the water and beheld a salmon tail that a bear had bitten off. The flesh was still pink in color, so apparently the bear had been feeding there not more than an hour before. He had been feeding directly in front of my blind.

Later in the evening, I went back to the estuary when the tide was in and the pinks were milling but there were no bear. For the first time, I have the feeling that I am trespassing. It's the bears' turn to take over their claim.

In the afternoon there were no pink salmon in my log blind but the pool was full of coho young. By this time it was clouded over and it looked like a thunder shower coming up. I decided to hell with getting wet again, and I couldn't see dragging my raft up. So I didn't dive.

In the late afternoon on my third or fourth trip to the estuary I got involved in bringing the camera to the waterfall, wanting to stress on film the fact that the tide comes up to the waterfall. There was a lot of milling of the pinks in the basin below the waterfall, obviously in salt water, but they were breaking the salt water and going up into the fresh water, getting their first taste of fresh water since babyhood.

The baby coho, by the way aren't afraid of me. They have orange-yellow tails and I can stick a bottle or can down and they will swim right into it. They are a charming fish and seem to swarm around me when I'm diving.

What else happened? I did my exercises. Oh, yes. I could hear the noise of the logging camp.

## August 6

I went to the estuary in the early morning to see if there were any signs of the bear feeding. One bald eagle sat in a tree, and that was about it. The salmon remains were gone, so evidently I was again too late to see the bear fishing. I waded across the estuary to the gravel bar and noticed some tracks around the area I had been in the day before. Obviously bear tracks in the gravel. I also found a small portion of a salmon's intestine. I was convinced that there were bear feeding in the early morning. If I keep checking the times of the high tide, I will be able to locate the bear shortly. The bears, however, fish mostly at night.

I then thought I'd go on down to the ocean because I thought I had seen sea gulls and I wanted to see what their role is in the drama. There was a lot of tidal area exposed. One thing that came to mind while I was walking the beach is that this is a delta-type area which has been built up through the debris carried out by the Lake Eva system. There are a great many shells but they crush under your feet. They're not as hard as they are farther south.

Back at the cabin, I maintained a roof-watch and got very little usable footage on the pinks coming upstream. It's surprising how many eagle feathers there are on the stream, though. I think the eagles are really getting in the act now.

Society, the herd, is always operating under several different degrees of order and one is constantly hung up in the mechanics of depending on others. The more you depend upon others the less control you have of your life. More time is spent in repaying others and you have less and less time for yourself. You no longer can really live by yourself or operate as you originally planned to operate. Here I am getting hung up with society again and I really don't know why or how I got into it. Man is depriving himself of his sensory discomfort. I think the real issue is that we have to learn that in order to live we must be given time to be contemplative. The only way a person will be able to do this is to go off by himself . . . . This all came about because of a bald eagle, which represents power, and power is what everyone wants. Why? Because everyone wants to get out of the herd and the best way to manage that is to do something that will cause the herd to say: "You're so great we're going to put you on a pedestal." In the process of achieving power, we overlook the basic sacrifice involved, which is less time for ourselves. I think that of all the things I've gained out of the Lake Eva experience, one of the most important is the realization that a person can be

hurt and damaged by being around people too much. One becomes dependent upon others and never realizes his own total
value. While I sit here ruminating, right outside the window is a
beautiful Steller's jay—nature's creature—and this is the way I
think life should be. . . .

I wanted to catch the incoming tide to see what time the
pinks would run. I'm sure that the salmon don't traverse the
shallow area that runs from the upper estuary basin to the lower
estuary basin when the tide is low. The pinks come in when the
estuary fills. The only action on the pinks is early in the morning
or at night, when the bears wade in to fish. I think that the pink
salmon that are brought into the basin on high tide and do not
elect to go over the waterfall and up the stream are pulled back as
the tidal wedge retreats from the waterfall into the dishpan basin. They discover they're trapped and go this way and that. It's
impressive to watch. I believe the bear has a better chance in this
basin to fish. I feel fairly confident that I understand the mechanics of the salmon entering to the waterfall.

By 6:30 I was back at the cabin again, feeling extremely exhausted. I had some pork chops and beets. I didn't bother to
write up my film reports and went on to bed.


## August 7

As the days get shorter, the sun will have a limited time to
heat the lake and the water temperatures will be colder.

I was down at the estuary around 8:30 A.M. and the tide was
out. I set up the camera and there was some evidence of bear
having been there, but I was too late to see them. There was a
fresh salmon head there and the tissues still showed color. It was
awesome. I'm wondering if bear eat only the middle of the salmon or if they eat it all. When I looked down at the bottom of the
water it was very obvious that the bear had been fishing down
there. The rocks and stones were turned over in his fishing. I
hope I can get the film of the salmon out of the way before I come
across a bear. In a way I'm glad the bear are letting the tension
grow in me because it enables me to study the salmon. I think
that I am just about set to meet Mr. Bear. Hopefully, in a day or
two, I will see him.

I made five trips to the estuary, wanting to witness the tidal
cycle with the onset of the pink migration because I really don't

think I understand it. I have been increasingly aware that the bear are beginning to work the waterfall area. I am convinced now that the salmon come in only on the high tide. The pinks that came in were all small ones. I now realize that the pinks, after reaching the estuary, school very tightly, and move upstream. They are in the stream only when the tide has come in enough to deepen the stream. The most striking thing, as the fish come up the stream, is the way they are lifted up as they get into the current flow. They're too light and they get rid of the lightness by spitting air. I've seen fish doing this, trying to get their buoyancy down to that of fresh water. The ones that don't adjust their buoyancy are pulled back downstream and into the estuary basin where they stay until the next high tide. Another observation that has come out of my exploration is that there is a marked tendency for the salmon to linger around the mouths of the little tributaries that come in. A number of the tributaries are too shallow for the pinks but they do linger around the mouths of them.

The salmon activity that I've filmed to date includes resting and swimming, as well as passing the waterfall, and I need to try to film them spawning. I feel that I understand their activity fairly well now, after spending a week of study on the salmon, but how it compares to the knowledge of fishery specialists, I just don't know.

## August 8

The first thing that caught my attention at the lake was a floating sockeye salmon corpse. I made some passes with the boat and took still pictures, but it was gruesome. At the delta there were very few sockeyes in evidence, but there was a large school of Dolly Varden trout, each one about 2 feet long, tremendously big. I also found a small school of Dolly Varden among the weeds at the exit to the lake.

I then went to the beach in the bay to the south of the delta and landed next to a tree that was lying parallel to the beach. One of the problems I've been having is diarrhea, because of all the berries I've been eating, so I went alongside the log hunting for something that could function as toilet paper. I was just ready to appropriate a devil's club leaf when I made the horrible discovery of thorns on the underside of the leaf, so I had to settle for a smaller salmonberry leaf.

I heard a tremendous rumble in the bushes, which must have been a bear, but I didn't see him. There are now more signs of bear. I think that the bear will work the places where the salmon are spawning.

On the spawning of the pinks: they are fighting over the females. The males drive off the lesser males. The females come to rest upstream from the pool and in very shallow water. The males that are chasing others away from the female are doing so with their dorsal fin partly out of water. I also noticed that I could go down and stand not more than 15 feet away from them. So now, rather than being panicked by my presence, they are so preoccupied with the spawning action that they don't seem to mind.

## August 9

I am unhappy today because it's so windy that I find it irritating to be out in the forest. One of the things that I become very conscious of as I get more and more involved with the forest is the fact that hearing is my essential sense. On a day when the wind is blowing through the trees the noise completely destroys hearing. Only meaningless noise comes in, and my system is psychologically irritated by it. I'm also conscious that the bears are now out, and moving more and more into this area. I have the feeling that when I'm out in the woods, away from the estuary and waterfall area where the bear feeds, he hears me in the forest and makes the first evasive move, but I'm really not too sure.

It is a frustrating day because along with the wind the rain continues. I sat at the window in the morning trying to think just what goes with the pink salmon. I really haven't figured the animal out. I get the distinct impression that they do not dig a nest. Also most of the pinks spawn upstream on one of the mounds of gravel. The females get forward of the crest of this and maintain station there and the males work their way up to her, generally from the rear, and then roll over on their sides and squirt golden colored (not white) sperm into the water. It's a sizable squirt and it spreads out into a big cloud, about 4 or 5 feet in length, and 6 inches to a foot wide. The male on it's side releases the sperm with a tremor of the body and generally just in front of the female.

In the area in front of the cabin there is a great deal of courting going on. A female will be followed by a group of six or seven males that seem to run her around until she has had enough of them. Then she goes over to the top of the little hummocks and settles down. At least, that is the way it looks to me. The gravel is crushed there and not, in my mind, the best place to lay the eggs. It is apparent that these creatures move from one animal to another and there is lot of running around, staying in the area but following the female. When the female elects to settle down on one of the hummocks, the males chase each other. I don't know if the females also nip other females to keep them away when they are laying or not, but I see a lot of male dorsal fins sticking up out of the water right now.

I've often seen the animals depositing either eggs or sperm without a partner and I just don't understand it. I hope to get some clues about this underwater. I get the impression that the female lays her eggs generally on the upstream side of the shoaling gravel beds. This undoubtedly is the case. I can't help feeling that there is a negative pressure field in the gravel bed which sucks the eggs and sperm down in gravel spaces. If anything, this extremely shallow area must create a pumping action which is drawing water into the gravel from upstream. This is probably what brings the eggs down into the gravel. I don't get the impression that the female is digging to project the eggs into the gravel. It's going to be fun trying to get this all pinned down accurately.

The activity is much more frenzied today than it was yesterday. Yesterday it was possible for me to get in among the salmon and see what was going on. Today, I find that the fish are much more jumpy when I get into the water. A puzzling thing.

Last night about 10:00 o'clock I heard chirping and went out to investigate. The mother otter and her two babies swam under the logjam and surfaced this side of it. Without warning, the mother otter stood up out of the water. All three pretended nothing was wrong and that they didn't see me. They swam around, pretending to inspect the island, and then they bolted. The three of them began rushing through the water as if in total panic. They came up under the undercut of the bank and proceeded to run up the bank and into the woods. About 30 minutes later I heard then again in the stream just down from the cabin. I didn't move during the time they were there, so I don't think they were panicked by me. They have studied me before at very close range, so maybe the mother spotted something more basic. Another puzzling episode.

I spent the afternoon watching the salmon intently and I'm

now aware that the cloud of golden-brown material that comes forth is nothing more than the debris flushed from the gravel by the female as she rolls over on her side and strikes the bottom with her tail. It appeared that there were other activities going on: males fighting, and eight or nine fish chasing the female. I also have the impression that the courting and spawning goes on all the time. I could hear them swishing around out there all night long.

## August 10

This morning, except for putting my notes together and cleaning up the cabin, I spent on the roof watching the salmon. The interaction of the males and their positioning of themselves with respect to each other and to the female, is quite complicated and ever-changing. Apparently there is a dominant male who lingers right behind or slightly on the flank of the female and the other males group themselves almost like a wedge. All the males push one or another, each trying to drive the lesser male away. Meanwhile another male will work his way to the side of the female. It would appear that the female becomes excited by this and will go forward of her nest, roll over on her side, open her mouth, and slap her tail very hard against the bottom. This is the cleaning of the gravel sediment.

I think that the spawning sites are now free of algae, and although salmon are attempting to set up spawning sites on the heavier rock, rocks that are 6 to 8 inches across, I just can't understand how they are going to clean these sites. Obviously, I should compare the gravel compositional vertically in the two sites. When a male salmon is going toward the female or after another male, the dorsal fin is erected stiff and sticks up out of the water.

## August 11

At the estuary the pink salmon were beginning to collect in the pool above the waterfall and some appeared to be establishing next sites right at the brink of the waterfall, which was quite exciting because it was in an area where I had filmed the Dolly Varden. I was very much surprised to see the pinks going up the waterfall when the tide was out. The logic of the salmon going upstream on high tide seemed to be a genuine one but I was really shocked to see this. In general there was no jumping and the scene was unique in that the pinks are so big, their backs are out of the water, as they swim up the shallowest portion. It seems to be a long process, and they lodge themselves at the top of each of the "stairs."

I suspect that the bear that are working the estuary come down from the north side and work their way to the gravel area.

## August 12

First I filmed the waterfall to see if I could locate passage of salmon at a time other than when the tide was in. I think the salmon that go over the waterfall at this time are those that have presoaked in the pool below or in the estuary basin in the last low-tide period. I was intrigued with a school of pink salmon spawning at the lip of the waterfall brink. I thought it would be fine to record that imagery as a means of getting across the idea that the pink is a strong fish and not wiped out by the strong current there. I was surprised to see that some of the pink do get carried over the waterfall, but they come right back up. I think the number of males around a female has to do with the attractiveness of the spawning site and not the female. The poorest sites seem to be held by the smaller females, and very commonly in these situations only one male will be in attendance.

About 10:40 A.M., I made a snorkel dive at the center of the stream near the cabin where I had lodged several logs for a hiding place and something to hang onto. I went in to see what it looked like and to see what the behavior of the salmon would be toward my presence.

The stream appeared to be up, thus permitting a dive and the fish were approachable and not too bothered by me. The visibility was very poor, but it seemed as though the female who was the subject of all the activity I saw had apparently laid all her eggs. This raised the question: How come the males are still hanging around her? I can't explain it. I get the impression that the males work from one spawning site to another, but this may be wishful thinking. The water was quite cold and I found myself fairly uncomfortable as the dive went on.

I crawled around exploring the bottom and noticed that my

kicking the gravel created a sound that appeared to frighten the fish. This is the cue to which the salmon are most sensitive.

The final bit of activity was a boat trip up Wahinee Creek at the upper end of the lake to see if there were serious obstructions across it. It began to rain more and more heavily, making the trip anything but easy. The stream runs fast and deep, and there is an awkwardness in keeping the boat in adequate depths of water. I was delighted to find the sockeye salmon spawning here. They are a very colorful fish. They seemed to be guarding a site where they had already spawned. It is clear that they dig the gravel and make a small U-shaped trench. They have to pick a spawning site in which the eggs can be well distributed and well mixed down to considerable depth by current action, so that there will be sufficient flow rate to oxygenate the eggs and keep them alive.

In the evening I visited the estuary and had the quiet pleasure of watching a solitary otter swim.

## August 13

I'm getting more and more interested to know if the pink salmon run is indeed beginning to diminish. In the week just passing it's apparent that the population just above the waterfall has gone on and that the new fish at that site are few in number. Although the pink salmon are capable of traversing shallow water, they are not able to do so when they first come in from the sea. The pink's ability to operate in shallow water is enhanced as spawning time approaches. It becomes apparent that the fish fresh in from the sea do prefer deeper water, and the retreat of the marine water from the base of the waterfall as the tide goes out is a stimulus for the fish to go out as well. Once the upper estuary basin begins to fill sufficiently, the fish will move in. Evidence of this is the tremendous build up of rather large gravity waves which have a source point directly over the body of the school of fish. The more linear the layout of the group of fish, the more likely there will be a train of gravity waves going out over the total body of the school. In general, the schools as they come into the estuary are narrow. Once the fish work their way up to the waterfall they are in a two-current system. Above, the fresh incoming water of Eva Creek slides out over the top. This is the normal situation until such time as the salt water reaches the base

COURTING AND SPAWNING 135

of the waterfall. It is in evidence at the waterfall on the highest tides. The final portion of Eva Creek, the lower portion of the waterfall, is dammed by the influx of seawater, so there is an appreciable sill of fresh water flowing out on top. I get the feeling that the salmon are aware of this and make their way up into it. They suddenly discover they are being borne up and they react by diving, in the process of which they kick their tails up and make a disturbance. This is one area I've not attempted to dive in yet.

The final phase of the pink's traversing the waterfall involves the fish not in just one quick run through the center, but, usually, in working its way up the edges of the stream (although I have seen fish going up a steeper and deeper portion).

I can assume that the activity of the bear on the stream at night has already engendered in the fish a learning experience in which it has differentiated objects from above and objects such as rocks which give off noise. The fish seem most disquieted by the transient rock sounds which come from rocks bumping together.

I made a dive at the cabin which was a repeat of the dive of August 12. The fish were more skittish. There isn't enough water for me to swim so maybe this is the reason I chill so easily. I have to remember not to clean the face-plate frequently because that scares the salmon, and I have to keep clear of the bottom so I don't clank. I have a great blind in which I'm operating in no more than 3 feet of water. I once thought that when the female makes her nest she is very frenzied and digs at the bottom, but I now see this is not the case. She swipes at the bottom only when she is agitated. I have yet to witness the deposition of eggs and sperm. It's just a matter of getting in and waiting it out and the real issue, as I say, is the cold. My dive lasted about 45 minutes and I did get one good shot of a pink male biting another male.

I think that as the spawning sites begin to be taken up by the spawning activity the salmon will spawn in sites of lesser quality. I was intrigued to see the number of young coho salmon. The little parr that are a couple inches long are now out and around the big fish. The fewer fish involved in a spawning site the more difficult it is to approach and the more prone are the fish to leave the area. I wish there were some way to warm the temperature of the stream around me so I could stay in all day with the fish.

On both the 11th and 12th I had a view of the mother merganser with her thirteen babies. On the 13th there were only seven babies left, without the mother, so it appeared that an eagle or bear or otter got hold of the mother. I felt depressed wondering how successful those babies would be without the mother. The big family of mergansers is dwindling away, and this is the way nature would have it, I suppose.

## August 14

Filming today gave some good views of the female and male pinks. The fish are a lot more weary today and I think this is a consequence of the sound of the gravity waves created by the wind. There were long waits for the footage but I think I got some meaningful shots. One was of a male coming up alongside the female and quivering. The males appear to bite the female on the tail, whereas they bite other males wherever they can get a hold.

Now it appears to me that the activity of getting the spawning site ready is taken up mostly with driving the other fish out. This is energy-consuming. I have noted that the males get more and more scuffed up in this enterprise and that soon disease begins to overtake them. They lay-up next to a log and just do nothing.

It's becoming more and more apparent that at the waterfall there is a bear stomp. The coarse grass is all pushed down but there is little activity of the salmon there. On the way back to the cabin I went across the stream, and it frightened the salmon there. I am becoming more aware that the fish are upset by outside activity and they really take off. I also found a male pink salmon that had just died. As I was putting him at the estuary he let loose with sperm on my waders. I felt a little sad that here I was giving the last rites to a male salmon and he let loose with the sperm, which is milky white and spreads immediately, just to show the sperm had not all been used up in the spawning activity.

I returned to the estuary after supper to see how my salmon corpse was doing and if anyone had spotted it and carried it off. There has been a very marked shortening of the day, which makes me think that the water will be quite cold by the time I'm finished with the spawning activity of the salmon. When I got back to the cabin I was pleased to see a rainbow, which I thought would mean a good day for the 15th. I went to bed about 10:00, after doing some exercises.

## August 15

What the rainbow heralded was a rainy day.

I wanted to film the behavior of the female in cleaning the nest. I got a fire going and then got into my wet-suit and went out into the stream at 1:00 and came out at 1:30 badly cold — my feet as if they were frostbitten. I attempted to put myself in the general area where the nest-building takes place. It became apparent that the salmon would not stay when I was there trying to film. I think they are being negatively conditioned by the nocturnal feeding of the bear. They are certainly more difficult to be around now than they were earlier. I finally moved up in the same area that I filmed before and was very much aware that the salmon had been digging at the site because of the tremendous amount of uprooted plants. The clue to the spawning site is freshly dug gravel. I also noticed that as a result of the female's digging at the gravel with the tail, there are abrasions on her tail. Another observation: lurking around the spawning beds are a fair number of young coho parr that look very fat and very successful. I'm sure they're feeding on the spawn, which suggests the interesting feature that the eggs of the pink are providing for the growth of coho young.

A solitary heron flew across and the otter came through this morning, kicking up a good-sized gravity wave. I heard his chirping.

## August 16

It was much the same as the 15th. The storm continued. I spent the morning largely on chores, working again on the generator. The cabin was down to 43° and the air was down to 33°. Water was about 54°. The pink salmon activity continues but it doesn't appear to be so intense and the spawning groups are fewer. It's been my experience in diving with these fish that each day it gets tougher. One thing that I may not have mentioned is that very commonly, when a female holding down a nesting site is distracted by the arrival of another female, she gives chase, whereupon another female quickly goes into the nest site and goes through the cleaning action. I can't guess how many tail beats are used in cleaning the nest, but there is an actual digging in which a pit or groove is dug. It may be that the number of eggs that can be locked in the gravel is nominal. I don't really know if the eggs are placed in this groove.

The lack of visual contact with the bear is distressing to me. It's apparent that there aren't too many here, perhaps because the stream is located on a lake. Maybe if we had picked a stream without a lake we would have been better able to film this food chain—I just don't know.

One thing that is not clear to me yet is how the behavior of the female changes when she is satisfied that her nest is completed. Nest-cleaning females appear to be a brown, faded color, quite different from the color of females that have already deposited their eggs and are guarding them. These females are quite a bit darker, green in color. As the spawning goes on the males appear to develop a long ribbon of white along the top of the back, in front of and behind the dorsal fin.

One would like to speculate whether the success of the spawning is proportional to the nesting site. The current was stronger on the 15th, which enabled a lot of sediment to move from the nesting sites.

I made a dive at the cabin but I did not, by any means, finish this adventure. I did get some activity of the female cleaning out the nest and the interactions of the attending males. I am still an irritating factor and the fish are agitated by my presence. The unique thing about this dive happened while I was filming the dominant female cleaning the nest. Along came another female, one that was spent. She got right in front of me and cleaned. She repeatedly got very close to me, sticking her tail out in front of me. I reached out and touched her and she did not recoil. I then put my hand around her tail, in front of the tail fin, and held on. She swam a little bit away but there was no violent escape reaction.

I made two more trips to the estuary in the evening. I turned up more evidence of the bear at the waterfall area. Piled up on the rock was a dead male pink where the bear had stopped feeding, maybe having heard me come down the trail. I really don't know. It's becoming more irritating that I haven't seen a bear yet. I did observe one pink going up over the waterfall, but that was about all the activity there. I went back to the cabin and had a steak dinner, and felt moderately well.

About dusk I made my second trip to the estuary, but again no bear. I did see a few bald eagles, which are beginning to look quite ratty with some feathers missing. The great blue heron was also down there. A few pinks were making their way up to the waterfall. I came back to the cabin and turned in about 10:00.

# 11

# THE NEST
# AND THE SPENT
# AND DYING

*August 17*

I heard the otter chirp and quickly moved the Big Ear out in the direction of the logjam. The otters were playing between the two logs of the logjam, and without any warning the mother surfaced with a salmon in her mouth. The two babies got up on one of the logs and were really chirping. It was much too early to film, and I feel the less I bother the animals at the logjam the more willing they will be to come back. They were there about 20 minutes. One can really get fond of this animal.

I was in the water by 11:30 and stayed in for a little over an hour. The female that was cleaning her nest yesterday had spent her eggs and was busy keeping the other females out. I was aware that there were a great number of male pinks up next to a log blind and I stayed on the back side of the log, using it for a tripod. I was excited by the males. The object of their attention was a female with eggs who was building a nest.

The unique thing about the dive today was that the female made one very strong effort to stir up the bottom and then a lesser effort. I can generally spot when the female is going to work on her nest. She becomes restless and then moves either backward or forward. As far as I can tell the nests are not used twice.

The female seems to guard the nest about two days and then moves away. The dominant fish is building a nest and most of the time is not sought after by the males. She is a pale color and the males don't seem to crowd her while she's building the nest. It became apparent to me throughout the dive that she was releasing some eggs because she was getting that concave look. Now whether the quiver is in releasing the sperm or if it's just a courtship action I can't be sure at this time.

Today I filmed the courtship and there was biting, not only between males but between females and males. I could hear for the first time today the power of the impact of the tail on the gravel. I feel that I need more of the male-female interaction. The building of a nest is a long, drawn-out process, taking all of 24 hours to complete. Some of the males also go into a nest-cleaning action, going forward of the female. The male does this as he runs ahead, while the female does it by arching her body so her head comes out of the water and remaining stationary. What the significance of this is I don't know. I feel now that when the female vacates her station she has heard a female building a nest close to her and she wants to run the other fish off.

Later, at the estuary, the tide was in and again mixing with the waterfall, but there were no fish going up it. I think the fish make it up the waterfall the minute they have adjusted their buoyancy. I have been maintaining a watch at the waterfall at the wrong time; they seem to go up the waterfall just before a high tide. I thought that at a high tide the fish would go up because of the water depth and they wouldn't have to jump. So this concept has been misleading me. The number of salmon that came into the waterfall was very small. I was aware that the place was beginning to smell on the sour side.

The devil's club fruits are beginning to turn red and just crying to be photographed. Also the twisted stock fruits are beginning to ripen. The colors of the twisted stock vary from orange to dark red when fully ripe and for the first time since flowering they are conspicuous. It's amazing how certain plants are in evidence only when flowering or in fruit. In the old days people used to go out and pick berries with the idea of making jam. I remember with great pleasure my boyhood days of berry-picking when the whole family would load up in a Model-T Ford and go berrying. I can remember so well the smell of the berries after they had been cooked.

## August 18

I cut up two timbers last night and another one this morning. So I'm beginning to lay in my winter supply of wood. I delayed firing up the generator until after breakfast, which means that I ate in a dark, gloomy cabin. I heard a chorus of swifts and hope I have this recorded. I was down at the landing about three times for water, and hoping I would see an otter. Around 7:00 I looked out to see a salmon minus his head on the logjam, so I know the otters came in.

The pinks are still in the area, but the intensity of spawning action has lessened. It is easy to tell which are the spent fish. The tails are very white and rough, so this must be the most damaged part. It's amazing how the fish reposition themselves and clean the same area because most of the available spawning sites have been used before.

In the process of firing up the radio yesterday I heard two fishermen talking back and forth. One said that he had caught only thirty-two fish that day and mentioned some ungodly sum that he had caught the day before. It seems hard to believe that in this stream there are only about 1,000 fish, and out of the approximately 2,000 eggs that are spawned per female, only two will survive. One noticeable thing about this spawning is that virtually every site chosen has been one in which there is a raised ridge. The fish elects to work the little basin in front of it, which means that the eggs are deposited in an area in which the current flushes the nest. I have the feeling that the fish measures this. They have to have an area where there is a good flow of water through the nest so that the current does not deposit debris on the eggs.

## August 19

I worked with the monopod and extended it out in the direction of a female pink. Without any warning she charged the monopod and grabbed it by the rubber bottom, actually hanging onto it and shaking it. After she let go she never touched it again. The males are more cowardly and run away.

I must confess that I'm feeling a little edgy when it starts to get dusk and I can't see footprints any more, neither mine nor the bear's. That's when my imagination takes over. There was no bear activity at the estuary. The tide was low and the pinks were working their way up from the lower estuary. You can hear them as they move on up and, of course, their backs are out of the water. I found two fresh bear kills at the waterfall area. The funny thing is that the bear didn't eat the male pink he had caught. He had bitten it in the tail and apparently didn't care for the rest of it.

I think that when the female fish gets into the stream there is a two- or three-day wait before she gets worked up enough to want to spawn. She will spend a day cleaning the site and the next day she is spent, and then she guards her nest for God knows how long. I think that the bears find it easier to catch the females because of their nest-building.

I couldn't help thinking as I walked to the estuary and through my skunk cabbage hollows, noting that all the skunk cabbages have laid down their leaves, that I have an abiding admiration for this plant. It grows in an area which, you would think, it could not tolerate. I now begin to suspect that it won't be too long before the leaves will start to decay. The bracken is about to give up too, and the berries of the other plants are very much in evidence everywhere. I found a fresh bear track in the skunk cabbage. The bear had gone down to the marshy area.

The false lily of the valley isn't dying completely. It apparently has a disease in which the leaves are sprinkled with rust, and it stays that way. The most brilliantly colored shrub in the fall is the devil's club, which is a bright orange and yellow and is just delightful. The Oregon crabapple has quit shedding leaves, and it still has some left.

Now the male pinks don't have to drive the females into the spawning act, and they don't have any trouble finding a female. The only thing that the males do is an occasional cleaning of the nest and the quivering, which I think is probably the sperm release.

## August 20

I heard a chirp from the otter down at the estuary and I could see the mother otter with two babies. I sneaked out of the blind and sat behind a tree looking into the point where the estuary and stream come together. Suddenly the mother and one baby took a look at me and panicked, diving to the other bank where they surfaced. Along came the other little baby, about 15 feet away from me, and proceeded to eat one or two fish right in front of me. The baby then became a little nervous and chirped, whereupon the mother immediately left the far bank and swam over to the baby—and growled at me. Then the babies joined up and swam by me in full view. They and the mother went on over to the other side of the bank and started out of the water. I heard their chirping going off into the distance, but soon, coming down the same trail they had just used, the mother and two babies returned, along with three adults. They all started swimming up the estuary and up the waterfall. I sat quite awhile pondering the fact that the mothers will protect their babies even though they themselves are panicked. More and more I find I'm getting involved with the otter.

I had been down to the estuary earlier this morning. The water covered the bank and the pinks were wandering up over the coarse-grass area, near death. When fish are near death they lose their ability to maintain themselves in a group and they go about solitarily. They wander about and generally begin to station themselves in an area where the current is strongest, which is interesting. The only explanation I have of this is that possibly the fish is so near death that its respiratory need is greater and the fish finds it necessary to maintain a higher flow of water over the gill. The easiest way to do this is to hold a position where the current is strong. I was somewhat stunned by the appearance of the two female pinks that have been guarding their nests. One of them is beginning to give up.

For the past week I've been delighted by the depletion of the mosquitoes but I am being irritated by the gnats. I ran into a spotted sandpiper, but the ravens aren't coming any more. I also had a close view of a great blue heron that flew up the stream. It was strikingly beautiful.

## August 21

When I got up it was apparent that the pink school was made up mostly of old males whose white backs are very prominent. The females are in varying conditions, from good to not-so-good. I had an interesting experience while washing dishes in the stream last night. One pink salmon came up, took a gasp of air, then dived again—and seconds later rolled over on its side and floated to the surface and on down the stream. There were two other corpses of males lodged in the stream.

I think that there are three things that have to be right for the nests: (1) the right gradient, meaning that it must have a substrate of large and small rocks, with the depth and width of the basin correct for sufficient waterflow; (2) a mixture of fine and coarse rock in the area; if it's too fine the eggs can't get into the gravel; these areas are cleaned of sediment; (3) an interaction of females and males; for without this the eggs will not be deposited or fertilized, even though the nests have been prepared. Now the males are virtually all out of business; they are apparently dying with a yellowish fungus.

I made a dive of two and a half hours and several important facts emerged. I got out there to find the fish vanished. I waited and waited and finally the female came back. I became aware that these fish are apprehensive and I think most of this is due to the males being in a sickened condition. They are more irritable, but their behavior is no longer drawn to the female as the primary object.

I had to be at the landing at 7:30 for Channel Flying so I left the cabin around 7:00. As I started off across the landing, right out, halfway, was laying a fresh fish head, that of a female pink that had been holding down a nest site at the same place the day before. It had been killed by bear. I think the bear are coming in to feed at night, and the only way to get the fish is to get them on the nesting sites. Bears prey on these sites, and the fish most likely to be there is the female. It was irritating to think that here the bear had come into my own private stock of pink salmon and had been working on them. This probably explains why the peripheral banks had suddenly lost their females.

I got the boat and started on up to the lake, aware as I went of the bear walks going out onto a small delta where the bear would go into the water to fish and then bring its catch back to the delta to eat. There is a very distinct rotting smell on these deltas and I was surprised to see the jays on these areas working over salmon remains.

When I was going along into an area where the pinks were spawning I was very impressed by enormous footprints of the brown bear in the gravel under water. That was wild.

The plane came in while I was in the boat so the pilot didn't have to come up to the landing. While the pilot and I were talking two migrating flocks of about twenty-four Canada geese flew up the lake. The pilot was telling me that I should be down one more bay. Fishermen are going in there and poaching, and one of them got hurt and had to be taken out, leaving the camp unguarded. When they came back the following day the bears had moved in and torn the tent to bits. So apparently the bear has been extraordinarily nice to me not to have got into the stuff I have cached in my supply tent at the lake. The location of the camp that the bears attacked was only about five minutes away from here on a stream that didn't have a lake on it, which I think must bring in more salmon.

I had a lovely view of the great blue heron going up over the top of the waterfall. I then went on over to the estuary, hoping to find some otters, but there were none.

The hydroponic experiment is beginning to shape up and leaves are out on most of them. I have lost several dishes of radishes from either drying out or too much water, I'm not quite sure which.

I had a lot of trouble with the young coho swimming around my head and I was pretty cold and tired but I shot quite a few stills of the adult pink. One could ponder why so many salmon are dying off during the spawning, but keep in mind that they are not feeding and the activity of building a nest, along with fighting off the others, makes them vulnerable to disease. I think the mucus on the fish keeps their bodies clean and provides a layer foreign material will find difficult to penetrate.

The stream has a definite smell of death about it and it is being littered by fragments of fish, the heads and tail fins that are left by the bears. There are also numerous dead pink males on the bottom that are pinned down by such things as roots.

I'm looking forward to the fall. I had a fire going this afternoon after I came out of my dive. The temperature of the stream is dropping almost daily because so little radiant heat is going into the lake.

I should point out that I am practicing on my little recorder in the evening, playing a folk tune, and I am cheered by the thought that my blowing is much easier than it was before I came up here. I like to think that that is a consequence of my being out of the noise and confusion of the city.


## August 22

One grows enamored of the long day, and when the long day starts to pull into night the consciousness comes that time for getting things done is short. The feeling of this is already beginning

*e cabin seen from the trail on
posite side of the creek.*

*Potbellied stove in kitchen partially
hidden by drying blocks of fuel.*

The waterfalls of Eva Creek are
nearly obliterated by an extreme high
tide which impounds the estuary
back to the upper level of the
waterfall. Salmon take advantage of
this natural lock to avoid jumping
the cataract.

*A female pink salmon hovering over her nest.*

*Eva Creek above the upper rapids.*

The remains of a male pink, which
had been fed on by a bald eagle. The
eagles consume only the salmon's
liver, making an incision behind the gill.

Female salmon
maintains guard over her nest

to seep into my nervous system. The male salmon are nearly spent and the activity of the females is about all I can film. The fish are much more weary than they were a few days ago and some are spawning in about 8 inches of water.

I filmed a female pink with three male escorts. The female has been digging all day, resting between nest building. Occasionally a stray female wandered in, which she would chase away. This role is interesting. The dominant fish is the biggest one and also the one that has done the most fighting and is further along toward death, with the abrasions showing. The dominant male turns to another smaller male and chases him off and then, in turn, that male turns to another smaller male and chases him off.

As I go along the stream I am overwhelmed by the death of the pink salmon. This salmon comes into fresh water only to lay its eggs in the gravel. When the fry are hatched in the spring they immediately take to the ocean, which means that the pink salmon is the least dependent on fresh water for its life cycle. They don't spend any time at all in the fresh water as young, whereas the coho young are in the stream from one to two years.

According to a man from Sitka, the bald eagle will take a salmon and just pull his liver out and that is all. I began looking around and, sure enough, there were a lot of salmon with the liver sticking out. I had previously thought this was the bear's doing.

I find myself getting to be more and more old-maidish, developing idiosyncrasies about neatness, like keeping the lid of the john down. Another thing that I have noted about loneliness is that one tends to get over being a hypochondriac. You may feel tired or have a headache, but you can't complain to anyone and in a few minutes your symptoms tend to disappear.

I watered my radishes today and I have the feeling I'm not giving them enough light. I have to feed them about twice a week to keep them from drying out.

Spawning ritual is still being carried on by the group of four. I'm at the landing now and the dominant male is keeping station directly above the nest. The female just came back, having chased another female. The dominant male just turned and drove off the second male, and now the third male. The second male is in much better condition than the dominant male. The smallest male returns and now another small male, so we have picked up the fourth male, which is almost as big as the other one. I think he is migrating up stream. When the female gets ready to work the nest, she works her jaw once or twice and then moves forward to clean, pulsating with her tail, which strikes at the bottom. At this moment the males come in, so there must be a chemical substance released in the water, either from the cleansing of the nest or the release of eggs, which excites the males and they dart in. There follows a flurry of activity as the males attempt to reestablish their positions. These groups seem to do best with two or three males. With any more, there is a great deal of time spent fighting and time away from the nest. Right now there is a tremendous amount of this activity going on. The dominant male is pretty tired and the other males are trying to go in. Now the female is lying very quietly, oh, a male is coming in and now she's driving him out! Now the female is holding station away from the nest, which makes it appear that the nesting is over.

This nest area is lined by large rocks and the fine gravel in the middle. Now she's moving back into the nest and she's starting to clean again. The males are moving in again. The female is beginning to clean again and this time the smallest male charged in, which required the other males to break rank and drive him out. She is cleaning again. She has a black streak on her side and her fins are metallic. As she cleans she bends her back and her whole body eventually comes up nearly to the surface. Oh, one male has hold of the smallest male's tail and he won't let go—that was wild! I think when the female goes down in a quiescent position right after she's been cleaning that she's very likely laying eggs, but I can't prove it. She just cleaned again, and the second and third males are at it again. Now they're back in position again. When the female is cleaning she opens her mouth slightly. I think in the morning light I could film this nicely because I'm not more than 10 feet away from them at the moment. I don't think this is an ideal nest site, because they have to work to clean this station and the female is not bothered by other females. Now I think that when the female, after she cleans, wags her tail and moves away, she is depositing her eggs; because it drives the males absolutely crazy and they all rush into the nest. There, a male came in and attempted to clean. There are four males now and the female has moved off to the side. The female is off the nest and the males are driving one another off.

*August 23*

This morning, when I got up at 6:30, the great blue heron put in an appearance and I tried my hardest to get a shot of him but he took off. He is elegant. A flock of Canada geese flew up the stream and over the trees. The ferns are turning various colors of brown. Also, the bunchberry is changing color now and I defy anybody to find two leaves that have the same color. It has a beautiful cluster of orange berries.

The bears didn't seem to take too heavy a toll on my salmon last night.

I went to the estuary and came back about 11:15. The tide was out but had just cleared the upper basin of the estuary and the rapids were beginning to show. But, again, no bear. I never see the eagles perched there watching the main basin, which, of course, carries all the fish. Instead, they appear to work at the junction of the two basins. I think that is a dead end and when the tide is high a few of the fish get caught in there. I see a few pink salmon with their eyes and livers pecked out.

I had about a two-hour dive, with three hot-water bottles, and I was cold when I got out. I worked the two blind areas that I worked before. It is apparent to me now that the male salmon are the timid ones. I filmed a few nest-building areas but most of the pictures were of the females that were spent and trying to hold down nesting sites. I was impressed by the way the females chased out obvious egg predators, the Dolly Varden and the little cohos. It's very interesting to see a little trout or a little salmon with an egg in it's mouth. I wanted to get a picture of the release of the salmon eggs and how they are clustered at the back of the nest with the female at the front. I really have to learn how long a female will get the nest ready before she deposits the eggs. I inhibit a lot of the fish activity by my presence. I was surprised to see how easy the eggs were to find. I can see how someone walking along through the nest would just wipe out eggs right and left.

Late in the afternoon I walked to the estuary, hoping to see a bear but of course I didn't. The single otter was down there, but only his head was showing. I gave him my best otter chirp. He stared back. I decided I'd go on out to the ocean, which was just beautiful in the twilight hours. I came back very happy, very rested, very content. I threaded my way back to camp, through the stream. I noticed a dog salmon trying to court a male pink salmon, and this was amazing. I also couldn't help noticing the tremendous mortality of the pinks that has occurred already down at the estuary. The males that spawned about a week ago are beginning to show fungus infections around the tail. The pinks coming in now are trying to spawn just anywhere, the waterfall or wherever. Now they are coming into the stream already in spawning condition.

## August 24

I devoted the morning to a dive, that proved to be the most successful dive of the series. I was experimenting by lying on my side. The only thing this does is flood out my snorkel and I have to blow it out. Also, I can't lie just anywhere in the stream because the males scatter and then I can't really see what I want to see. There was a female working between two logs, and it was eerie being right down there watching her and the males work. I made the observations in a little tunnel under a log, looking through the opening.

The female had cleaned out a pit in the bottom, and the pit-like structure was filled with 3- to 5-inch stones. This female kept sliding down into the pit and I could see that the area where the eggs are released is swollen. I was watching as she was cleaning the nest and occasionally touching this area when suddenly a male dropped a little sperm, an off-colored cream, and it clung to the bottom and expanded. As it expanded the female rolled over and the next thing I knew I was looking right down her open mouth. She looked for all the world like one of the Hollywood sex stars in one of the sex movies, right in the middle of an orgasm with her mouth open. The female then immediately turned over and began to cover the eggs. I didn't see the eggs being deposited because I was on the wrong side. But she continued, as rapidly as she could, to cover the pit and I observed her until it was over. When I left, the pit was completely covered. I feel very strongly that I saw the typical subsequent action of the female, which is to cover the eggs. I suspect that it takes a fish about a day or a day and a half to prepare the nest. I don't think that the big dominant male was the one that released the sperm. The sperm were laid down behind the female and she seemed to slide back into the area of the sperm; I don't know how she sensed that the sperm was there. . . .

The estuary was completely blank — there was nothing there. I went on over the trail to the ocean and noted a few huckleberries and blueberries. There was nothing at the ocean, however, but the fourth species of salmon, chum salmon, are beginning to come in and they are really feisty. I think they'll want to use the same spawning places as the pinks. They are a much more slender fish, faster and torpedo-shaped, and terribly afraid of people. I haven't been able to get close to them. They have black tails and are very fast swimming. I'm anxious to see them in a dive.

## August 25

The bald eagle sat on my log blind. There was a pink salmon at the estuary that was close to death. I went on over by the old cabin and I heard a noise that sounded like a bear. I did go on up to the ocean and walked up a little creek there where an old boat is tied up. It has the strangest oars I've ever seen. I thought it had been there for a long, long time when I first saw it. This morning, however, it wasn't there.

When I got into the dive the sun was to the west, which meant I couldn't see anything. I was sitting out in front of the fish so they could see me. I went from one group to another and each group unobligingly moved over to another site out of camera range. I had one 30-minute session with a group of three males and a female. One female would have nothing to do with me and promptly vacated the site, while the males thought that was where she should be and they did not vacate the site. The only male that really stood his ground was the dominant one.

When I got to the log blind I discovered that the visibility wasn't very good. I'm not certain if I can sort out all the salmon down there. There are supposedly three species, coho, pink, and chum.

One thing I forgot to mention: when I was walking up to the lake, I encountered some very fresh bear droppings which were still almost entirely moss. On the way back I encountered a lot of bear dung which was old but consisted mostly of berries. The bear, when he's eating the berries, apparently doesn't bother to sort them out. He eats the twigs, leaves, and berries, so the twigs were still there. They were huckleberries. Also, there was a bear walk right on the single island where a bear had been fishing in the night. There were still some traces left by him in the form of a fish head.

I thought I'd prepare a spawning bed in the stream in a manner in which I think the salmon would not be repelled, so I laid out a series of rocks for a blind and put in some current deflectors. I can film from any of the different openings but I have no fish using it as yet, so *I* probably laid an egg.

## August 26

I was trying to wait out a female that had spawned but wanted to spawn more. She was in a quiescent position on the nest, very rarely making a nest-cleaning motion with her tail but feeling the bottom a lot. She still had three to five males who lay back from her. Occasionally one would get bold and would come up beside her and quiver. She was spawning right alongside one of the rock piles I had placed. I found that I could place the camera out between the opening of the rock pile so that it was about at her vent. It was one of those unlucky breaks, though. She had nearly finished spawning and what she had left was insufficient to generate the final act. I didn't see any sperm released but I'm sure there would have been had she released the eggs. I don't really know if the males see her release the eggs, but I've been thinking about the possibility.

Her fins are a metallic yellow-green, all of them, and she has a red lesion on her tail. The two largest male fish were dark in color, whereas the third in size was much lighter colored, almost an olive-green.

The female would move away if I made the slightest noise; when she felt the danger was over she'd move back to her nest. I spent two hours waiting for the female to lay her eggs. The male must come in and deposit the sperm to a cue and I'm not sure what the cue is: whether he sees the eggs being released or smells an odor that the female puts into the water or if he responds to an attitude of the female. This female didn't chase the other females. She was mostly involved with rubbing her vent in the pit of the bottom. I should mention that there are not a great many fish spawning right now. There are a large number of females cleaning a nest that have no males in attendance. I don't know if there aren't enough males to go around or if these females are, in some way, not attractive to the male.

When I was concerned about the predators not being on the stream day after day, I came to the very logical conclusion that the animals can be taught and if the predator stays off the stream for a few days the fish become unconditioned. I throw that in on the side.

Another thought came to me again about the large bear trail on the north bank of Eva Creek that has numerous offshoot trails coming down to the stream. One can ponder the fact that there are only two or three bears using the stream and wonder if it's always been this way. I just don't know. I've had the feeling that ever since man has been after the salmon, man has been in competition with the bear. I can't believe that the salmon were designed for man to exploit in the open sea to the degree that he does. As a consequence of man there is a dwindling supply of salmon, and I would be willing to bet that the bear population has responded in turn, because there's no other way for a bear to make a living. He can't go on welfare, he can't hack out another type of life. Nature has tailored him to this available food supply. When you see all the cans of salmon coming out of a cannery, you realize how far and wide man's "food chain" extends thanks to transportation and preserving. I think the bears are not as abundant as they used to be, not because they are afraid of man but because man has gradually taken over their territory. As the Forest Service chops more and more, and as more and more tracts are being developed, there will be less and less bear. I just can't believe that these animals will flourish in any way other than they do now, and it's too bad that they're going to go. I think the writing is on the hemlocks—that's my wall up here. I really think that we don't see bear at Lake Eva because there are fewer bear. As you can plainly see, everything is working against the salmon here. So the Alaskan brown bear is suffering a diminished food supply because of man. And so it goes.

It's too bad. Man is oriented only to man, and he looks at animals merely as a source of amusement or something for his own use, not as a means of keeping the environment healthy, that is, in ecological balance. Anytime you take out one of the wheels or gears, there are a lot of repercussions, and a lot of mechanisms suffer or become impaired.

## August 27

I made my dive at 10:30 because I thought there would be a supply drop in the late afternoon. I got the hot-water bottle much too hot and I was in utter agony after pouring it into my suit. I rushed to shore and added cold water to the hot, so the dive didn't start out too well.

I went to one of the sites I had set up the day before, and a female was there that had more eggs than any other female I've seen. The males definitely know who's going to deliver and who isn't and they aren't hanging around any female that's in the early stages of digging a nest. Today's dive was a two-hour one, and there were just too many males. I have the feeling that once you have an egg-laying situation the nipping and biting of the males is diminished and they go into a panic. I think that the female is just as surprised as the males because when she has to go she has to go. It's almost like labor. The dive again resulted in a spawning, again the sperm was sticking to the bottom and the female lay on the bottom as if she were frozen. Her mouth was rigidly open. As soon as she released the eggs she was up and covering them over, about a five-minute operation. Then she started to protect the area.

## August 28

I filmed the fish with the light shining through the fins this morning. I was pleased to get this large group. There are three types of agitation with the males: the dominant male, who is agitated when the female is gone from the nest; the number two male, who is busy chasing away the other males; and the other males, who are extremely clever at getting in when the sperm needs to be released. It was hard to get some pictures of the biting.

I came in at 1:00 and went through the hassel of reloading the camera. It took me about 20 minutes to get out and into the water again. With this roll I was shooting primarily the female. The second roll went through in about an hour and still no eggs. She was doing very little nest-cleaning, mostly feeling the bottom with the vental area. I thought I'd better get another roll done, and I made up my mind to shoot four rolls. By this time it was 3:00 but I went back into the water and waited and waited, getting more selective. I really don't have the vaguest notion as to what I shot. At the end of roll three, I was so stiff and numb that I just lay there. By lying in the water and allowing the current to push against me I was able to get up onto my knees and then I got out. I reloaded the camera on the back landing, but it was starting to get dark so I decided three rolls was quite enough. I had made three dives but didn't get the underwater release of sperm or eggs. I have a feeling that she is spawned out and won't be there again.

## August 29

I noticed a lot of new fish milling around the site I had built the night before so I wandered over there, and lo, the males were lined up three and four abreast and the female was in the process of laying the eggs. I couldn't see any sperm because there were fish between me and the female; nor could I see the female's mouth-open position as she pushes the eggs out in the gravel. I filmed as much of it as I could and when things began to simmer down, there were several trout in the nest with their heads buried down into the gravel about 2 or 3 inches, obviously feeding on eggs that had been deposited. It was fantastic. Again, I don't know how they sense that this is the moment they have been waiting for.

When I came back out of the dive I was cold and it was cloudy and rainy but I felt very fortunate to have witnessed the nest-robbing by the predators. I was also happy to have seen one of the big mating parties as opposed to the smaller ones I've been watching in the past. I don't know how much longer I can push my luck, because I was weak and tired after the dive.

I get the feeling, in watching the females cleaning a nest, that they don't spawn twice in the same place. I think the cleaning action and the cleaning away of dirty material is a necessary sensory action. If it's already cleaned the female gets an improper sensory reading of this, whether through smell or sight or tail or what I can't be sure.

I find that when I come out of a dive I'm punchy and stupid. Everything is against me. I'm insecure of my footing and have to watch my footing. I find myself very much weakened physically and unable to maintain my balance. I'm uneven in my walking. I guess I'm suffering carbon dioxide poisoning. Being in the water for more than two rolls of film is really pushing it. When I got up this morning I was depressed by the amount of tasks I had left undone last night. I had bad dreams about the salmon and constantly woke up. I slept very badly. I charged up the battery this morning and started a fire. I'm very upset. But I have observed the building of the nest, the releasing of the sperm, and the small and large groups of salmon spawning. I have also observed much dying.

There are a lot of things to deal with in the bottom of a stream.

CHAPTER

# 12

# BEARS
# AND THE
# TOADSTOOL
# PRINTS

### August 30

I came back into the cabin and I heard a sound. I looked out the window and much to my surprise saw an Alaskan brown bear tramping up the stream. It was medium-brown with very thick fur and its hump was tremendous. It looked very big. I just couldn't believe it. Here was the brown bear and I couldn't have picked a nicer place to see it than from my window. The bear turned toward the bank and I decided I'd better get some film on it. I grabbed a camera—I'm not even sure which one—and went out the front door and up the stream in the direction of the bear. Now, however, I couldn't hear or see him. I then went around the side of the cabin. I heard a snorting sound. I then thought it would be better if I filmed him from my porch in the back. So I dashed through the front door, and on through to the back door. By this time the bear had gone up the bank and was sitting in the bushes between the porch and the path. I must admit I was frightened and my heart was racing. The bear was making a snorting sound that sounds like a blast, not soft or gentle. I had the feeling that the bear was aware he was in a location that had a lot of human odor and that was why he was snorting. I said something—perhaps "Hi, Bear"—and very abruptly the bear stood up on his legs,

157

turned his head, and looked straight at me. I was on the top of the porch, which is raised at least two feet off the ground, and the bear was tall enough that its eyes were at the height of my eyes.

At that moment there was more snorting and noise, and two cubs pulled into view. One of them stood up. I began to get a little nervous because this bear wasn't more than 25 feet from me and I didn't know whether she would charge me or not. I felt like Peter with the Wolf. I really don't know what I did, I didn't know what to do, shut the door or what. Mother Bear got down on all fours and started on down the trail to the tributary, her cubs behind. I decided that was well enough, I wasn't about to play games with her. It was a fantastic experience and I am a lucky man. I don't think in retrospect I could have the guts or presence of mind to shoot one if one charged me. Having seen the animal, I can assure you that it is very, very big.

I then went out, after I was sure she had gone quite a ways, to see where she had come up. She came up a little path that runs from the corner of my cabin back downstream but on a 45° angle on a bank that is like a cliff. She went down the trail that I've walked many, many times to the little tributary. I looked over the trail very carefully and could hardly tell that that bear had gone over it with her two cubs.

I went back and had supper and afterward decided I'd better go to the estuary to see how things were doing. I walked along the south bank of the two islands, and bear had been tramping along the edge right across the place where I had done the diving scene for the camera crew. I looked up toward the rapids and saw a tremendous area that had been tramped down since yesterday. I walked up there and it looked like a drive-in theater, about 150- to 200-foot frontage had been tramped down. There were also about four places where the bear had gone in and sat down. There had been a lot of bear activity the night before, and a lot of dead salmon were evident. One dead salmon had maggots crawling all over the head. Apparently bears like eating the brain. I must get some pictures of that, showing the food chain.

I didn't find much excitement at the estuary. There was a great blue heron alone with a fair amount of salmon that are trapped in the basin after the tide goes out. It was 7:15 when I got down there and by 8:00 I could hardly see a thing.

I did bring back some toadstools from the estuary, and I am beginning to make some mushroom prints. I cut off the stock of the mushroom and lay the umbrella, with the gills underneath, on a piece of gray paper. In a short time, there will be an accumulation of spores on the piece of paper. Some of the spores are white, and soon you get beautiful patterns of different colors.

I made a horrible discovery. About half of my hydroponic experiment is ruined because I didn't water soon enough.

## August 31

I was up at 8:30, very groggy, and it took me a long time to get breakfast. I heard the otters chirping so I rushed down to the landing and waited, but nothing happened. I could hear the otters up on the bank but they didn't come down. It began to rain so I brought in the Big Ear and the tape recorder with the camera. I heard the otters chirping again. This time the otters came up to the logjam and peered out at me. The mother came out of the water onto the log and sniffed. The male otter came out on a log behind the one the mother was on and sniffed the log and then sprayed it. After that I could hear them in the bushes right next to me and then they ran over to the island in a great rush.

The otter is in the skunk family. They all have anal glands and all advertise their trails and territory by spraying, like a cat. I'm anxious to get out and see exactly what the otter's spray smells like.

I went out on the logjam after pruning the bracken fern and alders. I got out on to the log the male had sprayed, but I couldn't find anything skunklike. There was a rather distinctive odor close to where the urine or whatever had sprayed down, but I'm not quite sure if this was otter, because it was almost pleasant. I also found a lot of otter dung on the log, which has a slightly fishy odor. I also noticed that the otter doesn't completely digest the salmon eggs — there are also a lot of rib bones and things. A lot of my log blinds were knocked over so apparently the bear were there also.

About 3:00 I went up to the landing to get some gasoline for the generator. On the way, it struck me that autumn is really here. The skunk cabbage leaves are lying on the ground and beginning to turn yellow. The twi-blade are a yellow-lemon color and I took pictures of all the things that really took my eye. Then I heard a snorting sound, which I had heard only once before, when I encountered the bear, so I realized that on the other side of a log was an Alaskan brown bear that I had apparently waked up. Needless to say, T.J. didn't hang around to see if his prediction was right. I picked up some toadstools to make my prints and came on back to the cabin. There were about eight kinds and I was delighted with the great variety of colors. I brought the toadstools in and was getting ready to take a picture when I heard the worst sound outside, a loud hissing sound. I dashed out and across the bank on the other side was a bald eagle that evidently had something. I rushed back in to get the camera and went across, but he took off into the trees. I looked to see what he had, and it was the great blue heron that I had become so enamored of in the past six weeks. So one of my cast of characters is gone.

The spawning is beginning to decline, but I think the fish that has the greatest effect on the fertilization of the eggs is the big dominant male. He is probably involved in several spawnings before he is exhausted by the effort. The number two male is the one most involved in the chasing. The large males probably get into fights with others of equal size and once the dominant male has been picked by means of a fight between them, the others fall in ranks as to size. I would say that probably the dominant male is the one to get sperm on top of the eggs, because he is with the female almost constantly. He is also the one who comes up and quivers alongside her. The quivering is not the release of sperm, but I think it's a sign to the female to reassure her that he's there.

## September 1

It was raining hard when I got up, but I went ahead with the dive. I didn't get too much. Two groups of salmon are going through spawning activities by the logjam, but the area was too shallow to film in, and the fish are very spooked. I could hear the rain in the middle of my dive and see it on the surface. The water got very turbulent and visibility went way down. I did see a cutthroat trout, which came close to me, with a toad in his mouth. He was really protecting it, much like a dog protecting a bone for fear other dogs will grab it away from him.

The tide was in when I went to the estuary after my dive, but there isn't much to report. For the first time I observed fairly large schools of pink salmon that were milling around near the surface as the tide came in, so there should be a pretty good run coming in.

The Oregon crabapple is now yellow with various blotches of brown, and so lovely that I played the camera over it. I also noted quite a few dead salmon beginning to come up from the estuary, along with quite a few jellyfish on the bottom. The dead blue heron is still on the bank where it was left by the eagle; and the fish, as I mentioned, are very wary.

I'm playing the recorder and I'm happy to report that I have some tunes pretty well down.

## September 2

I was cabin-bound virtually all morning by the storm that has renewed its vigor, with the wind coming in from the east. I didn't go to bed last night until midnight, and had prepared the kindling for the fire. I stayed in bed until 8:00 this morning. The stream had risen again.

I logged in the temperature and looked out the window. Coming out of the stream to the bank was a great black-and-gray Alaskan brown bear. I immediately grabbed the camera and returned to the window. By this time he had gone to the shore, where he paused. At that moment a brown cub came into view, nipping at the fish. I opened the door and got out on the landing. There was so much noise from the wind that I couldn't believe the animal would hear me start to film. But as I framed in on the young one, the adult looked at me and, after a minute, both disappeared through the bushes. I'm now irritated by the fact that the bear stopped doing what he was going to do because of curiosity about me.

As I set my fire, I began to realize that the bear knew I was there because, even though the rain is moving to the west, there is a cross-wind. I had no sooner finished breakfast when I heard a quack, and thirteen mergansers proceeded upstream chasing the young cohos that have been fattened on the salmon eggs. One of these merganser had caught a fish that it apparently couldn't swallow and I watched the other twelve mergansers chasing it out into the middle of the stream.

I spent quite a bit of time this morning looking over the toadstool prints. The spore colors are white, yellow-brown, pink, and purple-brown. Most are white and a fair percentage are yellow-brown, which must be their beginning stage. At the moment I have twenty mushrooms spread out for prints. I find that while these are lying there, they are being eaten away by a very primitive form of collembolan arthropod called springtail.

On the way up to the landing I saw the mate to the great blue heron; I wondered if she had young and if they would survive and not be prey to the bald eagle.

Most people don't realize that as the noise level goes up, one's ears tend to turn down the volume in the brain so one doesn't hear the sounds nearly as well as they should. This means that both the bear and T. J. Walker are at a disadvantage during a rain, so I'm not going down to the estuary until the rain stops.

## September 3

I set the alarm for 6:00 and the bears came around the cabin at 7:00. I got out the camera and shot from the back porch. I don't know what I got on the camera—probably their tail ends. The bears went on up the stream toward the island. One was the big black-and-gray mother bear. I then tried to shoot from the front door but they must have heard me because they went on up the creek. I went down to the landing to see if I could get another look at them. I discovered that the female had gone over the island, to the area near where I have the blind between the two islands, and she was standing on her legs watching me very intently and snorting. I began to realize this bear could play peek-a-boo very adroitly, and all the time she was focused on me. I don't know if my scent was coming to her or not. They worked their way up almost to the trail where you come to the upper rapids, and again she watched me very intently. It's most eerie.

I came into the cabin and headed for the back porch. There was just enough noise that the bear cub, who is a beautiful shade of brown, looked up at the cabin and went up the stream out of sight. I think the idea of my playing games with the mother or the cub is most hazardous. The alertness of the female has impressed me enormously. A bear is as much in a position to hunt you as you are to hunt it. Today I tried very hard not to make any sound in the cabin, but I suspect they were very much aware of my presence anyway.

The fish have diminished here. There are only about fifteen now. I was at the estuary from 10:00 to 1:00. I checked the island where the bears had been playing peek-a-boo at me and I noticed that there were fresh salmon remains at the corner of the island.

A male pink salmon fresh from the sea, beginning to develop breeding color and hump.

*Three male pinks yawning.*

*Two male pinks. The cream-colored blotches mark a fungus disease, a factor in the decline and death of post-spawn salmon. Fungus enters fish on part of body exposed to air when fish works water too shallow to cover the body.*

A log garden, Lake Eva, consists of grasses, self-heal, a mint, and ferns, which are able to root in the rotting wood and obtain nourishment from the lake water which splashes over during windy days.

Marsh sedges favor the brackish soils of the estuary margin, and the plants and flowering head here pictured are periodically inundated by the tide.

Marestail, an emergent aquatic, roots in 5 to 15 feet of water surfacing to expose its tiny weedlike flowers for pollination.

Salmonberry fruit, a choice item for the Alaskan brown bear.

Many fish are heavily covered with fungi now; and much of the final attempts by the salmon to spawn are not very effective.

I saw the female great blue heron flying up the stream in a slow, labored flight.

Back at the cabin, I found myself a little on the tired side, and it is a pleasant feeling to feel tired and not being pushed. I could hear the raven calling in what I call the "tolling of the bell" because it has a bell-like quality with a rich undertone. I also heard some squirrels chirping, which is slightly suggestive of the chirping of the otter. I have an Indian summer feeling today. I've seen quite a few migrating birds, and these migrants give me a feeling of homesickness. Since they're on their way, I feel I should be going.

## September 4

Two female pink salmon continue to build nests, although their tails are beaten up. It appears that the pink salmon migration is finished. The pathetic thing is that the poor, beat-up females are still going through the motions of nest-cleaning, even though they have no eggs.

## September 5

The fungi continue to pop up all over and I can't begin to tell you the names. One of the things I have been mulling over in my mind is the fact that a stream flows by gravity, ranging from the slopes at either a steep gradient or a slow gradient. A fish can't afford to swim in a stream at the speed with which the water is flowing by it. Which brings us to the specializations that the trout and other fish have, namely, that they have learned that in the flow of water there is a good deal of power, and this power is essentially falling. The fish has learned that, in the flow of water down the stream, discontinuities occur in the cross-sectional areas of the stream because of objects on the bottom. These objects are mechanical, fixed structures which cause the water to be mixed and stirred. Out of the process of water mixing and being stopped and turned and tumbled, emerges the remarkable condition where at certain spots water is going upstream, and at other spots it is stationary. The fish take advantage of all these mixing discontinuities to obtain a force which carries them against the current with a nominal amount of swimming.

In my dives I tried to see the consequences of pushing a fish out of one of these mixing spots into the current. The minute I got one out into the current, I could see it swimming terrifically hard. A fisherman is very much aware of this and casts into these areas of discontinuity. I think that the remarkable success of a fish in the stream is due to the fact that it is able to sense quickly the consequences of getting out of its little orbit of water.

Another thing people don't realize is that the stream essentially makes these discontinuities and also destroys them. It's all a matter of how successfully a stream is able to cut away, smooth out, the discontinuities. Streams do begin to develop, in time, an even gradient and to carry the erodable materials out to make a delta. A stream generates along its length a variety of habitats in which the substrate, the floor of the stream, ranges from mud, sand, fine and firm gravel to stones of different size and shape each resulting from a specific velocity.

What I'm saying is that a stream consists of a variety of velocities depending upon the slope of the stream at particular points. I look out the window here at a point where the cross-sectional area is very large, and as a result the flow of water is very slow. The salmon is an oversized fish to be using these perches where the discontinuities are; I, too, took advantage of the discontinuity of flow generated by my stone blind. Both the fish and I used the discontinuities that were large so we didn't have to fight the current.

I'm afraid that, if the studio wants some bear pictures in the few weeks left, they will have to work it out with the Forest Service and take me along to get into the pictures. I am really caught up with the variations of the bottom of the stream and the trout.

So, here I sit having got through the salmon-spawning miracle. It's raining constantly and the stream is way up.

# ALICE

*September 6*

My main involvement today was a chat with a family fishing on the stream. The man's name was Sollar and he was with his two children and another man who is a commercial fisherman. He was on his way to fish for halibut in Glacier Bay, and they were fishing and exploring as they went. It was indescribably delightful because I was a little upset with the diminution of biological activity. It started to rain and we headed for the ocean, They invited me to come on board and see their boat, so I did. We had coffee and cake and chatted about two hours until they took me back. What drew me to them was that they enjoyed the country and were spending so much time in it, fishing and hunting, that they had to be fairly decent people. They had a Siamese cat and two dogs aboard their boat.

This man, Sollar, said that virtually every person in Sitka hates the brown bear and almost every family in Sitka has had some member either killed or maimed. He said the large majority of these attacks are on hunters who are after deer, and the bear jumps the man when he is bringing out his deer. This makes good sense to me. Of course, he admitted, the female bear with a cub is very dangerous because of the mother instinct. Then he talked about all the places that he thought were good bear haunts. There is a feature common to all the bear sites: that there be two runs of salmon to feed on, for example, the pink and the chum. The chum spawn close to the sea and in the streams that are not lake-fed but have a delta on them.

I came back from my two-hour visit aboard the halibut boat with a very keen sense of what draws people to Alaska and why they are in a sense lucky people: some of them truly have a love for their land and they know how to use it in a recreational sense. A recreational sense to me is not a goofing-off sense but using this country for picnicking, camping, fishing, and hunting with a sense of appropriateness and in moderation. The country here is used in moderation for the simple reason that there just are not many people up here. They all learn to be fairly good boatsmen. The boat is the magic carpet enabling them to poke their way into all these places.

I think people should be brought into this kind of wilderness experience in a subtle way, not through a Coney Island style camping ground, which most national parks are today. The solution is to evolve a system of making these natural areas available in a way in which people are separated into small functional units. I think the one-family dwelling, such as those along the lakes in Minnesota, afford the best way for people to learn to understand and to love and to properly use the outdoors. The minute the lakeshore fills up with cabins crowded together, the magic is gone.

I ran into my merganser friends, now seven in number. The other five may be operating in a group, but I haven't run into them. I watched these seven as they made their way from the estuary to the waterfall, fishing as they went. They are beginning to stretch and flap their wings, so it won't be long before they take off.


## September 7

To be somehow caught up in as much of every moment as possible is one of the most subtle aspects of living.

There is more to living than constantly digging through the garbage dump of knowledge. I honestly believe that deep down in my heart I have put my finger on the most grievous error of the twentieth century, and that is the insane aftermath of the printing press and the invention of modern communicative and propaganda techniques, which have converted the human being into a captive. . . .

The skulls of all the salmon kills that have been accumulating are now being partly eaten—the brains and much of the skull gone, leaving only the jaws and a bit of the gills. It would appear that some animal or bird is coming in and cutting these things open to feed on the brain. My inclination is to suspect the otter or mice. I'm not so inclined to think it would be birds, but I can't prove that. I also found that a number of the salmon that wash ashore dead or dying do fall prey to the eagle. You find the incision the eagle makes to take the liver out just back of the pectoral fin. Generally the eye is out, but it is my impression that the eagles do not turn the fish over and remove both eyes, although I can't be sure. I was surprised at the thoroughness of the eagle in this matter. They were doing this on fish that had been dead for several days and coated with fungus.

At one of the basins of the estuary, where the salmon fall prey to the bear, there is a gravel bar through which the stream percolates. The tide was just going out and it had cleared this area, and lying there was a fairly well-preserved male pink salmon. I filmed him gasping and he was so weak that he couldn't flap or do anything other than breathe. This male was still there much later when I came back after making my tour of the estuary basin to the south, and I thought I would move him out of the exposed gravel section of the stream draining that basin. I worked him down with my foot, carefully pushing him into the estuary proper and I got him down to where he could swim. He showed no signs of being able to right himself, so I left him there, figuring that he was too far gone to think about. I went back up the bank and proceeded to do some still photography of the fall color in some of the plants along the estuary.

I should have pointed out that I came down here planning to film all the fish activity and damage. I had filmed the salmon that was lying there breathing it's last. I filmed it a number of ways and then I had a camera jam. Much to my horror, the film in the camera had gone around the second sprocket drive at the base of the mechanism twice, and there was film all over the magazine. I would have to take the camera back to the cabin for fixing.

I gathered up my gear and was all set to start back to the cabin. I looked out and I could see that the salmon had righted itself and was weakly trying to go back up to the same place I'd rescued it from. How annoying! I still felt the fish was extremely susceptible to the eagles. There were three or four of them perched around the area.

Before heading for the cabin I got in the way of the salmon, turned it around, and saw it weakly swimming. I worked it out of the shallow part and got it headed in the general direction of the rapids that connect the upper estuary to the lower. The last I saw of him, he had gone back into the system; so I feel a little proud of myself that I was able to rescue one salmon for a few more days of activity. I didn't think to squeeze it to see if it had active sperm. It had the hump and was in breeding colors.

I was starting up the trail toward the cabin when I heard a huge sound, almost like an explosion. Three other shots followed and I suddenly realized there was someone coming into shore. It dawned on me this was the big weekend [Labor Day] and it was logical that someone from the lumber camp would be coming ashore. I didn't hang around to see, but went on to the cabin. When I got there, I looked out the window and saw two young men walking by with fishing poles and guns. They proceeded up to the rapids and began to fish. I thought I'd seen them here before, so I went over and chatted with them. They were fishing intently and were obviously very good fishermen. They said they were from Sitka, and had come in about 8:00 A.M. in a cabin cruiser. One of them, twenty-three or twenty-four years old, worked in the pulp mill at Sitka. They apparently get over here quite a bit. I started talking to them about bears and they recommended Crab Bay or Kadashan Bay, which is near Tenakee, an old canning town. They thought Lake Eva was a marginal area for bears. They had hunted bears and had respect for them—they fire guns when they go ashore to let the bears know they've arrived. According to them, a bear can go through the woods and never let you know he's there. He goes through like a cat, which didn't help me in my thinking about the bears.

Channel Flying flew over the cabin later on, circled twice, and then went to the lake. Here I was at the estuary, so I had to cross over and get to the trail. I hurried as fast as I could and when I reached the landing I looked down to see a fresh bear print. I heard rustling in the bracken fern just in front of me and the characteristic snorting of the bear. I couldn't see them but knew they weren't 25 feet from me—the mother and a cub, big prints and little prints. I decided I'd go back to the cabin to get the other pack, and give them a chance to get away.

I thought I'd better go up to the lake for the supplies, whether

I wanted to or not. For the first time, I took the shotgun off the wall and put a cartridge in the chamber. I started across the stream, feeling very tense. I went on up the trail all the way following the mother and baby bear prints. For the first time I was able to smell the odor of the bear. It is not unpleasant, but distinctive. There were bear prints all the way up to the landing so I rushed up the stream into the lake with the boat. By this time the plane had taken off, but there were two boxes of groceries. I hurried across the landing, down the trail, and into the cabin with the supplies. I was grateful not to have had a serious encounter.

## September 8

Despite my sightings and all the tracks, the bears here are very infrequent and will have to be filmed elsewhere. I hope we can do this in an adjacent area, probably Tenakee, which has sixty or seventy retired people living there, a few supplementing their income through tourists. Everyone is friendly and nosey. It is a typical 1900 country village. I think it would be fun to work out of there and I hope the studio goes along with it.

At the point where I cross the estuary to get on the trail going to the cabin I spotted a dead male salmon today. I think it is the one I tried to rescue yesterday. He was obviously obsessed with going up there. I also found a female stranded in exactly the same place, pointing in the same direction up this dead-end, gravel shallow leading to the part-stream, part-estuary basin, and I rescued this one. I didn't work this one down with my feet, however. I picked her up and carried her and she didn't struggle at all. I finally got her down into water deep enough to give her a fair chance of outrunning a bird, if this was her intent.

Then I came up the trail, and as I started across the estuary and looked northward, I saw the most exquisite rainbow, one end of it in the estuary and the other end in the trees, very low. In the arch of the rainbow between the trees and end were three violet rainbows, three bands of violet. It was just beautiful. The trees were sheathed in the rain and it was a magnificent way to remember the little estuary at Lake Eva. . . .

It's now 3:45 in the afternoon and I think I'll do that camera scene of me falling into the hole. The coloration of the ferns has now turned from green to brown, so it's a rather different looking scene and I'm terribly sorry we didn't get it the way it originally was, but the studio has requested the scene so I'm going to go ahead and execute it this afternoon. It all reminds me of Alice in Wonderland.

I just returned from a mile walk to the lake and back, a leisurely walk that I started in a heavy rain. As I came back the sun broke out. The air was warm and it felt like summer, even though the forest floor tells me fall is here. It made me feel like a kid again—out in the forest.

I'm again fatigued and I guess the fatigue is the stress of people. It makes me wonder how I'm going to make the adjustment back to civilization. When I was a kid my best friend's father was a miner and he'd come into town for maybe a week, and then go back to his cabin. I never felt that he was happy in town, and I never knew why. His son became a metallurgist and I can remember so vividly asking how he could go into those mines. What if they collapsed?

Yesterday I finally saw a brown creeper for the first time. That is a tiny bird that goes up and down the trunks of trees, associated with the bark of the tree. I remember it very vividly from my college days in Montana, where birding and mountain-climbing were my two big hobbies when I wasn't wound up in books. It's curious to think how I would perform in college today, with all the turmoil.

I'd better get over and set up that falling-in-the-hole scene the studio wants, if I'm going to do it. It's now 4:00 P.M. and I wonder if Channel Flying has called the studio yet to let them know that T.J. is no longer in communication. I'll bet the radio circuit is happy not to have me on the line always wanting to know the time and asking for supplies.

I'm going to quit this chit-chat and go out and play games. Falling in a hole!

I find in general on the days people are in here it isn't easy to work, and I wonder if I should have stayed in the cabin and looked out the window. Was the hour I spent walking down to the estuary worth anything other than the comfort it gives me? I find that it keeps me busy and happy in a way, and thinking and reflecting and soaking up the charm and serenity and calm that pervades this place. Perhaps, in the long run, this is all that any of us can hope to gain from nature. Nature is so complex and subtle in it's activity that most of its activity is like coals smoldering. You are aware of a little smoke coming off the fire, but you don't *see* much, and that's the way a lot of this activity is. For instance, the biochemical activity leading to a tremendous capture of carbon dioxide, and oxygen being manipulated in water—and out of these raw materials comes this remarkable thing called a plant. Then the plants spin off in various ways and this energy reappears in the atmosphere in carbon and oxygen.

I did the scene that the studio requested: I walked happily down the trail and suddenly I fell into a hole.

# CHAPTER 14

# AVENUE
# OF THE OTTERS
# AND THE
# CUTTHROAT VILLAIN

*September 9*

I stood watch for the bears this morning but they didn't show. I guess bringing out the gun was too much for them. I went to the estuary about 10:00 with the thought of searching along the estuary for bear signs to see if they were working the ocean. I had just crossed the creek and started down the trail leading to the abandoned cabin when a canoe with several people in it pulled up from nowhere onto the gravel bar. They waved at me so I walked over and introduced myself. One man, named Larry Calvin, owns the Sitka dive shop and also runs a building-supplies business for homeowners and do-it-yourselfers. He was already fishing by the time I got across to him. I asked a lot of questions about the bear, and he put his pole down and started talking. He says there is a lot to the bear. The bear doesn't like human beings one little bit, and the likelihood is that I have converted Lake Eva from a bear haunt to a place shunned by bears. In all my walks I have left my scent, which remains for days, and the bears, according to Calvin, have picked it up and are avoiding it. The one exception to this bear/man relationship is in the lumber camps, where you have the tourist/bear problem because the lumber people dump their wasted food. The bears learn that this is an easy food chain, easier than beating the stream for salmon.

The more I talked to Calvin, the more interesting he became. He used to be a guide and a hunter, living in Sitka 37 years, and has been involved in a lot of things. He said he gave up the guide business because he doesn't like hunters, especially the tourists who come to Alaska to hunt. The people who live up here and hunt do so for meat, and it's not a big thing; it's part of living. But, he said, every place has bears, they're everywhere; of course, if you were to go to a place to find a bear with the idea he was going to be there, the chances are he won't be, at least not in the time framework you have. Apparently they are the most mobile of game animals, capable of walking up one mountain ridge to another, constantly moving around. He said there was one place he could recommend if I wanted to come back next year, a place that people don't know about and that he learned about from the Indians. It has a sockeye run in July and August, and is crawling with bears. But that's an opportunity that no longer exists this year. We chatted on and he told about one of his wildest experiences of all, when he had been on Eva Creek fishing. An Alaskan brown bear was in the water above the waterfall with only it's head showing, swimming back and forth and fishing. Calvin stood on the trail watching all this for about half an hour.

Mrs. Calvin was fishing all the time her husband and I were talking. They decided to go on up to the waterfall and try the little pool there. I quizzed him on salmon in general, the kinds and how they react, and so on. There again, he said, streams run hot and cold. Without any warning a stream will be alive with fish. This particular stream is considered a cutthroat stream, and that's why people come in here and fish. This year has been the poorest of all, Calvin said. Two winters ago a heavy, deep snow virtually destroyed the Sitka deer population, and they still haven't recovered.

We also talked about bear attacks. "I've never killed a bear," Calvin said, "and I hope I never have to. I like bears, but there are some bears that are nice and others that aren't, just like human beings." In general, he added, bear fatalities are caused because a hunter has left some game out, and he is attacked when he goes back for it to pack it up. "If you leave meat out, drying, curing," Calvin explained, "you can almost bet that a bear will find it."

I picked up quite a bit of information from this man. He was not optimistic about my chances for the bear, but he wished me luck. The conversation gave me pause for thought. Maybe because I've been out so much I have diminished the chances of adequately filming the bear. Should I stay cooped up in the cabin? Heaven forbid! Before many days I'd be climbing the ceiling. I think I won't use this trail so much any more; I'll use some new ones and let this one cool off a little. . . . . We went back to Larry Calvin's canoe at the estuary and he offered to take me out to his boat for lunch, so I knelt in his canoe and we went on out to sea to their cabin cruiser. He said that almost everyone in Alaska who likes the out-of-doors owns a cabin cruiser, or owns a share of one, and they take turns using them. We had some egg spread and salami sandwiches and some very good cookies. It's really odd how much pleasure there is in eating someone else's food.

Later I went to the estuary's dead-end but there was no sign of bear activity. I think my persistence in walking that trail three days in a row made the bear vanish. I'm sure now there aren't more than four bears here and they very cleverly get off the trail when they see me coming, and have probably seen me 100 times.

My otters were chirping over on the south bank area when I came up the trail. Calvin, by the way, described an otter mating which I'm anxious to put on record. He said that the female is mounted successively three times by two males. Each male has his turn, as it were; they mate with the male on top as the female swims in a lake. Calvin has had a tremendous experience in Alaska, having worked his way through college and spending a lot of time on the lakes and exploring. According to him, October is a wet, dark month, and I'll be lucky to get two hours of filming a day. In fact, he considered this was the worst summer ever in terms of weather.

We also discussed how many salmon a bear would put away in a day. Between the two of us we came to the conclusion that maybe five salmon was a good haul for a bear. He said they sometimes take an hour or two just to catch one salmon. Salmon-fishing isn't always red hot and bears have to work hard at it. Certainly the ones around here aren't getting five a day at the moment.

When the fishermen and hunters come in here they take potshots at bears if they see them from the beach. So naturally, Calvin said, the bears have shied away from that area.

You can tell where the bears are from the odor of rotting fish, although I thought it would be a worse smell than it is. I meant to comment on the droppings of the bear who is feeding on fish and berries. Most of the bulk appears to be due to berry, and what's left of the droppings is a greenish-black residue with a fair number of fish bones, the fine, riblike bones. That's unlike bear droppings in the spring, when the bears were entirely on vegetation. It's now almost entirely berry, although we're beginning to get a mixture.

I was amazed to see the white back of a pink salmon working in the little embayment. It swam in and then out. I didn't realize what was going on there, and as I started across the bank, the salmon swam out of the embayment and headed upcurrent toward me, and then turned into another embayment. I looked under there and saw a dying male pink salmon, very big and quite ugly, with a grotesque head, which is what happens when they are near death. I'm happy in a way that we have had the pink salmon. I've become quite fond of them and it hurts me to see them wasting away, and to know that soon there won't be any in the stream. I guess it will be back to the cutthroat and the Dolly Varden, then.

I was delighted to have a small brown bat performing right on the bow of the boat, not more than 5 feet from me. He was working over the gnats that cluster on the stream.


*September 10*

I was very much surprised to see a merganser at my waterfall, feeding in a fashion similar to the mallards, which is to up-end and feed off the bottom. This was quite unlike the way mergansers normally feed. Their bill is not really suited to this way of feeding. The pinks had moved out of the spot where the merganser was parked. It was right on the redd (the spawning site) and was obviously feeding on the eggs. It finally spotted me and abandoned the area, pretending that it didn't see me. I don't know if anyone has commented on the fact that the merganser could and would rob a salmon nest, but this was what it was doing.

I had no sooner finished filming this when I looked upstream and saw along the bank a mother otter with two babies. About 3:00 this morning those rascals had been chirping right by the cabin. On my way to the estuary in the morning I saw evidence that the otters had been there—a half-eaten salmon; they left the pelvic region, which is still on the log. When they got almost abeam of me they spotted me and took off into the shrubs. Then they came back again and I filmed that reentry from the woods. They left the water and went up a second time. Without any warning, they scooted down the bank into the stream and boldly struck up along the edge of the waterfall on the north side, and made their way on upstream. I filmed it all. It shows the use the otter makes of the forest for escaping when it needs to. That's also the first time I've seen them sliding, and I suppose that's a classical part of the otter's repertoire.

I thought I heard a bear as I came back along the crossing here, but now and then my ears play tricks on me. I think one's hearing gets extraordinarily keen. Also, I find my nose is functioning a lot better now that I've smelled a bear.

*September 11*

The stream has gone down to its nearly lowest level, and the island's coarse grass is now once again above water. With it are a tremendous number of dead salmon. It's peculiar that when the salmon begin to die they beach themselves and get turned around into the counter-circulation of the stream, so they are carried into the little embayments.

I hoped, when the supply drop came in, to fly over to Tenakee and Kadashan Bay to see what we would get there. I did take off in the airplane and, in a sense, abandoned my home for the afternoon and looked over the landscape. It was a beautiful day. Not a cloud in the sky. There are some clouds to the west in the evening, but I'm sure I'll have one more day of good sunshine. The lake appeared deserted with no wind blowing on it. There were a few mergansers up to the delta. I didn't see any bears on the stream, or any concentration of the salmon. The people at Tenakee were of the opinion that the bears were in Kadashan Bay, and in goodly numbers. It's up to the studio now and the Forest Service as to what we do next in terms of bears. I was in the small community of Tenakee about five minutes. It is astonishing how much escapes the ordinary tourist. He essentially expects the world to be built around him, but he never pokes into the real subtleties of any one place. I'm sure you could spend a week in Tenakee and have a marvelous time listening to people talk, and seeing the town, and learning about the countryside from the people who live there. This kind of traveling is unheard of; yet anyone can do it, and it is easy and cheap compared to putting up at the fancy hotel.

I went to the estuary in the evening, after getting back, and there was a bald eagle. He was watching me on the trail, so I stopped and watched him on the gravel island working over a dead fish. Everything was fine until I reached into my pocket for my glasses. As soon as I did that he took off with the bald-eagle cry that sounds like a cuss-word.

The bear is a rather remarkable animal, when you think about it, who has, by the technique of hibernation, been able to tolerate a rather inclement habitat and is able to make a go of it on the food it harvests essentially from April to November. It sleeps from November to April, so it's up and going seven months and out of commission five. By being both a hibernator and omnivorous in respect to plant and animal tissue, it is able to make a living in a relatively hostile environment. The amazing thing is that the animal is basically a forest animal, very timid and afraid to expose itself in the open. In general it is furtive.

I forgot to mention I'm very much of the opinion that the pink salmon spawning on the estuary are probably a genetic throwback of the base history of the species, when the species was less adapted to fresh water. I would be willing to bet that much of their spawn is left to the predation of marine isopods, which are everywhere in the gravel of the estuary.


## September 12

I went toward the stream, after waiting long enough to make sure a group of mergansers weren't coming down, and I began picking up fresh signs of bear. Just as I started to move along, I heard a few twigs snap in a huge thicket of salmonberry bushes and devil's club that lies on the slope of the stream, between the stream and the trees on the south bank. This is where the Alaska Fish and Game had dropped those 200 and some oil drums they used in the two years they kept this place warm. I'm sure there was a bear in there. It would move a little and then stop, and I didn't want to force the issue. I suspect that is where the bear sleeps. Tomorrow I will try to get into that blind area and check this out. There were two fresh bear kills of salmon there; one of the salmon had just been freshly bitten into, but one of the eyes was out.

It's an ominous day. The sun is shining, but weakening, and the light intensity is way down. There is a feeling of winter and my hands are cold. The transition from summer to fall has been swift and dramatic, generated by a flow of Arctic air from the north, which is already in the throes of winter. The whole area here now has the powerful aspect of fall.

The first thing I did this afternoon was to walk along the bear trail on this side of the stream down toward the tributary that cuts into Eva Creek. When I looked down on one of the side trails, I saw a fresh pile of bear dung. Obviously fish color, it was black and very homogenous. I went down and looked at it. It was in the shape of a pie, and was diarrheic. Even so, it was fresh, having been dropped last night or this morning. I noticed on the surface a lot of tapeworms. I can't be sure if these were from the gut of the salmon, but they were suggestive of the tapeworm fragments that I'd seen deposited on the delta when the sockeyes were there. I don't know what the implication of this may be. I took a dive near the log blind and was very disappointed with the poor visibility. The stream looks as though it has been completely turned over by a bulldozer. Every 3 feet of the stream bed all the way across and down is pocked with depressions made by spawning pink salmon. I was tremendously impressed by how high they heap the gravel in the shallowing areas. There are still quite a few salmon attempting to spawn in the stream, but they are for the most part sick and dying and not likely to produce an effective spawn. About halfway through this dive I was delighted to have a small school of Dolly Varden swim by, with the adult cohos directly behind. The coho is really an impressive-looking salmon. When they turn and the light hits them, I see that they are already beginning to darken. They turn a dark purple.

I was also struck by the dirtiness of the water. I think the explanation is the tremendous activity of so many fish laying their eggs and cleaning and reworking the gravel. The stream receives a tremendous cleansing, as it were, by the salmon, and the sediment is swept out by the cleaning action of the female pinks.

It's hard to believe that I've been five months at Lake Eva. No, not hard to believe. It has been a long while and this month is a month that will offer another test of my ability to live alone. I find myself more prone to depression and sadness now, and more easily frustrated. The few remaining salmon are spawning haphazardly and are unwilling to let me near them.

## September 13

Yes, I've been spurned once again by my otters, who have flashed by without giving me a chance to film them. You might ask, Why don't you go with them? If you go with them you're chasing them, you're following them, and bugging them, and that isn't my intent. Let me give you an example, and perhaps the example this morning is a cover-up for my laziness and inability to go along with the otter. You see, this stream is an avenue, a highway, and it's a very easy highway for the otter because the otter swims. It is a highway which offers the otter considerable security because it has an overgrown bank of shrubs. If I elect to go up the stream, I can't swim; the current is much too swift and the water is too shallow, and the only way to go is by wading, which is slow hard work. When I get to the rapids the going is impossible. I could no more keep up with the otters than fly. The likelihood is that the otters went into the waterfall area and then over into the swampy area, which is a myriad of channels and tunnels, completely overgrown with bracken and devil's club and a lot of mucky dangerous substrate. And I can't see anyway. So I can't go in there to snoop, and I think this is why the otters goes in there.

My techniques are your techniques. In other words, I'm not doing anything that is fancy and requires a lot of elaborate equipment. I'll not load you down with a lot of images of microscopic plants and animals, because we have no way of filming them in their real environment. Sure we can go out and collect a drop of water and put it under a covered glass and look at it with a microscope. It wiggles around, but is that its way of life? The answer is probably, No, that isn't the habitat in which it was originally, and it's not where we would normally see it. And so it goes. . . .

As I started up over the ridge where the waterfall develops, I could see three fishermen there. I noted they all had guns. I went over and talked to one of them who was changing tackle. He was a delightful person, a physical therapist from Sitka. So T. J. spent the afternoon being a gadabout. They came in from Angoon. Of the other two, one was a surgeon, and one an internist. They had just arrived and were not very happy with the small size of the fish they were getting. I said the people who fish the stream a lot go on to the rapids area by my cabin. They were game for that and gathered up their things, and we set off. They were real fishermen. When they got to the rapids they didn't budge the whole afternoon. I brought out a round of beers for them, and just sat there and had the fun of watching them fish.

They were the kind of fishermen that bang the fish on the head when they catch them so they don't toss around and suffocate or become unconscious. They were banging away and one said "This girl is ready to lay eggs." I remarked that they were very big eggs for that fish. It was a 14-inch cutthroat, and its mouth was full of salmon eggs that it had obviously eaten. The eggs had embryos. This cutthroat had been brooding around in a salmon nest. So I learned from watching the fishermen that the cutthroats are still working those nests, and a lot of the nests are situated in a place where the trout might station itself. Most of the people who fish here fish the two large holes in the stream at the foot of the waterfall and this one at the rapids. All the fish that you catch anywhere else are considerably smaller than the ones in these areas.

The fishermen stayed until about 5:30 and in the meantime I did some exploring on my own. I started upstream in my waders, heading for the bank where we had filmed the sequence of my playing the recorder, and had crawled up on a log. The log got loose and I found myself horizontal, falling through space. I landed on my back in 3 or 4 inches of water. It was a nasty fall. I hit on my back but slightly on the left side, so I was wet all the way. I excused myself and went back to the cabin to change clothes. The fishermen fished the rapids until 6:00 P.M., and then we all headed in the direction of their boat. They weren't eager to go back and the young doctor, who was not as skillful a fisherman as the surgeon, told me about the people in Angoon. It was his opinion that we would do very well with bears there. They are common around Angoon, and, according to him, one man had all the bears named. It is a possibility, anyway, and we walked down to the boat and across the estuary.

I showed them the way across the estuary. I had expected to see their boat anchored in the middle of Hanus Bay (I knew they had come ashore in the little skiff), but they had anchored it in the lower estuary, so we scrambled down there. What fun! The tide had gone out and the boat was sitting high and dry. It was a good-sized boat, seventeen years old, they said, with a 154-horsepower Mercury. It was two and one-half hours to Sitka, but it was obvious that the next two and one-half hours would be spent waiting for the tide to come in. We had a good laugh and then they offered me lunch and brought out some potato salad, homemade bread, chocolate cake, home-fried chicken, and a can of beer to wash it down. We chatted, and I said I should break away about 8:00 because that was when I turn my Coleman lantern on.

It was suddenly 9:00. I excused myself and we shook hands. With that I headed up through the bramble where I have a feeling the bears congregate and went over the estuary. The forest was really dark and I kept my ears up and my nose up and made my way across the landing and into the cabin without any untoward collisions. By this time my back was throbbing wildly. I had fallen on the left side of my buttock and it was sorely bruised.

## September 14

The cohos were down at the log blind and I think I saw the first signs of possible courtship. I'm not positive but a couple were circling each other and now and then one broke water, supposedly loosening up the eggs or sperm—but I'm very skeptical of that last notion. The estuary itself didn't have much on it. There were four or five mergansers on the middle part, and they didn't show much awareness of me. There were two new salmon along the south end of the estuary, although no signs of bear kill but very fresh evidence of digging in the area of my polliwog pond.

Supper tonight consisted of oyster stew and two slices of whole wheat bread with a tag end of jam. I'm beginning to clean up all the odds and ends so there won't be a lot of leftover food.

I did find the spring amanita, which is the death mushroom, but something is breaking it off and eating it.

## September 15

I had planned to dive today, and one group of salmon was spawning, but in very shallow water so it was hard to film. I dug myself a trench where the fish were spawning and planted the movie and still cameras and the strobe in the channel area so the fish would get used to them. When they did, I suited up. When I got to my trench, the fish took off and wouldn't come back. I stayed about an hour until my patience ran out. Since then I've pretty well determined what happened. I built the blind by digging a trench off to the side. In the process of doing this I opened an easy way for the water to flow through Eva Creek, which brought a strong flow of water into the spawning. Lying in that trench and allowing the water to flow over me did the trick. I'm sure it was carrying my odor all the way through that nest, and as a consequence the fish wouldn't go back into it until I left it. As soon as I did, they returned and this morning they have completed their spawning.

I moved over to another group of fish that had been spawning, and I got the usual cold shoulder. These fish also moved away. But I was intrigued as I lay there waiting for them, for there was a very large, fat, oversized, overstuffed cutthroat trout. He went to the bottom and into the nest, eating eggs and spitting out stones. Out of curiosity, I pushed the stones aside to see what kind of pickings he was getting. The place was loaded with eggs. If ever there was a handsome villain, this cutthroat trout was it. Shortly afterward, the salmon males came back, took one look at the cutthroat, and drove him out. It was extraordinary to watch the cutthroat sort out those eggs. His jaw was a little bruised, indicating that digging in the rocks wasn't really what a trout was intended to do. It's amazing to think that the salmon color is derived from the eggs, not the color of the salmon. The salmon's skin color changes dramatically as the animal goes from sea to fresh water and develops its final death color, which is also, ironically enough, its nuptial colors.

My otters came in this morning when it was still darkish. The two big ones got up on the log and went the full length of it sniffing. Then they came back and sprayed; they do it with a twitching action, and they pull their tail up high and hold it rather stiffly. The liquid comes out in a strong squirt. I have that in pictures, I think, with the sun light going through the ejected spray. I've been out on the log and sniffed the area, and I note that the moss is being killed so I think they consider that log theirs.

# 15

# HOOD BAY

*September 16*

S eptember 16 is the day on which the pattern of life, a pattern of living that I had been experiencing for five months, was brought to a rather abrupt end by the arrival around 2:00 in the afternoon of Bill Young, the production manager. He and the pilot, Mike, and the golden retriever, Goldy, pulled into view as I was making preparations for a dive. It was exciting and good news to know that we were going to take a positive stand with the bears, and try to work the bears in an area where they are more plentiful. Bill had been in Juneau discussing the matter with the Forest Service and Fish and Game. They offered us the use of their cabin on their fish weir at Hood Bay. Bill was in no great hurry to get out of here and while he and I pondered what we should take for the expedition, the pilot began to fish. In a couple of hours we managed to get everything loaded up and tied to the pack frames, and made the two trips across the stream and up to the landing. The boat was nearly overflowing with equipment. It was a rainy afternoon and I felt a little sad as I left the cabin. I was finally faced with the reality of leaving, of going somewhere else. Although it might speed up the passage of time, I find in general that, when I move into a new kind of activity, the days seem to extend themselves and the time doesn't pass any faster.

I was surprised at how short a trip it was to Juneau. As soon as we taxied up, it was almost as if I had never been away from the place. All the images I had remembered of Juneau appeared as if it were yesterday. We got to the Baranof Hotel and made some phone calls. I wasn't caught up in the excitement of seeing people—male or female. It was just the way I remembered it. I soaked in a tub and remember the surprise of feeling hot water over my body and being in a room that was heated by radiators. We charged up batteries for the trip, and then went down to the restaurant and had a very good meal. We thought about going to a movie in the evening, but we'd seen all that were in town.

When we first got into town I suddenly realized that I didn't have any shoes. All I had was waders and I couldn't walk into a restaurant in fishing boots. So we went into a men's store and they outfitted me. I also remember the pleasure of sitting in the restaurant and having someone serve me. It was my first green salad and predinner drink in five months. Back at the hotel, we watched television for awhile and then we hit the sack. The sounds were really oppressive to me because my hearing has become so acute, and I slept very badly. The sounds were right on top of me, the sounds of people and automobiles. I kept thinking they should be a long way off, and every sound I heard during the night was associated with animals.

## September 17

We got the plane loaded, took along the two Forest Service people, and started off for Hood Bay in nasty weather. I was looking forward to being on another island, and the stream there reportedly had a large run of chum salmon. We finally got over to the bay on a high tide and the pilot was able to fly right up to the fish weir where the Alaska Fish and Game count the Dolly Varden trout and the salmon. Water reached almost to the cabin door.

It was not a great surprise to me upon arriving at this place to discover that it was a mess. Although the cabin was larger and more lavish than mine at Eva Creek, it gave me a chance to envision how my cabin must have looked in the heyday of the five-year investigation carried out by Alaska Fish and Game at Lake

Eva. I was shocked by the tremendous accumulation of debris, long forgotten. The building was overladen with trash and junk. There was just barely room for a person to function. I was terrifically depressed with the amount of paraphernalia and scientific gear that had no function.

I had forgotten to bring along a toilet kit, insect repellent, hairbrush, toothbrush, and so on, so in the entire experience I was further irritated by constantly being reminded, by people and necessity, that I didn't have this or that. At least, it meant a *little* less clutter.

Three people were using the cabin and they seemed not to share the enthusiasm of their superiors who had wished us off on them. There was, for instance, the annoyance of having to wait in line to cook supper. We had to get our meals in without conflicting with theirs. I detected pinpricks of hostility in the air.

The principal difference between Hood Bay and Eva Creek is the lack of a true estuary at Hood Bay. What estuary exists is actually a small portion of the stream. When we came into Hood Bay it was a very high tide, as I stated, and the water was coming up over the weir. The fish came in across the top of it whether they liked it or not. There was a constant sea gull noise, which I found weirdly disconcerting. There were two types of salmon, the pinks and the chums. The pink run was heavy, about 10 times as many as at Eva. The stream itself was not particularly distinctive. It was a little more swift and probably has a greater amount of gravel than Eva Creek. It is stony, with mudbanks and stones covered with algae. The abundance of the chum salmon was also very evident at Hood Bay; at Eva Creek there are only a few.

When you begin to know an organism you begin to manipulate it in a way in which you demonstrate your superiority to the world at large by claiming to understand how the scene of nature can be improved upon. The fish weirs do this. Man is attempting to limit a species of salmon which is less desirable than another. Frankly, I find in that a contemptible arrogance. I fear that if man goes on thinking he is number one and has the potential of immortality by virtue of his brain, there will be a great havoc sometime.

My back hurt and I felt cruel taking the only remaining bed with a mattress on it. The others had a little conference, hoping that soon the bear footage would be shot and Bill and Kevin, the cameraman, could return to Hollywood, and I could return to

Lake Eva. It didn't turn out that way, and the reason, I think, is a matter of a certain amount of poor luck and inexperience on our part. Clearly also our impatience.

This attempt to gain further dimension to our task of filming the bear by going into areas where the bears are plentiful was a valid one. I think it was a unique experience, and a costly one for the studio. Had we been a few weeks earlier, I think we would have succeeded. Unfortunately, the runs of salmon are not spaced out in time sequentially in the different streams. The sockeye run on most streams was in July and the pink run was in August, and we were simply too late. Also, I think that our group was too large effectively to film the Alaskan brown bear. Sig Olsen, the regional biologist with the Forest Service, said that he preferred to run into the bears and not wait them out, and we were under his guidance.

## September 18

The Forest Service had been most anxious that I know Sig Olsen, whom I had met briefly when I first talked with them about where to carry out my investigation. Sig was our gun-bearer, along with another young man. We started up the trail from the field station around 9:00 in the morning, not too early. The party consisted of Bill Young and myself, Kevin Duffy the cameraman, and the two Forest Service people. The Alaska Fish and Game people had been up from midnight on, servicing their fish weir, which tends to clog up with the tremendous population of pinks and chums. The weak and dying salmon are unable to maintain station, so the Forest Service has to go in and remove these from the screens.

We had barely left the area of the cabin and had just come out on the stream proper when Sig stopped us. From the bracken fern ahead came the characteristic snorting of the Alaskan brown bear. Sig was disturbed by this and stopped and waited. The sound grew fainter and the bears retreated. We continued up the stream until we came out on a rather high bank that afforded us a distant view, both upstream and downstream. It was decided that this would be a good place to bring our cameras into action without being hindered by heavy brush. So we waited to see if the bears would come. I judged we were about half a mile from the cabin.

The day went slowly; it was rainy and cloudy and we waited and waited and waited—and nothing is more lethal to the spirits than to constantly expect something to happen which doesn't. We waited all day, until about 7:15 in the evening.

If you cluster five people in one spot, there is bound to be a certain amount of whispering, and moving, and scratching, and coughing, and other inadvertent and occasionally rude noises.

The point is, we waited all day and nothing happened. I remember feeling quite a relief when it got too dark to film. It wasn't a great disappointment, at least to me, to get the kind of treatment from Hood Bay that I've been getting at Eva Creek. So, the first day we came within earshot but we didn't see any bear. I think the Alaskan brown bear isn't terribly willing to let a person see it. If at all possible, it will take cover, unless it is drawn into contact by some sort of a food chain. Probably many of these so-called attacks of the brown bear on humans have been the result of repeated exposure to people, like encounters at the garbage dump. I suspect that the hunting activity is how the bear identifies man, and I wouldn't be at all surprised if the number of bear attacks goes up rather than down, and the bear will be gradually eliminated from the scene.

We had hoped to solve the cinematic problem by moving to an area in which bears were plentiful, but so far no dice. We returned to the cabin then and, having spent a day in the frustrating activity known as waiting, we waited again in the evening until the Alaska Fish and Game people had finished their supper.

## September 19

We decided to try a new tactic, namely, to reduce the number of people. The group that was to search for brown bears consisted of myself, Sig Olsen, his friend, and the cameraman, Kevin. Going farther upstream, we again had the same unfortunate result. No bears. We covered more ground; I got a stronger impression as to the abundance of bears; Kevin the cameraman did a lot of camera work of me following bear trails leading through the heavy bracken. We found a bear skeleton along the edge of the stream minus its skull—killed last spring by a trophy hunter, we assumed. It was an awesome sight.

In the evening we came back to camp and cooked supper, A council of war was held and it was decided, on the basis of Bill

Young's activities at the seashore and the fact that he'd been up another stream with one of the Fish and Game people and had been impressed by bear signs there, that we might logically work that area the next day.

## September 20

Bill and the cameraman, Kevin, elected to go out and search for a killer whale and a humpback whale combat, which the two Alaska Fish and Game men had observed the night before. I decided not to do that. It was Sunday and the day that Sig Olsen and his associate decided they had to be back in Juneau. They planned that Jack Culbreth would come out to replace them. We had a meeting last night and Bill was pushing to go to Pack Creek. He was of the opinion that, as a consequence of Sam Price and his wife having fed all the animals, they had managed to tame several of the Alaskan brown bears. These bears had actually hibernated under their house and had raised several cubs, and it was these bears that most of the wildlife photographers up here had been filming at very close range.

The first order of business today was Sig Olsen's departure, along with one of the three Fish and Game people. Bill and Kevin went out in the morning and came back after lunch with no success as far as the whales were concerned. We decided to try the other stream, and it was a cold, wet trip across the bay. We saw a fresh bear kill of salmon. We went into the area where we thought we could get the best cinematic effect, and we waited and waited and waited. No bears. It was a beautiful place, too, with alders flanking the stream and the leaves coming down in showers.

At Hood Bay, it was my impression that at night I'd wake up and hear bears walking by.

The final day at Hood Bay, Young, Kevin, and I decided we might succeed on this stream because we were down to three; therefore, the whispering was less and we should be seeing bears. The stream had a small run of salmon in it, and bears are like human beings in that they are always where the action is. And the action for a bear is where he can fill his stomach with as little time and trouble as possible. The idea has always been that the bears have territory, hold real estate, and everyone accepts the idea that the biggest bear is entitled to fish this point. He is at the stream for only a nominal amount of time, but no one esti- mates how many hours a bear is involved in fishing. You'd think a bear scientist would measure this. We didn't see bears. Return- ing to the cabin, we decided to get out of there, and the quicker the better.

# 16

# PACK CREEK

*September 21*

Bill already must have been thinking seriously about Pack Creek, a place I had not been aware of. But Pack Creek, I gather, is a stream that flows into a wilderness area, the Glacier National Forest. A couple live there, a prospector and his wife named Price, in their seventies and retired. They are living, not quite on the land, but on a raft which they have pulled into a cove. Their principal occupation is to keep alive, and this means that, since they're living in the wilderness, they have to cut their wood and grow their food. Their hobby is to be friends with animals, and it's a unique hobby because they have been friends to the Alaskan brown bear, which is, of course, a man-killer and a nasty, dangerous animal. This couple have had the bears hibernating in their shed.

On the way back to Juneau we had a conference. Bill wanted to stop in at Pack Creek and talk to the Prices and see if the tamed bears are there. To try the possibility had been one of his reasons for leaving Hood Bay. Being production manager, he was haunted by the economics of the alternate solution: to charter a boat for $250 a day, plus a hunter and all the rest of it, with no guarantee that we would see bears. So we put in at Pack Creek and Bill and I got out. It was a miserable, windy day. The plane taxied back into the bay to avoid being blown against the shore, and we walked up to the cabin and knocked. Nothing happened so we walked around the house. As I mentioned before, Price has built his house on a raft tied up to the shore. He has a garden onshore alongside the raft. The Prices are a unique, rugged couple who in a sense are running a semi-professional zoo with semi-domesticated animals. They devote their effort to raising food for the animals and have a sizable population of deer there. Also, the brown bear they've tamed, the marten, and so on.

We walked around the house and saw inside an elderly man sitting at his radio. He looked up and came to the door. He was very friendly and very sharp, and it was a real pleasure to meet him. I felt instant empathy with him and I wish there were more people like him in the world. His wife was in Juneau and would be coming home that night at 6:00. We asked about the bear and he said he hadn't seen the bears for a while because there weren't any salmon on the stream. He said maybe Suzi, (or whatever her name was) and her cubs would bed down in the shed this winter again. They come to the creek when the cohos are beginning to run and, he said, the cohos were just starting to enter the stream. He also said the bears can't catch what they choose when the salmon are fresh in the stream because they are just too fast and too alert—and I agree. I've been trying to dive on them.

Mr. Price thought some bears might still be on the stream and he suggested that we take some bread with us and saturate it with beer and honey. The bears go absolutely crazy over this and they will come for miles. It's like Pandora's box, and why not open the box and see if he is right? Bill thought it was worth trying and I added my two cents' worth about getting some of the other uncertainties of Eva Creek out of the way, namely the deer. I indicated the marten also because he is truly an animal of the forests of southeast Alaska. We asked if we could stay, and Mr. Price said, "Sure. We'll find space for you and you can take advantage of our cooking. You people can sleep on our front porch, it's glassed in and it's a workshop." Jack thought he would like to sleep out in the open under one of the sheds, which primarily protect their wood supply. We looked at the garden that night and Bill was anxious to go up the trail, so we went as far as the tree-house bear lookout the Forest Service had built in 1932.

About 8:30 we returned to the cabin and had a nice visit with the Prices. In addition to their front porch they have a back porch, which is essentially a room they have made available to their animals. It has a hole in the floor that the martens come up through. The window was open so the Steller's jays could come in and out. They have eight or ten jays and the marten. It was a welcome change of pace, after the filthy, cluttered biological station at Hood Bay, with the not too friendly technicians, to find ourselves with these remarkable people whose whole life is the animals.

## September 22

Despite the Prices' amazing preoccupation with and devotion to animals — not without parallel in the history of mankind, I'm sure — Mr. Price was once attacked by a bear that he thought was his friend.

Mr. Price was knocked down. He had a walking stick — an old pool cue, I think — and, looking up at the bear, he socked it in the nose as hard as he could. Apparently this was so painful to the bear that the animal broke off his attack and almost passed out from pain and left. Mr. Price's recommendation to those who are attacked by bears is to poke them in the nose.

This is all very well, but bears attack generally with rapidity and a good many people I'm sure would have an emotional blackout or could be killed just by being struck down. Sig Olsen described an attack on one of their men. The man was attacked from the rear and, although he survived, he had been hit with such force that about six months later he developed a heart murmur. It turned out to be a rupture of some of the blood vessels in the heart tissue as a consequence of the terrific force with which the bear had struck him from behind. So the man actually had a small heart attack, undiagnosed for six months, in addition to all the physical trauma and damage the bear did to him. This same type of injury occurs with people who are in head-on automobile accidents or in accidents where the car stops very suddenly and the driver is thrown up against the steering column.

## September 23

After breakfast we walked up to the tree-house observatory and laid out the bear lure of beer and honey. Mr. Price wished us a pleasant day and went back to his cabin and his company, and we climbed up to the observatory. Deer made their way up the stream, but it was another one of those drawn-out, nasty days in which we really didn't achieve very much. At least we went through the motions again of being quiet and waiting out the bear.

For the first time on the trip I was extremely cold. I seem to be much more sensitive to the cold than others from warmer climates.

We stayed the day out and again at the witching hour, I guess about 7:00 in the evening, we made our way back to the cabin and of course were treated to an excellent supper. I can't say enough about the friendliness and hospitality of the Prices' to us who were for all practical purposes strangers. I have a suspicion that all people in Alaska are a little overcome by lack of human contact, and people coming out to visit them and stay with them and talk with them provide a very rich experience, one which they cherish deeply. I noticed the same behavior with the foresters and miners. People who lead isolated lives are generally curious about other people and are very warm hosts. Farmers have much the same attributes, at least they did when I was a kid.

## September 24

On our second day at Pack Creek we were extremely disheartened not to find any bears despite our bear-baiting technique and sitting in the tree house all day. We decided instead of working the bear to get to the matter of working the deer. We wandered out to a meadow area where some six deer had been lined up along the banks sunning themselves. On this grassy meadow, which is really a delta of Pack Creek, we waited for our deer. We lay down and waited and waited. Again, I found myself feeling the chill of the day and Jack came to my rescue and wrapped me in a thermo blanket. Finally a young deer showed up and we attempted to photograph it. It retreated behind some trees. We followed it, and it turned out to be the fawn of the Prices' tame deer and had a bell and orange ribbon on its neck.

Around noon, two deer appeared out of the woods and came over into the meadow, so I sprang into action, pretending to film the deer while the studio photographer filmed me in my pretense. It turned out that these were also tame deer, and they were heading to the Price cabin for lunch. Mr. Price feeds them a mixture of grain. He also gives them potatoes, cabbages, and rutabagas, and even goes out into the woods during the winter and gathers up the deer for feeding. I suppose he is oversupplying the deer and therefore there is an overpopulation of deer here.

No doubt the population specialists of the Fish and Game shake their heads in disgust. They like to think that the hunter is necessary to keep deer in check. The other predators on the island are in short supply because there are no coyotes and wolf. The Alaskan brown bear only work on the carcasses of the deer in the spring months because they are hibernating during the winter. All the able-bodied men in Alaska hunt deer to their limit, which I think is four, because it is a necessary element to *their* food supply.

The normal technique for getting close to a wild deer is to imitate a fawn in distress by blowing through grass. All the deer for miles around show up to rescue the fawn.

Ken, the pilot, picked us up and proposed a wager: we would pay him $9 a bear for every bear that he showed us, and he would pay the cost of flying us back to Juneau if he didn't find any bear for us. We declined, but Ken took the plane up to the mountains anyway, to the Young Range. He said that the bears were sitting along the timberline of the ridge alongside their dens—he had counted fifteen on his way down. He flew along the ridge, close to the tip, so it was an awesome flight. Sure enough, he pointed out a bear that was sitting on its haunches, and soon another one appeared. By this time Bill was getting upset by the up-and-down motion of the plane and the turbulence. He indicated to Ken that he had made his point, and let's fly back to Juneau.

On the way back we overflew a solitary humpback whale. The pilot circled it two or three times so that I got a good look at it. It was the first time I had seen a humpback whale from the air.

*September 25*

I stayed in bed all day in Juneau, and that is that.

The delta of the stream supplying
Lake Eva from the valley above
provides a rest site for mergansers
as well as a shoal over which bald
eagles fish for spawning sockeyes
and Dolly Varden trout.

A pair of harlequin ducks. The male's
discontinuous color pattern makes it
inconspicuous at a distance.

*Stellar sea lions on a rocky offshore
reef near Hanus Bay.*

—

# WINDING DOWN

## September 26

It is strange being back in the cabin at Lake Eva, after being away for ten days. As yet the bear has remained elusive. I feel as though I'd been away for months. It's hard to explain this involvement with Lake Eva. It has grown on me and become oddly possessive of me.

The most ironic thing about my ten days away from the cabin was to find on my return a tremendous pile of bear dung on the landing halfway up the steps to the cabin. It was apparent that the bear had been on the front porch and had gathered a fair proportion of the hydroponic experiment with the radishes in the petri dishes. Further investigation showed that the bear had been all the way around the cabin but had left the cooler on the back porch alone. He had worked over the can of bacon grease which I had left for the jays and had left two nice teeth marks. The big can of grease completely disappeared.

It is quite apparent that the bears have been in the skunk cabbage hollows digging out and eating the roots. The excretion of the bears has been more a green color, which I think is due to the addition of the skunk cabbage in their diet. You might think of the excretion as being color-coded.

The stream has a forlorn look because the pink salmon are virtually all gone. There are a great number of pink salmon operculae (the gill covers), which are not eaten, and backbones. I really don't think there is much allure to the stream for the bears now. There is very little of the smell of death so apparent when I left here.

At the estuary things were pretty much the same. A fair amount of waterfowl swam on the estuary and were very timid. I stayed about ten minutes (it was pouring rain). There was a bald eagle perched over the blind area and several sea gulls. I came back to the cabin feeling a little out of adjustment. I couldn't help feeling that I was not acoustically in tune. When I started up the trail from the estuary I became aware that I really wasn't hearing much of it. It was distressing to think that in ten days I had grown tense, impatient and, in short, fallen back into the old jangling ways.

So I'm back and it seems strange to be by myself.

## September 27

I heard a very big thump and got up to find out what it was. After a little observation I discovered this was from the spruce cones which a squirrel was busy cutting above and letting fall on the tin roof of the outhouse.

There was no sign of the otters, just some chirping at the lake and down at the estuary. Even the jays are timid. It is really very dull because of the absence of spawning fish. I'm beginning to feel a loneliness which I'm sure will grow as winter approaches.

## September 28

It has been raining since the middle of the night and it is a hard downpour. The cabin is 50°, water 50°, and air 37°. All day long the water has been rising. I got up at 7:00, which leaves one in darkness now. The birds didn't start singing until 8:00 when I turned my generator on. There is quite a difference in the pitch, the time, and the amount of the varied thrush's singing.

One of the remarkable features of the salmon is that the salmon returning to the stream are the exact ones that left. Each stream system appears to serve a salmon population made up almost entirely of the offspring of the salmon that spawned there, so each stream's population contributes only to its own replenishment. With the demands of man's expanding economy and population for more protein and therefore more fishing, and with the constant exploitation in the areas where salmon abound, the salmon populations are finding it rough going and there appears to be an ever-diminishing number. I can't envision a very rosy future for the salmon.

At 4:00 P.M. I went to the estuary to review the situation. The trail was literally running with water, across and down the trail into the creek. The water was pouring off the trees and the total effect of this inundation was to plunge me into a deep depression.

## September 29

I slept very badly all night because of the sound of the rain on the roof. I was psychologically troubled by the thought that I probably wouldn't be able to ford the stream. This morning the stream is overflowing, filled with ugly brown water, and there is no suggestion of the quiet placid creek. The water is well over the landing and it would be foolish to wade it. All the coarse grass is down along with the bracken and the flow of water is swift and churning fast. The logjam is completely covered. It was very dark, even black, when I got up.

I looked out the door a few minutes later and saw a brilliant white object coming down in the current at the tip of the north island. I actually thought it was a swan so I grabbed my binoculars and looked again and saw it was one of my gasoline drums from up the stream where we have the boat. I was dumbfounded. This leaves me with a very uneasy feeling as to whether or not my landing has been carried away. If it has it means the loss of quite a lot of material plus the loss of the boat and the gas supply. I can't get across the stream to check but think I will traverse the bear trail on this side of the stream. It is obviously a flood.

I put on the rain gear and fought my way through endless thickets of huckleberry and blueberries and wandered in and out along the bear trail. Even though I had a strong sense of the location of the landing, by taking the easy way through areas I found myself angling off at odd distances to the stream, which shows the extreme danger of wandering around in the woods without a compass. The boat was still there and the six tanks of gas are still in a box. I do think I've lost about 30 gallons of white gas.

Few city people have experienced this feeling of going in circles in the woods, unable to break loose and find the way out. The danger is a real one, although I think a human being has just a suggestion of a compass built within him. It's unbelievable, the endless variety in terms of little clearings and trails that come and break and go in and out of the woods; and one has no signposts, absolutely none. The distance from my cabin to the boat landing is not more than ¼ mile. I left the cabin at 10:00 and got back at 11:30. It took me one and a half hours to go ¼ mile using fragments of an old bear trail, and I didn't waste any time. In the process of doing this, if I hadn't kept my wits about me and listened carefully, in a matter of moments I would have been lost even though I was in a very narrow valley. The stream dropped 2 or 3 inches by afternoon and had the muddy greenness that one associates with the Missouri River. The trip up the bear trail was grueling also, and I came back exhausted.

Floods mean many things to many people, whether generated by a hurricane or a massive and quick spring thaw. Or one can think of the major river systems which generally flood in the spring because of high temperatures and snow melting off the mountains too fast. As a child I remember wondering why, since they know about the possibility of flooding, people risk all their businesses and homes by building in the valley floor. Of course, one of the things the government does is to try to fool nature by flood control, and the government likes to appear in this as though it is succeeding.

The signs are very clear that human beings are in trouble, and I think the lesson is clear. If there is only one point to be drawn from all this, I think it is simply this: we are all exceedingly frail and hung up in a world we have made too complicated. We have been too abstract and we've finally come around to a crisis, in education and in living. It's difficult for an individual to see the forest for the trees.

It continued to rain all day, and I was still bound to only one side of the stream.

## September 30

I got a little better insight into how things are beginning to look, particularly the skunk cabbage hollows which lie between here and the boat landing. The glorious, magnificent, reliable, underrated skunk cabbages are on their last leaves and, woe, the bracken fern have overgrown them, but they are now brown and beautiful and autumnal.

I must point out that the huckleberries apparently drop their leaves two at a time, and right now looking out the window of the cabin, I am aware of the comparison I made this spring of the gradual obliteration of the mossy coating on the upped roots and downed logs by the leafing-out of the huckleberries.

I would like to go on record and say the last plant to bloom up here is the lace flower. I also made the observation that the autumnal color of the bunchberry varies, depending upon how much light it is exposed to. I noted that bunchberries in the shade all have a pale yellow cast whereas those out in the open are oranges, reds, and purples, just a riot of color. I'm beginning to think the color a plant develops in the shade is a consequence of light.

## October 1

The devil's club plants are still quite colorful, but have a collapsed look. The huckleberries continue to drop leaves and the skunk cabbage are almost out of the scene now. There was a brief appearance of the dipper at the stream, and yesterday I noted two of them trying to mate. I think these animals tend to nest in January or February so this mating activity may be very normal for them. The water temperature was down to 47°, which makes me believe there was snow at the higher elevations.

I seem to be dragging my feet all day.

## October 2

I set the alarm for 7:00. It was still dark and black but I got up and turned the heat on to warm some water. The cabin was 52°, air was 34°, and water was 47°. The stream still has a brown color to it but has gone down sufficiently. I thought it might be a sunny day, but there were clouds around the mountains. I checked in with Channel Flying and overheard some fishermen talking on the radio and saying the winds were up to 40 to 50 knots. I can see my islands again and they don't have that terrible drenched look. I was surprised to see that the coarse grass is up again, and along the stream some of the shrubs are in fall color. Some are still a bright green. It is a brave effect.

A lot of the leaves were stripped from the plants and have been carried downstream. It is quiet. I don't have the morning chorus of birds, as if nature is saying that it's going to play a trick on T.J. and keep the day in suspense. But no tricks. It remained dark and gray and sullen.

(I don't know when I'll be leaving, next week or the week after, or in November. I guess that's part of the game. Keep the hero guessing.)

In the twentieth century there are so many, many ugly things, but there are also things that are to be enjoyed and savored. I can't help thinking that each and every one of us should function as himself and shouldn't be intimidated by what doctors, professors, musicians, and so on know. There are areas of knowledge that have a big payoff and that payoff, in my judgment, should be the same for all professions. I don't see any reason why a person should get any more or any less because he spent so much time learning the profession. The tragedy of the way that it's done now is that the clever people and selfish people are people without talent and oftentimes get into a profession and push themselves around and do the organizing. We have so much minutia in the paper work and the coffee breaks, but how many of us come home happy about what we did?

(Eva Creek is flowing to the sea and I'm wondering what to do, what to do.)


## October 3

I suddenly saw an Alaskan brown bear come out at the crossing, coming out behind a hemlock tree, and of course I stood there watching it and I thought he was watching me. I went into the other room to get the camera and when I came back the bear was gone. I stood there a little annoyed and hoped he would come out again but he never did.

Suddenly a mother bear came out of the bushes and then proceeded on up the trail and a few seconds later out came a darling little cub following it's mother, but I just left well enough alone and didn't go out to get the footage of them. I just sat there and pondered them and filled my eyes, absolutely thrilled.

Man has really competed with the Alaskan brown bear by fishing for the salmon and, thus, not so many bear are around. I found a clipping in a newspaper that said the packing of the cases of salmon was well over last year's level, about 90,000 tons of salmon. The average weight of the salmon packed is about 10 pounds. I think now of 18,000,000 salmon going to the human being. It isn't at all surprising that the bear are in short supply.

I'm beginning to see the telltale signs of the fungus on the coho salmon that have already spawned, but there are very, very few in this stream. Of course these fish stay in the streams the longest and possibly feed off their own young. I'm taken up with the bear and I begin to wonder, since we are turning back quite a few fish that we hook on our line, why we can't use a colored dye or something instead of bullets and not really kill these animals.

I have been exposed to the bear and I have drawn one conclusion. The bear eats the salmon and leaves the ends, and this sloppiness actually has benefit to the animal because I would say that in the weeks that have transpired, during the ten days I was away, the bear goes around and very tidily eats the fragments he left. I'm sure the bear is going through and cleaning up the last of the salmon and the last of the berries.

I have one bad confession to make, and it is a very bad one. I discovered that the mother bear and two cubs had been on the trail this morning sometime. I went across the stream this afternoon and laid out a cardboard box, thoroughly soaking in beer, and made a sacrifice of a half can of sockeye salmon and some maple syrup, cleaning out my pantry and trying out Mr. Price's theory that the bear liked this combination. I then put some peanut butter on the box. I left this peace offering for the bear. The box will probably be visited by deer or by the squirrels, which are in the immediate area, or the jays. But tomorrow I will go back and see what happened. I really feel I'm cheating, trying to lure the bear and tempt him and being sneaky.

## October 4

I went to the estuary at 9:45 and there were no marks on the trail other than my own footprints. The peace offering was all still sitting thére and the bald eagle flew back and forth in front of me instead of staying on the other side of the estuary. I didn't have the camera and was quite surprised to have him flying around me. I went on across the estuary and noted a killed salmon there which still had some meat on him so I left it and will probably go back later and get a souvenir of a jawbone. I went on to the ocean and the tide was way out. It was really a beautiful day with long, yellow shadows and the atmosphere saturated with moisture. There was no wind and it was moderately warm.

What first struck me on this trip is that as I walked along where the tide had gone, I saw bear prints loud and clear. I also forgot to mention yesterday that I went up to the lake and there were bear prints all the way up the trail to the lake. The interesting point is that there is a mommy bear and two baby bears, and yet the bear that walks the trail 98% of the time is the two-year old cub. Apparently mommy and baby walk abreast and only occasionally do they get out on the trail.

I found some lily of the valley fruits. They are red, which is the color they will remain all winter. I was also surprised to see a foam-plastic cup in the intertidal area.

It was a good morning, a Sunday. I couldn't help thinking how better off people would be if instead of going to church they would go to a place in a forest where they could be alone and ponder. I'm sure they'd come back a little more beautiful.

## October 6

Each one of us needs time to think and time to reflect and time to be alone. I don't think one gets this in one's job, one's school, or even one's vacation, particularly if you are caught up in driving or flying here and there. This, I think, is one of the many tragedies of the twentieth century.

I'm here at Eva Creek and Lake Eva feeling all this and I'm aware in walking the trail that the leaves are quickly going from the tissue-paper look to no look at all and they're gone, and some of their molecules have gone to the earth beneath and been chemically absorbed. You wonder, how has life worked it's magic through us, and how does the animal kingdom represent evolution, and what *is* evolution anyway? There was a route through which change was supposed to have proceeded—I just don't know. So I'm about to hit the sack. That's one of the attributes of being at war, for in war, you learn to optimize your rest when the time comes because you never know. . . . So you go through the agony of war which is largely the agony of waiting. For what? For what? I suppose the mechanics of making this film involve the agony of waiting. But out of this will emerge, I hope, the accounting of ecology of streams and lakes and the memory of this will burn bright, like all good memories.

## October 7

Four goldeneyes paddled by in their winter plumage which is very handsome. They saw me but pretended not to notice, so they turned around and headed back downstream.

The stream has been carrying a lot of foam which is washing down. I think it is caused from nutrients which hit the air. These are the days of the inversion, which means if the air that overlays the water is chilled by the water, and whenever there isn't any wind, there will be a direct change of air to cold, and this air sits right on the water. The light that is on this cold air is bent and creates a lens which makes distant objects seem much higher. I get the illusion that things only 3 or 4 feet high are higher.

I now have the feeling it's about to snow and I play on my recorder a bit.

## October 8

Fog lies over the ocean and the length of the day is not long enough to keep the lake heated to 47°. Most of the submerged aquatic plants that live in the lake proper are declining, and their life cycle for this year is over.

I am very worried about the decreasing light situation.

I noticed that the otters haven't been in evidence for the last couple of days. The log they sprayed is showing a considerable amount of damage. The moss is killed off by the spray. I fed the jays in the morning and had Carnation Instant breakfast and a grapefruit. I was surprised to find that all the food was gone that

I put out before. The dippers were feeding on the gravel areas in the morning, kicking and scratching around along one of those salmon spawning sites. I noticed that the coho salmon are able to knock the gravel to either side of their tails and they're able to dig themselves a long trench or channel in a bed of heavier stones, under which the eggs are dropped. The pinks don't really get much of a channel dug, unless there is a large number of pinks. I still suspect that the shallower sites in this area are a consequence of the salmon digging over and over again each year and they've put this odd configuration in the stream bed. It is strictly a consequence of the salmon using the stream.

One of the jays is sitting on the hemlock branch eating pumpkin seeds. He jumped off the branch, shaking the water off as he did so, and jumped on down to the feeder. It is a tremendously real and intimate experience.

I went up on the roof and was drawn to the fact that the goldeneyes (ducks) were very close to the cabin. I get the impression from watching the goldeneyes that, even though they do look at me, they become upset by something that is going on in the water. I do hope the days will continue as they were today. Occasionally I do get a little depressed by the gloom and the shortness of the day but I've been fortunate that I haven't been penned up too much and am able to get out and stretch my legs.

(I've been mulling over my relationship with my son. I think I've learned a great deal from him — an understanding of a newer generation. This isn't to say he has been involved in all aspects of the new generation, but he has manifested many of its traits. I think my son took quite a beating in our home; first the mechanics of school, which he didn't go through with, and that generated a great deal of confusion between my wife and me. Then my son decided he was completely against war, a pacifist. He also elected to become a vegetarian. When the time came for him to be drafted, he went to Canada, which was a great shock in my mind and I did get terribly upset about it. It was a great emotional stress. In retrospect, this appears to be very courageous and perfectly honorable. I think I have learned from my son and his actions that his judgment was right and I think he saw much of what I, after six months at Lake Eva, have just now discovered. Much of what my son said and his ideas set the wheels turning in my mind. I'm sure that much of what I say is a carbon copy of what he thinks, but we have never really gone into this because, unfortunately, there is no dialogue between father and son in the twentieth century. No dialogue between the old and the young. But when I leave Lake Eva, I'll go visit him.)

## October 9

After I came back to the cabin and was sitting on the john I heard a chirp and five otters came up stream, working their way up to the rapids, but they didn't come out.

The question arose, as I was sitting there, If man is not happy within, what is wrong without? I think what's wrong is essentially that man has somehow misinterpreted what his education will bring him and assumed that because he has access to so much that no harm can befall him and no problem exists that an expert cannot solve. The human being feels that because he lives in an age of specialization and miracles, there are no problems, or at least none that a trip to the psychologist or group sessions will not resolve. It just isn't that way. One must learn to live alone. Come to think of it, most people are alone only when they're in their cars or on the john. What is it, this herding?

You may remember I left a box for the bears with a little salmon, peanut butter, and beer. Everything is gone, except the salmon, although someone had left a beer *can*. I picked it up and, much to my surprise, it was punctured with three or four good-sized bear holes.

## October 10

I took a long walk along the lake and discovered that my bears had been up there and had gone into the yellow plastic tent containing my diving gear, and had torn the trunk open. They didn't wreck the trunk but they scattered the contents all over and completely tore the tent apart. The group of bears that had visited the tent was the group of three, the mother and her two cubs. They had gone by the cabin on the other side of the stream sometime during the night. Their prints on the trail were filled with rainwater, so I knew they hadn't come by in the morning. The box in which I had my goodies was gone and I still haven't found it. The bears have obviously taken it and carted it off, so I decided to make up a new box, putting in a can of beer and the sockeye salmon and some syrup.

I waited up there until about 8:00 P.M., and I have to admit that I had a queasy feeling in my stomach on my way back. I would say that in general the bear has about, . . . let's say a large human being takes a size E or R shoe, . . . and the bear I would say has about size X width and about 20 in length, So it appears we're still playing games with our bears, but, as I say, I haven't seen them lately.

## October 11

I've been preoccupied with the thought that in the last couple of weeks I really haven't accomplished much. I used to ponder the behavior of the workingman, the laborer who does everything with his body. In my college days I did a few labor jobs and I think it gave me a feeling of kindness and appreciation of all people. I don't think I would have gained this without some honest, physical work.

I do think that hard work is something that all of us need. How much I don't know. I've often wondered how much the life expectancy is cut down among laborers by physical work. How much of it is cut down by sheer work and how much by some of the behavioral or sociological consequences of their occupations; smoking and drinking, for example. Many thoughts seem to enter my mind on a Sunday. It is Sunday, and I do feel I'm the keeper of Lake Eva.

I've thought about taking one gigantic slug out of here and carting it back home. But I think of all the feces that could possibly get loose and escape and cause agricultural problems forever after. To think that a biologist would perpetrate such a foolishness. Besides, I don't think I really have the right to cart this thing out of this wonder paradise, where it manages to produce its kind. To bring it back just to show someone how big these slugs are in southeast Alaska is rather silly.

## October 12

Someone will probably be up to take me back this weekend or the next, but there is no sense fretting. When they show up, they show up.

I'm slowly but surely nibbling away at things, and right now I'm running a soup kitchen. That's about all that is left in the cabin.

The goldeneyes are all gone now. They too took their share of salmon eggs already close to hatching.

# BUT WHAT
# DO OLD TREES
# DO?

*October 13*

Most of the trails in southeast Alaska were built during the Roosevelt administration, the days of WPA and CCC, but the economics of keeping them open are prohibitive, so gradually a good many of the trails have been allowed to fall into decay. None of them are cleaned out and made fresh each year. Very few of the lakes have trails. The Forest Service is going out of the trail business. They are all for roads.

In Alaska, there are very few roads and they don't go very far. One has to strike, it seems to me, a balance in which one allows opportunity to extend down to the lower levels of our economic family. The eternal motto of the Forest Service is multiple use, multiple use—we have to use our forests to the best advantage of everyone. I think this is a great idea if, in the process, we don't lose the forests.

Who eventually wins out, I think, depends upon the public relations department. Isn't that something? It's just human nature to defend what supports you. I can see how this timber industry in Juneau would be a welcome thing. It would be a real boost to merchants and to the economy of southeast Alaska. I would hate at the moment to say whose side I'm on. The thing

Alaskans don't realize is that although Alaska looks immense, and is immense, when you think about population potential, it isn't very much.

I'm essentially in what would be interpreted as an emergency situation. The next people to come out should be the studio, and that could be tomorrow. The biological dramas yet to be enacted here are few and my role is just about played out.

## October 14

This morning as I was walking along the bank by the bear trail leading down to the ocean on the cabin side of the stream, heading down to where the cohos were, I heard a low growl and on the side of a tree trunk was a marten. It was very dark and he came down the trail and trotted off across the forest. With that I went back to the cabin. Later, when I opened the door, there on the log on which I keep the bacon grease was the marten feeding on the grease. I grabbed for the camera but he darted off. I looked down, and lo, there were two of them. I fiddled around with them for about 30 minutes trying to get some good pictures. They never gave me a good chance to film them. While the martens were in the area the squirrels around here, who are reasonably tame, were up in the trees, chattering and carrying on immoderately. They seemed to be scolding the martens, but were not in the state of terror that you would expect. It was an exciting morning, all told.

I noted that a great many of the pine cones are floating on the stream and that the alder leaves are falling on the lake and floating down the stream to the sea, so here is one leaf that doesn't rot on land.

When I walked down the stream trying to find some coho I heard a loud splash in the water. I could see a surface disturbance, so I worked my way down to an area where I thought I could see bear, but I couldn't. I then heard the low characteristic growl of the otter and discovered they were right underneath me. I kept hearing a crunching sound and carefully worked my way to an overhanging tree, and there was an otter eating a fish.

I'm curious when the studio will come up and take me out of here. I could easily finish off these rolls of film in no time. I'm still perplexed as to what happened to the box I put out for the bears.

## October 15

I had a very bad night and didn't feel as though I slept at all. I was essentially cabin-bound by a very heavy rain. I didn't want to get caught with the awkwardness that I did with the last storm, so I moved the boat to the lake and put it up on higher ground. My plan was to get everything off the landing of value that could be washed away.

I am pondering another shortcoming of scientists in general, and that is that they build up an empire or bank account of knowledge and we tend to perpetuate people who are enamored with the minutia of this huge bank account of knowledge, which is overpowering in its content.

I had the radio on for a few minutes and the confusion in southeast Alaska seems to be the same as usual.

## October 16

I would say that about 90% of the biological activity that takes place in the drainage system of Eva Creek and Eva Lake is microscopic. . . .

If you had only one or two years to educate people, what would you want to give them? I think if we thought of this we would sort out and throw away a lot of the nonsense that is associated with learning.

At the age of sixteen or seventeen the child starts to rebel because he begins to feel he is an adult. Yet he continues to be dominated by the adults who tell him he has to go to school or to work or to war. Yet we go on modestly pretending we are more mature. We have erected a rather imperfect system in which there are abundant loopholes. (All through life there are loopholes.)

## October 17

In looking across the stream I find that the salmonberry and thimbleberry are just about running out of leaves. There is a marked difference between when the leaves are shed on the north side of the stream and when they are shed on the south side. The north side of the stream leafed out much earlier, but it

*Land otter resting after romp in the snow.*

*Devil's club fruit.*

*An Alaskan brown bear, ears erect,
testing the air for a foreign scent.*

*Huckleberry, fall color.*

Walker resting on elevated prop roots that buttress main trunk. Such roots are more evident when trees are shallow-rooted and standing in water-logged soil.

*Winter comes again.*

lost leaves faster. I would have never noticed this in the confusion of civilization.

The best way to measure the productivity of lakes is to tag the bicarbonate. You can use a radioactive carbon which counts electronically. This has been a spin-off of the atom bomb. So much for that.

## October 18

I did get out and shoot about 35 feet of the jays feeding at the feeder. It was a cold, cold day and I didn't really accomplish much. I feel much further down than I did or have during the past six months and have built myself into a state of emotional collapse, which hasn't really done much good.

I moved the boots up to the boat so that if the camera crew shows up, which I doubt, they will have boots. I also took a spill and got the feeling of what 40° water is like, because my boots got well flooded out and one boot was perforated by a tripod. I then discovered that I had brought up all the left-footed boots to the boat, which meant I had to go back and carry back the right-footed ones. The boot that I perforated was a left-footed one, so for the first time in my life I walked half a mile in the wrong-footed boot.

I was depressed because my Coleman heater isn't working very well. I just hate to waste my wood, so I went to bed early to get as much warmth as I could. I find it rather annoying to think that the studio would be so crass as to let me just sit here. Biologically, things are very slow.

## October 19

It was a wild night with a fair amount of wind and rain and I slept badly. My heater went out and that upset me. I also discovered that the carburetor of the generator is out and it doesn't mix the air and fuel. That means no radio and no lights and no batteries.

I've been here by myself a little over six months now and I think, in retrospect, I may not be an expert on the wilderness. I have, however, fully savored it. If I were a younger man and had a partner, I would be itching to see whether or not I could hike the valley to the bitter end and make my way up over the pass and down into one of the other valleys and out to the ocean and down into Sitka. This is the kind of adventure that I used to do all the time, but up here it's not quite so easy. There is a tremendous canopy of trees which hide your chances to see where you are. When it was raining last night and I heard the raindrops I thought that one thinks of an aquatic environment as beginning with a spring, and one could say that the aquatic environment of Lake Eva extends all the way to the top of the ridge. Here the gravitational force will divide the water and the stream is actually a gauge that tells you how much water has fallen. I'm sure this water is low in nutrient. There is a tremendous supply of nutrients in the bog areas and these are special habitats in which there is very little lime and very little carbon dioxide. But I have stayed out of that habitat because there are no trails which lead into it. Besides, bogs are the same the world over, and there are many, many of them.

(I think I'm really getting the urge to get out of here. The depressiveness of the long nights has finally got to me. I feel that I have lived up to my part of the bargain and the studio should get me out now.)


## October 20

Now that time is heavy on my hands again I feel myself as responsive to the music as I was when I first got here.

I was awake last night from 1:00 to 4:00 and was tempted to start a fire because my toes felt a little frostbitten in the boots, but I didn't do it. I have only a comfortable week's rations, no more and no less. I don't know if I will get any more or not.

There is a remote possibility that the camera crew will come in today or that I will have a supply drop. If I do get a supply drop I will go on into Sitka and see just what the story is. This present situation is almost untenable. I am wasting a lot of time.

One thing that really gets me is that most of the fighting between the birds and even the salmon is very short and quickly resolved, whereas humans get back at each other in a much more devious and long-drawn-out manner.

(Right now I feel as if I'm a prisoner here because I have no way of getting out by myself. This bothers me.)

## October 21

The supply drop came, miraculously. I was very tempted to hop in the plane and go to Juneau and get on the phone and tell the studio my problems. But I decided it was not in my best interest, and if the people in Juneau couldn't call and tell them I was out of film, light, and subjects, that there was no transmitter, and that the weather was definitely wintery, I probably couldn't do it either. I carried down the groceries that had been brought and was happy that I had some mail and that Channel Flying had come out on their own to see what happened to me. . . .

I get the feeling nature is very untidy and it is terribly gloomy in the forest right now. . . .

I'm encouraged that maybe I can keep the generator going and keep the lights in the cabin. I have been pondering the dilemma that has been facing me about what the studio is going to do and if the film I have taken captures the ambience of Lake Eva.

I just can't see that a road is the best way into nature's secrets. Frankly, if I had to fight one bad use of our planet I would fight the automobile and the road to the degree that they are now designed with minimum contact with the world around them. This generation continues to gobble up resources without regard to anything but making money. It seems sad that we are so much on the move that we don't really see anything. I think that trails are the logical way through these woods even though the Forest Service thinks they are too hard to maintain. I think I clearly appreciate the attitude of the fisherman and the hunter and feel they are entitled to some say in these things. You know, if you do want to conserve something, all the publicity won't do anything unless people see it. Basically, the Forest Service shouldn't be in the position of land management and *selling* natural resources. As long as the government has the power there is no recourse.

The big issue, it seems to me, is to what degree we need to cut the trees down and how much of what we're cutting down is going for trash and things of no value, and how much for things that are good for the world. I'm pretty sure that cutting the trees down botches up the watershed, and no amount of scientific double-talk by the experts will change my mind. It would seem to me that when the trees are cut down, the first thing to occupy this naked place would be the understory of the devil's club, alder, etc. If one is content to allow a lower plant form, you may get away with it, but is it worth it? I really don't know.


## October 22

I shot the last of the film yesterday and spent most of the footage on the dipper, which is a winning bird. As I was putting up the film and writing film reports, there was an attack on the dipper by a hawk. I have noted that most water birds, when they take flight, emit a call as they fly. But this bird flew upstream without a call and the hawk, a sharp-shinned hawk, flew up the stream also. I opened the door and rushed out. The hawk had disappeared. The dipper popped out of the water at the logjam and sat on the log for 30 minutes, fluffing it's feathers, safe, sound, and exhausted. I made a recording of the bird taking a bath and you can hear the rustle of the wind through its feathers as it bathes. That was unique experience, seeing that life wasn't a bowl of cherries for the dipper. The important thing about these food-chain relationships is that the moment of attack is brief, and when you witness one you should feel very lucky. If the animals want to stay alive they have to stay under cover and this makes it very hard to film them. If you're not the kind to sit and wait, you are not the kind for these experiences.

I would like to point out that the Forest Service has in their employ various specialists. These specialists mean well, but a natural system is very complex and the average ecologist is dealing with it in an abstract computer sense. He doesn't come into as much contact with it as you and I do when we go into the country.

Whenever you manipulate this environment and this planet of ours with the idea of using it for man above all, you are biased. Such bias is blinding. I deplore the constant warfare in our society between the various groups of vested interest. And I still basically don't understand what in hell we, our species, has against other animals.

The foresting has a lot of effects and the rate of flow is greater and changed and the stream characteristics are modified and the snow goes off at a much faster rate because there isn't that shade. The organisms in the stream are designed with the peculiarities of the stream and when you tamper with it you are changing it. I don't honestly think that any expert knows because it is such a complex system.

It is clear that the environment has had quite an effect on me in the last six months, and I feel it is because I'm not caught up with millions of people bustling around. I'm free. We live in a world which is varied and complex and are here and gone in this life, just like that.

We are all today caught up in a group reaction in which we make the food chains for each other. We have made our environment so much for man that it is hard to get out of it. We are stuck with each other's presence.

My sympathy is with youth. I'm trying to think of something that I could tangibly offer that isn't negative. My feeling is that we should not be putting kids into the educational situation as it is now constituted.

I would like to make it very clear that I am confused as to when I'm going to come back out of this. I'm sure when I do get back I will search for places where people are infrequent. I don't know how many books have been written with the title *Voice of the Wilderness*, but that really expresses what's here. As a child I can remember so vividly the people who were out of society and lived in tiny shacks without friends or contact with anyone, social outcasts. But who is to say what a social outcast is, if a person is living the way he wants to live and has the courage to live that way. So my heart reaches out and I feel very vividly the frustrations and inability of any of us to do a damn thing.

## October 23

On the trail down to the ocean I found someone's undershirt. Who would take an undershirt off and leave it there? I have to admit that I'm really not dressed for the coldness and my feet always feel chilly.

It's raining very hard and I wouldn't be surprised if, when the studio comes in, Walker will be down to his last can of soup. It's certainly not going to be fun packing up all this stuff and carting it down the trail. Pretty soon this trail will be too icy. The berries are still on the bushes and are drying up and dying. . . .

We are too caught up in trying to do more then convey ideas. We all are trying to be different when in reality we aren't all different, we are all basically the same. Certainly, there are people who have a flair for creating word textures which move, but this is a world where we want more than word pictures, more than symbols. We are so overfed with printed pages that we no longer care and turn ourselves away.

(I don't mean to talk about the problems that face me when I come out of this little cabin, which is now becoming musty. I will have to go back and face the reality of what I've said and filmed.)

It's been a grand experience.

(I don't know what to do today. All I'm doing is waiting for this to come to an end. I am a little worried and annoyed and fearful about going back into civilization.)


## October 24

It was clear when I got up and I almost fainted. I looked out the window and saw the moon without a cloud around it, and I looked forward to going down to the estuary in the morning. The stream is up and considerably browner than it was. Along the lake and the estuary the tributaries were all pouring down about 10 times their normal volume, indicating again that in the month of October the blotter reservoir is filled to overflowing. There is also plenty of snow along the ridge back of the lake.

Yesterday there were a lot of things going on, but nothing much to talk about. I made a trip to the lake to bail the water out of the boat and there were no new bear tracks there. I did notice the deer fern, which has the fertile and sterile leaves and is very delicate. I'll have to get some still pictures of this. I heard quite a commotion and just across the lake where I keep the boat were eight whistling swans. For the first time I realized how the big neck of the swan makes possible that beautiful song of the swan. It is ethereal, just ethereal. The swans were a yellow-white. I was so thrilled with seeing them that I didn't go down and drain the boat. I stood there looking. So I have a memory of something lovely that isn't down on film.

At the estuary I saw some hooded mergansers and went into my blind and spent about 20 minutes filming slides of lichens. I just finished that and was picking some blueberries when I heard three shots and coming into the estuary were two hunters shooting straight at me. All the ducks took off and I was just absolutely sick to my stomach and enraged. The utter nastiness of human beings. No wonder we run around in herds, because in herds you don't have to see the other guy die and everyone is safe. But are we? So I fled the scene. I couldn't go down and talk to these two fellows. I would have punched them in the nose or punctured their boat. We have put a man on the moon, so what? We haven't begun to scratch the beauty and mystery of the world around us and we never will. We're playing games with ourselves.

I have pondered the issue of cutting down trees and the effect on the watershed, and I think that we need to find out what kind of a blotter we do have underneath the tangled bush that comes up when the trees are cut away and what kind of a waterflow we will have in the stream below.

How many people have ever seen or want to see the some seventy different kinds of plankton that live in the stream? Even the studio says people don't want to see this. We are always trying to figure out what the mob wants. The mob is hungry for real things — real, real things. The miracle of television is seeing it for yourself. The naturalness of the organism isn't the way it is conceived in the eyes of the zoo and the eyes of the great museums. I don't know, maybe you see them for what they are. I can go around to museums of natural history and find many errors in their labels. If I were just a kid and knew what I now know, I would be perfectly happy to be just a bum. They've got more guts and more courage. They're the living ones and we're the dead ones. These people are free. So T.J. is going back from here a wiser person.

## October 25

Today was the last of the breakfast food and yesterday was the last coffee, so I'm running out of provisions. Yesterday evening I had a rather exciting time with the marten who came around within a matter of moments after I put the meat scraps out. It was almost dark and it was hard to see him.

Today the cabin was at 38°, air was 22°, and I didn't check the water. I find that my sinuses get initiated in sleeping in the cold air of the cabin. Mid-morning yesterday it started to snow. Toward the end the flakes were actually an inch across and I've never seen anything like it. It was beautiful.

I went to the boat and it took me about 20 minutes to bail the boat out. The lake was up and there were no birds on it. I went up around the lake and there were some fresh bear tracks, which I skirted. I heard a huge crunch and looked up to see a big branch of an old tree falling on other branches; thus nature prunes it's trees by wind.

When I got back I discovered I had had a visitor at the john. He hadn't used the john in the usual sense but he had carried the toilet paper off about 5 feet and got the roll all wet and chewed on it. I'm sure it was going to use the paper to line a nest and I'm sure it was a marten. He left his paw prints!

Yesterday I felt very bad because it was the first day I hadn't been able to feed the jays. I placed a pan of stew out on the bird-feeder and the jays were out there this morning pecking on it but not really liking it.

I have only four more cans of oil for the generator so will have to start preserving this. I'm sure that somehow out of all this something of value may come. You know the whole idea of this was that I was to be costarred with Alaskan brown bear—and in that sense, it's been a bummer. The bears are gone and the fruits hang on the bushes rotting away. . . .

Here is a forest that for twenty generations has been growing to maturity. There are downed trees here and there covered with mosses and fungi, and the whole is absolutely more beautiful than all of man's attempts to make things beautiful. It makes me think how nice it would be if we were to be eaten by the animals when we die, because that's the way it used to be.

## October 26

The trail was wet and soggy. I walked up to the lake and busied myself taking pictures. All at once the sun broke out of the clouds, and at the same time I could hear the distant rumble of a plane. Sure enough, in a matter of minutes the plane landed. I maneuvered the boat around to the side of the pontoons and the pilot handed me a small box of groceries. He said, "Well, we thought you ought to celebrate and we got you a New York cut steak instead of those humdrum old rib steaks."

I thanked him profusely for his kindness, and without more ado he took off and I was left alone. Why go back to the cabin, I thought. Let me instead take a final turn around my little lake. I took the boat to the small delta which had been built by the stream that supplies Lake Eva.

I can't deny that I have mixed feelings about leaving here. I think it would be foolhardy to stay much longer what with the state of winter-proofing on the cabin. I vividly remember the three sheds of wood that Mr. Price had cut and prepared to keep himself and his wife and their pets, the jays and the martens, warm through the winter. When you see the amount of wood that's involved in doing that, you can anticipate spending most of your time in bed. Even now I find myself taking a hot-water bottle to bed with me just to keep a little extra warmth in the cabin, or in the sleeping bag. I certainly wouldn't want to spend the winter in a sleeping bag, particularly with the little light that will be available here. . . .

There were seven swans on the lake that took off when the plane took off. I had that sinking feeling, man has done it again. This kindness to me has caused those swans to go up in the air to wait for things to subside, to wait until calm returns. Two of them came down in the distance. One of them was the nice white color and the other was the old dirty-gray color. I immediately remembered the Hans Christian Andersen story of the ugly duckling. There it was going through the molt and having the beautiful white plumage briefly before it was soiled by the business of living. Keep in mind that swans operate in a dirty muddy environment and they are oriented to the edge of the lake in the shallows where the coarse grass grows.

The swans took off again at the sound of my motor.

I did frighten them and I felt it was necessary. I wanted to go to the other end of the lake. It was my farewell to the lake. I knew that once the camera crew arrived, the utter confusion and the rush and the stress and strain of packing up and carting everything up the muddy trail to the lake for transport would nullify any feelings, nostalgic or otherwise. If I wanted to take my leave privately, it would have to be today.

The sun came out and the edging of the lake was beautiful with the colors, the somber colors of fall, subdued and smudged by reflection in the inky black water of Lake Eva. Most of the memory of that lake and my leave-taking was recorded on film, with all the imperfections of my art, or lack of art.

Truly, it was wild, the upper end of the lake. The mountains were revealed to me by a parting of the curtains and I suddenly gaped at an enormous stage with a hundred curtains between the back scene and the front. It was a ghostly interplay of space and light, clouds and mountain. The atmosphere was generative and dynamic, filled with caprice. What once appeared to be a sullen background abruptly shattered and fragmented into so many photographic planes. As I looked back over the lake and turned the boat around and sped to the landing on the stream, I could watch the lighting of the sun as it became momentarily obscured by the clouds, a wisp of clouds that was hanging and rising along the upper valley. So here was a great personage playing with a mask of humor which allowed the eager stagehand such pleasures and magic as the dramatic urgency of theatrical business would never allow. . . .

I must also mention that I scared off a flock of about 200 ducks and a flock of geese. They headed off to sea, down Eva Creek to the strait.

Little ugly me, the symbol of the nasty guns that bark and spit and litter the lakes and marshes and the ocean edge with the carcases of a million birds. I suppose what is so challenging to the hunter is the complexity of getting in for that awful revelation when your little cloud inflicts nasty holes and your nasty buckshot causes that bird to tumble. It is not a pretty picture. I don't care how one looks at it. All the propaganda of all the hunting magazines and all the mystique of all the hunters will never be able to shake my feeling that there is something more to life.

In all of my stay at Lake Eva, I have realized that there is more to life than writing and talking. You must experience it for yourself, even if it involves only an insect crawling across your lawn. . . .

We're in the age of insecticide. Nothing escapes us. We kill everything. For what? For us, and why not? That's the attitude!

It was kind of nature to pull the curtains aside so that I might view once more the pageantry and beauty that brought me here.

The world at large will think I am jousting with windmills, and yet I know the windmills are there. That's more than the rest of the group knows; but they may not even care. Someday those windmills will quit running and turning and it will all be in books and in museums. People have to see it on television and read about the "New Explorers." Pity, pity, pity. They will have to work fast to see any of the reality.

Ours was the lucky generation, a generation of truth. . . .

Civilization overstuffed, overfed. Affording, granting the best of everything, whenever you wanted it. Now nobody has a chance to want anything; everyone is pushed around in the maze of too many, too much.

This has been a marvelous experience, and I have learned so much and gained an understanding of myself in relation to the world. I'm not destructive and fighting civilization. I think man is a perfectly marvelous animal and he should be able to live in peace and harmony with his fellow man and with himself. Each of us should be able to live each day aware of what we are and expecting no more. We should not have to be involved in trotting off to church once a week in order to live a better life.

We add and we subtract and chance plays its ugly games. We come, we go. We all move, we all cry. We all are lonely.

I've come further than most. I look ahead, I look back, I look out the window. (There are the trees, swaying in the wind. Beautiful, beautiful trees.)

I look at the paper from Sitka and what does it say? "Young trees make more oxygen." Isn't that great?

But what do old trees make? They make wood, they make soil, they make lovely, lovely forests. They take care of themselves. They grow and die the same as you and I. What does it take? We are caught up in the widening circle of being born and dying.

There is much to do. Yet, is there, I wonder? I'm not sure I can operate much longer. . . .

It will be difficult to put this on paper. There's no reason to put it on paper. The rain is thumping down on the roof and no writing will ever capture it.

I'm ready to go back to society and the lovely world. . . .

We still every month gather up the sacrifice of the young and those who don't have any comprehension as to what war (or death) is or justification of it and pack them off to Indochina. We continue to scratch our rear-ends and sit on our asses. And the blacks are still oppressed. There just aren't enough food chains. We have the great this and the great that and the question is, Do we make what we've got go all the way around? We are at the same time getting more and more rigid and more and more planned. Our brave new world, our brave new world. . . .

## October 27

It's about 9:30 in the morning, my time. I don't know if that's 10:30 or 8:30. It looks as though it's going to be a beautiful day. It's cold—32° outdoors and 32° in the cabin. The removable pane that allows me to film out the window at the feeder came out last night (fortunately it didn't break or fall), and I can see my breath as I sit here talking. I haven't measured the water temperature. I've been down to get water this morning but I just didn't think to do it. I don't even have it written down here. God, I'm confused. I have a slight sore throat. I'm very tired. I stayed up late last night and then I thought I'd better clean up the cabin a little bit and put a few things in order, which I did.

For the first time in my life, I'm rather reluctant to think about going anywhere. I envision about a ten-day trip, being hither and yon, anything, any hither, any yon, but hither and yon as I work my way down the coast to my home. The first stopover at Prince Rupert then on into British Columbia to visit my son during the week. On that trip I'll be out in the woods, open country, prairie, Fraser River. My son, for a number of years, has been studying bighorn sheep. There are very few bighorn sheep in British Columbia, and this is one of the few herds that are left. He's become quite a remarkable naturalist and observer in spite of his reluctance to do anything in a professional way. He's very anxious to show me the sheep.

The dippers are still trying to mate. The female has that magnificent technique of now you see me, now you don't. She drops into the water in front of the male. Just fun and games, but it actually turns out to be the way they save their lives on occasion. Two of them out there. It's a clear day with patches of clouds. More patches than clear, but nonetheless I can see sunrise this morning. In fact I can still see it over the ridge to the south.

Yesterday I took a final look at my hydroponic experiment with the petri dishes. The radishes were still alive but a fox sparrow had come by the day before and had dug every one of them up. Now it looks like a typical fox-sparrow scratching—just a little chicken sparrow—a marvelous bird.

I'm so happy that it turned out to be a lovely day for the camera crew to come in. It will facilitate so much the transfer of all my equipment from the cabin to Lake Eva.

I hate the thought of saying goodbye to all of this, and I am saying goodbye to it. I'm terribly proud to have been allowed by you, the reader, the listener, the viewers of the TV special, to have this experience. I hope a little bit of my meditation and love of nature and moderate understanding of it has come across. I hope I haven't bored you or appeared overdrawn, over emotional. Any one of you could have done the same. A little training in the use of the camera. You can't miss with nature. Nature is all grace, all beauty, every picture everywhere. I defy anyone to take an awkward picture of a flower. You may not be technically skillful and you may not express the last nuance of the situation. You may photograph it under adverse conditions, but nonetheless. . . . I think one of the hang-ups of the old-time writer was the fact that he had to create the illusion of scenery, and you just *can't* generate the illusion of scenery. There's only one way to see it, and that is to see it. . . .

I just went down to the stream to get some water. There's a big, overpowering cumulonimbus cloud boiling up from the west, catching the morning sunrise, and it's brilliant yellow. Toward the estuary there's a mist and haze and another big blot of clouds. It, too, is gilded with the yellowing light, the fading, aging light, the much-filtered light that streaks through much too much atmosphere and much too much of man's pollution to remain uncolored. Like the lyric — it's a great big wonderful morning, and as I sit here with my hands squeezed tight, waiting for the camera crew, the ugly thought of having to say goodbye overwhelms me. But I will never be long removed from the mountains, the mountain streams and their magic music, the wind in the trees.

The wind here has been different from what I expected — not the blasting wind that I am used to. I guess this is a consequence of living on the ocean. The mountains in the center, the interior of the continents, are subject to a tremendous motion of air in and out of the mountains as a consequence of the flat plains heating and developing low pressures. The air settles and drains down through the mountain valley, creating a tremendous wind usually in the very early mornings. I missed that.

I am holding a cup of coffee here which is getting cold, as usual.

# INDEX

PT. MOS

ESTUARY

WATERFALL

WALKER'S
CABIN

LOG JAM

**EVA CREEK**

RAPIDS

LOC
BLIN

BLIND

CROSSIN

ISLANDS

**LAKE EVA**

BOAT LEFT HERE

TRAIL

**BARANOF
ISLAND**

LEAN-TO